GOOD MEN AND TRUE

The lives and tales of the shepherds of mid Wales

ERWYD HOWELLS

I dedicate this book to my parents, John and Elsa Howells, Dôl-carne, Ponterwyd for their support and encouragement, and also to my parents-in-law John and Margaret Griffiths, Ffynnongeitho, Llangeitho who gave such support and kindness when the need was greatest, and to my long-suffering children Elen and Gethin for their patience.

■ Erwyd, Elen and Gethin Howells at Glan-fred, Llandre with the faithful, true to type Welsh sheepdog bitch *Meg* in the foreground. As far as I am concerned, she will always be the key breeding bitch because of her invaluable contribution in producing good working stock. (Photo by Arvid Parry Jones, Talybont)

Contents

■ Cover photograph: Charles Abel, Cefn-brwyn (see page 104).

Published by Erwyd Howells, Capel Madog, Aberystwyth, Ceredigion.
First printing: August 2005.
Second printing: October 2005.

ISBN 0-9551736-0-4

Printed by Cambrian Printers, Aberystwyth.

Foreword

Dear Reader,

It is with a sense of trepidation that I first set pen to paper to record some of the stories, facts and adventures of the shepherds of mid-Wales. Having collected facts over many years from various sources, such as publications, tapes made of people who had first-hand knowledge, plus personal contact with many of the 'old' shepherds and their families, I have felt for quite some time that the lives and dedication of these people, who gave so much, for so little, deserve to be remembered. Many of them had lived in the ways of their forefathers, enveloping the rich culture that only a close-knit society can create.

Many of the stories within have been handed down by word of mouth only, and as society has taken a dramatic turn during the last forty to fifty years, a written record will ensure that they carry on for many generations to come. I would be the first to admit that some of these stories are of very little importance to the world and his wife. However, they may contain some little gems for the immediate family or descendants of these shepherds and some of them convey a great deal about the way life was in this area years ago.

Having left school at fourteen and English being my second language (the only word of English I had at seven years old was 'yes') there is no attempt to make this an intellectual book, but merely to safeguard what is rapidly disappearing from the hills of rural Wales. It was by hours of discourse around the family hearth that the tales and traditions of yesteryear were kept alive. Many occupations such as shearing have been speeded up to the degree that the joviality, and the number of people employed, has diminished to the extent that today it is a business to be finished as quickly as possible.

The characters within are recorded as I knew, or heard, of them. Some of the tales may have been slightly embroidered in passing from one person to the next. My gratitude is immense to so many people who, wittingly or unwittingly contributed by word or deed to material within this book. Not being the most methodical person by a long shot, many of the hundreds of articles and more importantly, photographs that I have collected over many years came from sources that I cannot remember, therefore I ask the original owners of photographs published to 'forgive me my trespasses' if I have done so without their consent. A list will appear of persons that have contributed in various ways, but will not be complete, as many were people whose names I did not even know.

Many questions will go unanswered because so many people did not ask the right questions to the right people years ago. It is the great wealth of my life to have lived and worked in a hill society and to have shared the company of so many wonderful people who are no longer with us, but have left a legacy which should be kept and treasured, yet shared. This is why I have written this book in English, so that it may enrich people's lives beyond the boundaries of Wales. I hope that it will serve as a window, through which to glimpse the past – when man, animals and their natural environment were very closely bonded.

Erwyd Howells

■ The ruins of Lluest-newydd.

Long, long are gone the hands that laid
These stones one upon the other
And proud to live within its walls
A father and a mother.

Their children ran, and played and laughed
Their world so full of freedom
This area and its rough terrain
Was their entire kingdom.

Long, long these stones they will remain
For a future generation
To think of us, who love this Vale
Long long gone to oblivion.

Introduction

The vast tract of mountains extending from the Elan Valley, including Pumlumon, to Machynlleth, has been called 'The Green Desert of Wales' and yet by someone else 'miles and miles of bugger all'. The Rev Richard Warner from Bath in his book *A walk through Wales* in August 1797 had seen very little life in the Elan Valley area 'except in two or three small hovels which occurred in the course of ten miles, and were inhabited by the joyless beings who tended the widely spread flocks that feed upon these mountains'.

I would like to focus on the people who controlled and looked after this beautiful, if sometimes inhospitable, area. Many changes have occurred within living memory, such as afforestation, erection of fences, depopulation, networks of roads and the swallowing up of many homesteads to make up larger units. My work as a shepherd has taken me right across this area, from the Elan Valley to Machynlleth. I also spent three years working in the Tregaron and Llanddewi Brefi hills, an area about which I knew nothing previously, but I came away from there enriched by having made many friends and having been steeped in a lot of local knowledge. John Buchan stated about Scottish shepherds that they were 'a creed both at once stalwart and merciful' and indeed there are many examples of rugged Welsh shepherds who had a gentle side to their character. The landscape in which many lived and worked called for a resolute nature, and yet the word shepherd is synonymous with caring.

Many of the early photographs of this area were taken by the local landed gentry, or well-to-do visitors. These photos captured a moment in time when things were so different – indeed, some are well over a hundred years old. My gratitude is immense to these unknown people. I wonder how many more early photographs of mid Wales are hidden away, unidentified, in some darkened drawer, within and without the boundaries of Wales? One thing is certain, many of them captured scenes that have been, gone, and will be no more.

Welsh phrases are shown in *italics*.

Dafydd Lewis

I would like to start with a man called David (or Dafydd) Lewis who was a shepherd at Glan-hirin, in the upper reaches of the Elan Valley, from 1892 to 1934. There is little question as regards the fact that he was the best hill shepherd ever. His control over his dogs was a legend, as was his management of the sheep. The Glan-hirin flock was, at this time, divided into seven lots and because of regular shepherding, he would be able to gather most of the 3000 acres with very little help. Many people still recall how he often had eight or nine dogs following behind him, and only the one he would name would leave the ranks to do whatever task he wanted. One story I have heard is that he and a friend were crossing a river when Dafydd gave a stop whistle to a dog working a good distance away. The friend noticed that the two dogs following behind actually lay down in the river in response. Dafydd would never boast about his dogs, and if somebody asked him about a certain dog, although it was a good one, he would say, 'He's very

■ From left to right: William Davies, Hirnant; Dafydd Lewis, Glan-hirin; Harold Hughes, Aber-glan-hirin; Arthur Evans, Llwyn-iorwerth. Front: Richard Davies, Hen-fron; Bill Morgan, Nanerth-ffrwd; Jack Lewis, Elan Village.

good round the food pot!' He was the eldest of seven children, born at Hafod, Llanwrthwl. His parents, Thomas and Elinor Lewis, later moved to Pencae-mawr, Abergwesyn. His brother Edward Lewis, under his pen-name 'Iorwerth Camarch', was an accomplished poet. Another brother – Evan Lewis, Pencae Mawr – was the author of an earmark book compiled around 1916. Evan's son Jim who lived at Troed-rhiw-ruddwen, Rhandir Mwyn was very much akin to his uncle in management of sheep, and especially dogs. Jim died on the 15th of October 1997 aged 78.

Dafydd Lewis married Sarah Ellen Lewis from Tymawr, Cwmystwyth, at Eglwys Newydd, Hafod, on the 28th of June 1893. He was 25 and she 21. I have heard that she was of a stern nature, and that there was not a lot of nonsense as far as she was involved. They had nine children (six boys and three girls) who survived into adulthood. Two children died young and were buried at Eglwys Newydd. One of their daughters, Annie, remembered when she was about six, asking her mother what was in a shoe-box, and being told that it was a baby, obviously still-born. James Lewis, their son died on the 7th of March 1931, aged 35. He was buried on the day he was to have been married. Rhys, another son, died through drowning on the 16th of January 1948, aged 48.

Life in these remote farms could be pretty grim at times of ill-health or confinement. One tale tells of Dafydd Lewis walking to Bwlchwallter (his wife's eldest brother lived there) on a very misty night, to ask one of them to go down to Pont-rhyd-y-groes to fetch a doctor, as his wife was going into labour. The most direct route to Glanhirin for the doctor would have been eight miles, over some rugged country, and the journey made doubly worse by misty conditions. Sarah was one of a large family and their circumstance was one of great hardship. I have heard that one of her elder brothers (David) was given £20 to pay the rent to the Hafod Estate (who owned Tymawr at the time) but saw a chance to better himself and took himself, plus cash, to America. He had got a local girl pregnant, but came back 18 years later, and married her. They went to live at Alltfedw, Llanfihangel-y-creuddyn.

I do not know as much as I would like about Dafydd Lewis, but the first mention I heard of him was that he used to visit his in-laws at Tymawr, very often on a Sunday morning, with eight or nine dogs at his heels. He would sit by the fire and sometimes, when his trousers were wet you could not see him for the cloud of steam as his clothes dried, yet for all this he lived to the ripe age of eighty-five when he died on the 17th of

■ Shearing at Glan-hirin c.1927.
There are about seventy-five people in the group.

August 1952. It was strongly reputed that he never wore an overcoat, no matter what the weather, and that his trousers fitted so tight over his boots that it was virtually waterproof. One of his favourite meals was dripping and butter-milk. One of the sounds that Dafydd Lewis was able to hear from Glan-hirin that is not heard today was that of the train at Strata Florida.

Another tale that I heard from his nephew John Lewis, Tymawr, was that Dafydd was out on the hill one day when suddenly, something black shot out of the peat hags and was caught by the dogs. It turned out to be a young pig which was taken home and eventually killed the following autumn. It was a great puzzle how a pig had got to the hill of Glan-hirin, but it transpired that the family from Nant-y-maen, Tregaron had been to the town, bought a weaner pig, and lost it on the way home! The little pig's journey would have taken it at least ten miles across rough country.

Glan-hirin was owned then, and still is, by the Birmingham Corporation who bought all the hills (45,000 acres) that form the catchment area for the Elan Valley reservoirs that supply Birmingham with its water. There is a tale of an old lady called Gwenno, who at one time worked as a seamstress in Nant-gwyllt, a small mansion now beneath the waters of the dams. She had 'seen' the machinery and dammed water a long time before they came. She had also foreseen her own death. Before she died she had instructed her son to prepare her by washing and dressing her, and that no other hand was to touch her. She also asked that her coffin was to be roped to the cart as she had foreseen an accident. Although she was a small lady, the coffin was very heavy. The bearers however omitted to rope the coffin and on the rough road, the cart overturned, and the coffin rolled down a slope. When the coffin was retrieved it was found to be the normal weight (*Welsh Gazette*, 1st of January 1948). Nant-gwyllt (turbulent stream) was bought in the late 1700s by a Thomas Grove, of Fern in Wiltshire. It was then an estate of 10,000 acres of wild hill and valleys. Two very good references to this area and era, are a poem of 350 lines, called *Coombe Ellan*, by the Reverend W. Lisle Bowles (1798), and a book called *The Vale of Nant-gwyllt*, by R. Eustace Tickel (1894), which mentions that the poet Shelley lived at Nant-gwyllt in 1812.

After Dafydd Lewis, a new shepherd took over at Glan-hirin in 1934. His name was Hughie Roberts, and he had been born in Ty'n Cwm, in Pont-rhyd-fendigaid, hailing from a long line of shepherds. Hughie remained there till 1938 when he moved to farm Pen-garreg, Elan Valley as tenant to the Birmingham Corporation. He moved later to farm Bryn-glas, in Llanddewi Brefi. During his stay at Pen-garreg he walked to his old home at Ty'n Cwm to attend a funeral. This was during the winter, and his riding pony was on tack. Having spent the night at Ty'n Cwm he set off next morning, but by the time he got to Claerwen it had started to snow in a big way. On he went for a good while till he found some footprints, and then realized that they were his own. He was now lost. He had however taken a big black dog with him called Fleet which had walked at his heels, but then the dog started walking in front of him. Hughie followed him, but had no idea where he was till they came to a fence at Hirnant, Elan Valley. This dog certainly proved he was man's best friend. Islwyn, Hughie's son, now farms at Bryn-glas.

Below are just a few notes on Glan-hirin in case they might be of interest to somebody, somewhere, in the future.

Glan-hirin was owned at one time by a gentleman called Loftus Otway, who was from a family of landed gentry from Presteigne, well known for their gifts to the needy of the area. Because of this connection, the pitch mark (after shearing) of Glan-hirin was an 'L' inside an 'O'. The same family aslo owned Hen-fron farm for which the pitch mark was 'LO'.

At a site on Glan-hirin called 'Cormwg' there is a dipping tub inside a shed. This was built by the Birmingham Corporation in 1915 as a communal dipping place for Claerwen, Hengae, Abergwngi, Glan-hirin, Lluest-aber-caethion, Aber-glan-hirin and Hirnant. Similar tubs were built at Blaen-methen, Rhiwnant, Marchnant, and at Kingsfield (near Upper Lan-fadog – so called because the King was there in 1904). These dipping baths served almost the whole of the Corporation Estate.

Many years ago, probably going back to the late 1700s, several hundred cattle came to graze over the summer months at Glan-hirin. They came from the Ffair-rhos, Pont-rhyd-fendigaid and Tregaron areas. They were mostly black cattle. As with sheep coming to a new area, these cattle had to be 'settled' at their new home, and they had to be watched for the first fortnight or so *day and night*, otherwise they would head back to where they had come from. Historically, it was a fact that prior to about 1750 there were more cattle on these hills than sheep.

The following tale about Glan-hirin, I heard from my mentor Tommy Hughes, Aber-glan-hirin. Directly in front of Glan-hirin house, heading straight for Hirnant there was a path called *Llwybr Rhys* (Rhys' path). It was quite distinct in years gone by, but by now is almost covered over by molinia grass. This Rhys was an exceptionally strong man. They had run short of hay one winter, and he walked over towards the Wye Valley to get some, having taken a rope with him to secure the bought hay. The farm he went to was Nant-llymysten (the brook of the sparrow-hawk). The people there, seeing this strong man, thought they would have a bit of fun at his expense, and put an enormous amount of hay in a heap, and tied it securely with the rope, hoping that he would have a job to lift it, let alone carry it, but Rhys put the load on his back, and proceeded to take it home. Anybody who has been to Nant-llymysten will know of the very steep hill he had to negotiate before going out of the valley towards his home, which was four miles away. Quite a feat.

On a personal note, my great-great grandfather Thomas Rees was born at Nant-llymysten on the 25th of May 1827. He later moved with the family to Foel-goch, Llangurig. He married Jane Rowlands from Allt-fedw, Llanfihangel-y-creuddyn, and they lived at Glan-yr-afon near Fagwr Fawr, Ponterwyd.

There are many tales of very strong men in years gone by. One such man was Isaac James, Diluw (near Nant-rhys), who used to walk to Aberystwyth, buy two sacks of grain, and carry them, one under each arm to his home, twenty miles away.

According to the 1841 census return for Glan-hirin a Rees Lewis (79) and his wife Margaret (66) lived there. A Rees Lewis and Margaret Lewis had married at Llansantffraid Cwmdauddwr Church on the 3rd of June 1797. They had children named Elizabeth (34), Ann (32), Rees (30) – probably the strong man – and John (28). A daughter called Abigail was baptized at Cwmdauddwr on the 20th of November 1817 for Rees and Margaret Lewis. By 1851 Rees and Margaret Lewis had moved to live at Pen-bryn, near Blaen-cwm, Cwmystwyth, and kept a small shop there. He and his son are described as 'flower dealer', which should have read 'flour dealer'. Rees Lewis (senior) died there aged 90, and was buried at Cwmdauddwr on the 19th of August

1851. I wonder if there are any descendants still around? A Rees Lewis died at Cwmdauddwr on the 4th of January 1887 aged 76. Could this be the strong man? So many questions, and only an uncertain span of life to try and find answers!

At Aber-glan-hirin there is a large white stone, which weighs nearly 300 pounds. Rhys was reputed to be able to lift this stone with ease above his head. Quite a character, and if it wasn't for people like Tommy, these tales would have gone into oblivion. Somebody called Newell Dwight Hills once said 'And these recollections are embalmed and transmitted as soul capital, legacies unspeakably precious'. Nothing could be truer of Tommy's recollections.

In 1951 a David Benjamin came to Glan-hirin to shepherd for Mr Arthur Evans. Arthur Evans (1902–1988) was a nephew to William Evans, Glan-serth whose family had been at Glan-hirin since c.1850. Arthur was 24 years old when he came to help his ageing uncle. David Benjamin and his family stayed at Glan-hirin till 1956 when they moved to farm Cae-mawr in Pont-rhyd-fendigaid. (He had worked in that area previously as a shepherd for Morgan Jones, Wern-felen at Ty'n Cwm.) Their stock were walked over the hills to their new home. William Benjamin, his son, continued as shepherd at Glan-hirin until 1969, making his home with Tommy and Nell Hughes at Aber-glan-hirin. Glan-hirin remained from 1969 till 1982 without a full-time shepherd, with Arthur Evans doing the best he could, with paid men coming in as and when they were needed. In 1982, Arthur Evans relinquished the tenancy, and the new tenants, Maldwyn and Ann Rogers and their family came there to live.

In 1839, during the Duke of Newcastle's time at Hafod Mansion, Pont-rhyd-y-groes, a count was made of Glan-hirin sheep and they numbered 1,498.

■ Mrs Dorothy Benjamin with her daughter Betty at Glan-hirin. These trusty steeds were their only means of transport from this isolated farm.

Thomas and William Pugh, Bodtalog

Thomas and William Pugh were brothers born at Bodtalog, a farm at the upper end of the Elan Valley on the boundary with Cardiganshire. They were the seventh generation of Pughs at Bodtalog, and the ninth in the area. It is one of my great regrets that I did not tape them, or ask more questions when they were around. Being able to own or afford a tape recorder was one of the furthest things in my mind at the time. William, or Bill, as he was generally known, had been with the 11th Hussars at Aldershot and was an expert horseman and one of his favourite recitations was this one which I believe to be from *A Cavalier's Toast*. The poem may be mis-quoted, but the general gist is:

> *Two things I love the most –*
> *A horse, and a beautiful woman.*
> *And when I die may my hide be tanned*
> *To make a lady's saddle,*
> *So that I can lie between*
> *The two things I love the most –*
> *A horse, and a beautiful woman.*

Bill Pugh, whom I remember as a cool personality who spoke with almost a drawl to his speech, said to me once that a shepherd should smoke and be married – probably implying that a contented mind helped a person living in an isolated situation to cope. He also said about his father (William Hugh Pugh, died 17th of May 1943, aged 81) that when he had been away from home either on horseback or pony and trap, he would whistle when nearing home, and woe betide if there was nobody there to meet him and unharness and stable the horse. Two things that his father could not resist buying if he got a chance were a new stallion or a new cockerel. When his father was housebound during his later years and a heavy fall of snow came, he would say 'Billy, you go to such and such a place, that's where the sheep are buried'. No matter where the wind blew he would know of the places of danger, which had come not only from his, but his forebearers' experience. When William Hugh Pugh was on his deathbed (1943), the council were making road improvements in the area and he stated that he did not want them to move the long stone on 'tro maen hir' (the bend of the long stone) and his wish was granted. Unfortunately, in the early 1990s, when a more enlightened attitude would have been expected, the stone was removed to the other side of the road. Thankfully it is undamaged, and I have a bee in my bonnet about putting it back in its rightful place, possibly standing. While I was shepherding at Ty-llwyd (grey house) Cwmystwyth in the late sixties, Tom and Bill Pugh became very good friends of mine and although there was a big age difference, they took me under their wing as it were, and advised me what

■ Y Maen Hir (the long stone, 13 feet in length, on Bodtalog land). Photo by Seiriol Dafydd.

to do and, probably more often, what not to do! They showed me kindness and gave me encouragement, for which I will respect their memory as long as I live.

I remember being very impressed by a dog called Lad that Bill Pugh once had. Lad would go up the main yard at Ty-llwyd, close to the stable wall, and cut out the exact amount of sheep that would go into the handling pen. All the sheep were caught by

■ William and Tom (mounted) Pugh, Bodtalog.

hand then, which makes people of my age group really appreciate the blessing of a sorting race, and I often wonder why people had not thought of this simple and effective device many years sooner.

When Bill was exchanging labour with other farms, he was always jovial and full of wit, but when there was work at Bodtalog he wasn't quite as happy and could be difficult to please at times. I remember him telling me one time 'These people would rather trip in the wool than pick it up'. There was an old saying 'You look after the loose wool, the loose wool will look after you' – probably from an era when the price of wool was more lucrative than it is now. It was Bill who taught me how to bleed a sheep that was not well, or suffered from photosensitivity – an affliction that makes the sheep's head swell up – by cutting through a vein below the eye. It may be called 'bush medicine' by some, but it was effective.

Tom Pugh and his brother Bill were some of the last Welsh speakers in the Elan Valley and the standard of their spoken Welsh was very high compared to what is spoken by many today, especially considering the amount spent on education. Tom moved in 1918 to farm at Gwar-dôlau, on the outskirts of Rhayader (the spelling of which I dislike, because it should be spelt Rhaeadr Gwy, meaning 'the falls of the Wye'). It is with great fondness that I remember going to visit Gwar-dôlau, especially in the long winter evenings, with Tom Pugh enjoying an evening conducted only in Welsh – something he didn't often get a chance to do – and Mrs Pugh plying us with refreshments to stop us drying up. Mrs Pugh (Agnes May, known as 'Babs') would go to Rhaeadr for errands and so forth on her bike. Somebody asked Tom one day if Mrs Pugh had been to a function held in the town. He replied in the affirmative and added with a chuckle, 'Mama ne'er miss much'. Tom was again an expert in handling dogs and sheep, yet he never boasted his dogs, but he let them boast themselves, and when you saw them working, you knew that he had something that he could have boasted about, but that was not his style.

There is a hill called Pen-rhiw-wen within four miles of Gwar-dôlau and it was onto this hill that many low-lying farms sent their sheep over the summer, about six different flocks in all. Tom used to go up on a regular basis to keep each lot on its own patch of ground, and it is stated that he got quite cross if a ewe from another lot got mixed with a particular lot that was being gathered, and not cross with anybody else, but cross with himself! While at this job one day he had an unusual experience in that his dogs put up a grey squirrel (on a bare hill), and in a desperate attempt to save its own skin, the squirrel ran up the horse's leg, and onto Tom's shoulder. The horse took fright and started off at a gallop, and Tom, in trying to dislodge the squirrel, lost his hat. What a commotion! When recounting such stories he had a very warm chuckle that seemed to come from deep down. He told his friend and protege, George Bates, from Rhaeadr years ago when they were gathering the Park sheep, 'When you and me have finished, all this [the sheep in Pen-rhiw-wen] will be one lot', and indeed by today, it's virtually true. I found him to be a natural gentleman. When about to tell a tale of a dubious nature, he would start by saying 'This one is a bit rough' and yet I cannot recall any tales that deserved the term 'rough', but that was his way. At the end of his days he went to live with his daughter at Rhaeadr, and also spent some time at the hospital in Llandrindod Wells, where he used to set off the fire alarms because of his pipe smoking! One thing that will stick with me always is the fact that I called to see him in his latter years, and was very disappointed to find that he could not remember me, considering that we had been such good friends.

It is gratifying to know that the children and grandchildren of Tom and Bill Pugh are still farming in the Elan Valley, with the bonus of great-granchildren, hopefully to follow in their footsteps.

Jim Pugh

Jim Pugh was a brother to Tom and Bill. He was a tall, smart character, who was very much a military man, described as a typical soldier. He served in the First and Second World Wars. He was married, and started farming, but alas, his marriage and farming enterprise went a bit pear-shaped, and thereafter, he spent his time in different jobs, mostly associated with Forestry. He spent his latter years helping his sister, Cissie (Elizabeth Eleanor) Evans, at Aber-gwngu. During the severe snowstorm in 1963 he was taken ill, and was taken by helicopter to Llanidloes Hospital. He made a recovery, and came home, but died in 1964 (a year to the day he was flown into hospital) in his mid-seventies. He had one son, who now lives in Southampton. One of Jim's memorable sayings came out as he was giving a friend a lift on his motor bike from Rhaeadr after closing time one night, 'It's hell or Lanfadog in five minutes!'

In Aber-gwngu, probably around 1850, there lived a Morgan Thomas, who was a shepherd for Mr Pugh, Abermad, Llanilar. Morgan was renown for training sheepdogs. His neighbours were Hughie, Thomas and John Pugh, Bodtalog, and they had a bull that was of a troublesome nature. This bull one day went to Aber-gwngu, and Morgan tried to send it back with a dog, but the bull went into a deep pool in the river Elan and stood under a bank, and would not budge from there. Morgan gave the dog a specific command and he leapt onto the animal's back, and savaged the bull to such an extent that it was very glad to escape and make its way home.

A group of out-of-work leadminers from the neighbouring areas made a decision to go to America, and Morgan Thomas went with them. He went to Liverpool, taking his dog with him, and somehow got him aboard without being seen. The dog was hidden for weeks, but somehow the officers came to know of this stowaway, and Morgan had to give account for his actions. The end result was that they threw the dog overboard, which must have been a devastating blow to his proud owner.

In the 1841 census, Morgan Thomas was aged 26. His wife was called Sarah, and they had a son called Lewis. According to the 1851 census, they had three other children called Sarah, Richard and Ellis. I am very much indebted to Mrs Eirionedd Baskerville, who works at the National Library of Wales, Aberystwyth for helping me trace official reference to many of these people.

Did Morgan become a shepherd/dog trainer in America? I would like to think so, but like a lot of my questions, I have no answer.

What has been lost forever with the passing away of Tom and Bill Pugh, Dafydd Lewis and another hill character, John Davies, Hirnant, Elan Valley, are the names that were used on the different areas of the hill. Every brook, every hillock, all the big stones and outcrops of rocks had names. It was stated by the Jervis family, who lived at Cefn-brwyn, Llangurig, that one of them could go onto the hill, leave his cap anywhere on that hill, and be able to direct another member of the family to go and find it.

> *But to the cultivated eye of taste,*
> *No rock is barren, and no wild is waste.*

Many of these names give us a strong clue as regards what had been in ages past. There is Nant yr Hydd (brook of the deer), Nant Iwrch (same meaning), Bryn Ieir (hillock of the hens). Many names contain 'Blaidd', meaning wolf and 'Arth', meaning bear. At the source of the Elan River there is the poetic name, Byrlymau Elan (the bubblings of the Elan). On the hill of Tymawr, Cwmystwyth, there is a spot called Bwlch Cynnydd (the huntman's pass). A note in passing before leaving the Bodtalog area – there is a bog called Gors Lwyd (Grey bog) nearby. Tradition has it that the waters of the young Elan once flowed, not towards the Elan Valley, but down to Cwmystwyth. The build-up of Gors Lwyd eventually turned it towards its present course.

On the boundary of Cardiganshire at the edge of Gors Lwyd there once stood a tollgate kept by an Eleanor Jones. During the Rebecca riots this tollgate was attacked on more than one occasion. A second attack took place on the 9th of October 1843 and the Chief Constable at the time reported as follows:

> *The attack on this gate took place on the 9th of October, 1843. The party arrived at the gate at about twelve o'clock, and having fastened the door of the toll-house proceeded to destroy the gate. The gate-keeper, Eleanor Jones, states she perceived from the window nine or ten men standing about the gate, with white shirts over their clothes; two of them were sawing down the posts and others were using axes...*

Robert Pugh, a farmer residing near Bodtalog, stated he was coming from Aberystwyth on the morning after the attack on the gate, between two and three o'clock, when about two miles from Bodtalog he saw a number of persons coming towards him, but who turned off the road when about one hundred yards from him. Then he counted nine persons and perceived that many had something white over their clothes. One of them had what appeared to be a large saw over his shoulders.'

All that is left now of the place is a slight indentation in the ground where the pigsty used to be. This spot is still called *Tyrpeg Neli* (Nellie's Turnpike). Another name for the same spot is Pen-rhiw-lwyd. When coming up from Blaen-cwm towards the Cardiganshire boundary, the old road (Rhiw-lwyd) can be seen set up on the hill to your right.

John Davies, Hirnant, Cwm Elan

A bubbling character full of wit, John Davies had a ready answer to all comments made to him, and set in his weathered features were two sparkling blue eyes full of mischief. He was born in the Tregaron area into a family with a strong shepherding background, who were of fairly poor circumstances. His mother was one of fourteen children.

The family home was called Glan-gors-fach, but was always referred to as 'Y Bwth' (pronounced 'booth', and short for *bwthyn*, which means cottage) and so in true country style, the young John was called 'Jack y Bwth'. John's grandmother – Bet y Bwth – is mentioned in a book by Cassie Davies called *Hwb i'r galon* (p.23). There she is described as a small lady, who was known to be meticulous in all that she undertook. She used to work on neighbouring farms in exchange for food and clothes for her large family. It is reputed that wherever she was, there was always merriment and laughter.

During this time, the little house was re-vamped, or re-built, and the old lady, John's grandmother, said of the new house, 'It looks like Buckingham Palace' such was the improvement, and the house thereafter was nicknamed 'Y Bucking', and John was re-named 'Jack y Bucking' – a name that stuck with him for the rest of his life.

He was initiated into shepherding from an early age and even took his sheepdog bitch with him to school, tying her in the toilet for the day, and then after school, going to help somebody with their sheep. This was a fairly common occurrence in days gone by. One of my relatives, David Rees (1891–1974) from Fagwr in Ponterwyd, started in the local school, and two of the dogs went with him. He was told that they were not welcome, and he had to take them to a nearby smallholding called Ty'n-bryn, to be tied up for the rest of the day. This happened on a regular basis for the duration of his schooling!

John Davies began his working career with an Evan Davies, who then lived at Bryn-glas, Camdwr, near Nant-y-maen, Tregaron. Evan Davies later lived at Tywi, where he died prematurely on the 12th of July 1949 (aged 63) from a cut he had sustained on his hand at a shearing, which later turned septic.

I have only a vague history thereafter of John, but I believe he worked for the Edwards family at Nantstalwen, then for the Jones family at Troed-rhiw-cymer, and for a short time with the George family at Nant-rhys. I think that the George family from Garth, Lledrod took over Nant-rhys, from Mr Waddingham, Hafod in 1918.

John, having worked in these outlying hill farms, would have gained an enormous amount of experience, and his knowledge of such a wide tract of land was second to none. He had memorised the names on these various mountains, and was probably the last to have retained them. Such a dreadful pity that nobody took enough interest to put

■ Mr and Mrs John Davies celebrating their Golden Wedding.

them down on a map, which means that these names, with enriched meanings that had survived for hundreds of years, have gone into oblivion.

In 1932, John married Annie Evans, from Gilfach, Blaen-Pennal, and lived at Troed-rhiw, Gors-neuadd, Tregaron before moving to live at Maes-glas and working for Mr William Jones. (Mr William Jones' grand-son, of the same name, farms Maes-glas today.) The family moved from Maes-glas to Glan-hirin in 1939, and to Hirnant in 1950. John and Annie had nine children. While at Glan-hirin (c.1942), they, like many others, had to abandon their isolated home because the area became a firing range for the army, and consequently they moved down to Aber-glan-hirin. They were shearing on a Friday and had to be out by Monday. They remained at Aber-glan-hirin till about 1948. In 1944 they went through the trauma of burying a set of twins, Nancy and John, who were born at Aber-glan-hirin. Annie was 40 when their youngest was born. I remember one son, David (Dai), who worked with a gang of hand-shearing contractors, at work in Glan-hirin in 1967. He cut the widest swaths that I have ever seen, and tidy to boot. He died in 1983, aged 47. John Davies was a dab hand as one could expect at training dogs and was especially good at starting youngsters.

I remember well him telling me in the late sixties when I was shepherding at Ty-llwyd, 'You'll have a job to understand these Radnorshire people'. He said with a chuckle 'they'll ask you after a gathering "How bist ye boy, have you any ship for we?"'

– meaning 'How are you boy, have you got any sheep for us?' A Capel Bangor youth, Alun Jenkins, who used to go up for the Elan Valley shearings, heard Tom Pugh say after a gathering at Bodtalog, when they were looking at the sheep in the field, 'Boy, boy, they be prime yows', and it took him a few seconds to work out that he meant the ewes were in good condition.

Around 1977, John and Annie left Hirnant to live at Pen-graig isaf, Ystrad Meurig, both within a few miles of where they were born. John continued to be active with his pony and dogs, tending to land he had at nearby Ty'n-graig and helping his neighbours. When they said that they would be doing something with the sheep the following day, the next morning John would have gone off early to gather their sheep, and they would be in the yard waiting! A truly good neighbour, a great character, and a person I wish I had questioned more when he was around. John Davies and his wife celebrated their Golden Wedding in December 1982. He passed away on the 18th of June 1987 aged 76 years. Annie died in January 1988 aged 80.

Prior to John Davies coming to Hirnant the place was shepherded by Jim Worthing. His father, John Worthing, was a tenant there. They were there before the 1st World War. After the death of his father, Jim took over the running of Hirnant. The family had a farm called Dôl-agored, near Builth Wells, and the sheep from Hirnant were walked down there to be shorn in the twenties and thirties.

Jim had ideas that differed from the Elan Valley farmers, and it was he who planted the ever-green trees that are seen by the roadside around Hirnant today. He also had a fetish for white stones, which he carried from good distances to incorporate in the walls around the farm. It was considered a lucky omen to have a white stone in the wall of a house years ago. White stones were also used to mark paths, which were especially useful when there was thick mist, or at night. There were such stones on a path leading from Claerddu to Ysbyty Ystwyth. Tom Jones, from Claerddu died in 1935, and was the last of the family that had been there for a hundred years. There is also a row of white stones from the foot-bridge crossing the Elan to the house at Aber-glan-hirin.

Jim took on the job of postman in the Elan Valley area before the coming of the mail van, to help supplement his income. There is nothing new in diversification, or conservation, as this man proved. His one wish had been that he would die on the road, saying that if he died in the house it might be a while before anybody found him. On his way home from Rhaeadr his last wish was fulfilled. Jim was a batchelor, and died c.1951, aged 68. Since none of John and Annie's children were born at Hirnant, and the fact that Jim Worthing was a batchelor, no-one can recollect a child being born at the present house until, on the 12th of July 2000, Morgan, the first son of the current occupants, Clive and Gail Hamer, was born, possibly making him the first child to be born in the present house.

Lewis Rees

Moving west to the Ystwyth Valley we come to the farm of Blaen-cwm, which until 1918, was the home of Lewis and Jane Rees. Lewis Rees was born in a place called Hafod Lydan in the Llangurig area, one of eight children. His father worked as a carrier for the Clochfaen Estate and his mother, born at Cwrt, Cwmystwyth, used to work at the Cwmystwyth lead mine when she was eight, for a penny a day. In the *Welsh Gazette* 11th of February 1926, it is stated that a Miss Ann Parry who died when 87 years old at Penpompren, Ysbyty Ystwyth, was the last woman to work in the lead mines. She was born at Dôlchgennog, Cwmystwyth.

Lewis, like a lot of his contemporaries, worked for a period in the coal mines of South Wales and in the local lead mine before becoming a shepherd at Blaen-cwm. Jane Rees was born at Penbryn, a row of seven houses just above Blaen-cwm – one of which was a shop at one time, and all of which have disappeared by now.

Lewis and his father were going to fetch sheep from a good way off when Lewis was a youngster and, passing through the village of Cwmbelan very early in the morning, Lewis caught the smell of somebody frying bacon and said to his father 'That smells good'. 'Well, draw on it my boy, that's all you'll get till tonight' was his father's reply! Many years later when Lewis was at Blaen-cwm, he was driving a fresh bunch of sheep to Ty-llwyd where shearing was in progress, and suddenly the shearers heard Lewis shout 'Help! Help!', and they all rushed out to see what was wrong, but it transpired that Lewis had bought a new dog – called 'Help!' During this time, Mrs Jane Rees had a set of stainless steel knives,

■ Lewis and Jane Rees, Blaen-cwm and Blaen-hafren.

when it was a rarity to have something new, and was obviously quite proud of them. When she was away one day, and Lewis left to his own devices as regards his food, he came across these knives and found them to be rather blunt, so he set about sharpening them, which put paid to their stainless quality, and he was justifiably scolded when his wife came home.

They moved in 1918 to Blaen-hafren in the Llanidloes area, a hill farm near the summit of Pumlumon. In his book *The Beauties of England and Wales* (1812), J. Evans wrote: '...we reached Blaen-hafren, a farm house, if such it can be called, occupied by a Mr Edward Rowlands, who has no enclosed land, but pays as an acknowledgement the sum of £10 per annum, the rent of the range of mountainous pasture for his sheep. These, apparently a peculiar race, are horned, slim in the carcase, small handsome faces, and remarkable for the size of their tails.'

Lewis was earning about 18 shillings a week at this time. Their daughter Martha (Matt or Mattie) who lived with them, was renown for her prowess with dogs and horses. A strong, strapping girl, who according to my information, had toothache and measles at the age of twenty-two, and was attended to by a Llanidloes doctor who, when asked to see her again, refused to come out. Mattie died soon after on the 26th of July 1932. As can be imagined, Lewis Rees felt very angry towards the doctor concerned, but in the latter years of his and Mrs Rees' life, only that doctor was deemed good enough to treat them. Forgiveness is a wonderful virtue. Lewis and Jane Rees moved from Blaen-hafren around 1934/35 to a farm called Belan Trybedd, and later to Lluest Las, Llangurig, where they lived until they passed away. Lewis died in 1958 aged 86. He was highly thought of as a shepherd, and his wife Jane, known for her hospitality. They were the last family to live at Blaen-hafren – of which there is now no trace except the site where it once stood – and the land has been incorporated as part of the 10,000 acres that the Forestry Commision has planted there. These outlying farms were very often visited by shepherds and farmers crossing from one area to another. The shepherd's dogs' barking was a cue for the wife to put the kettle to boil and prepare a meal for the hungry traveller. Times have changed, with visitors being offered today what I call an 'urban cup of tea', accompanied by nothing else!

Lewis and Jane had four other children – Margaret (Marged), Edward (Ned), Richard (Dick) and Jack.

■ Martha Rees at Blaen-hafren.

Margaret Jane Rees

Marged Jane, who I will always remember as a most beautiful character, started her working life in Lluest-dôl-gwiail, about two and a half miles from her home, towards Llangurig, with Evan Griffiths and his family. A tarred road was made to Lluest-dôl-gwiail in 1967/68 when the place was a ruin. I often wonder what a boon it would have been to the families that had lived there in the past, to have had a level metalled road along which to come and go.

Marged often related the tale of the Griffiths' two boys Evan Owen and John, when they were aged about five and three and a half, getting lost one evening, and she set out in the dark to get help from Blaen-cwm or Ty-llwyd, but met with a tramp who said he had seen two little boys who had obviously been crying but had left them alone in case they would be frightened of him. She took him back to Lluest and Mrs Griffiths asked if he could go back to the spot where he had seen them. He said he would if Marged would accompany him. She went with him, which must have taken a lot of courage as he was a rough looking stranger. After they had walked a good distance, they came upon a local farmer/dealer called Richard Morris of Rhos-y-rhiw, Pontrhydygroes, who had been to a fair at Llanidloes and he had both children on his pony. The tramp was as delighted as anybody to have found the children and was given food and shelter at Lluest that night. He was given two shillings to see him on his way next morning and, to show his genuine good nature, he gave the boys a penny each.

When the Griffiths family moved to Braich-y-fedw in the Staylittle area in 1916, Marged moved with them. She then moved to Glyn Hafren and was there for seventeen years with the Evans family and again moved with them to Oswestry on their retirement. She then moved to work with a branch of the same family in Ebnall Lodge at nearby Gobowen. The Raw family had several times asked her by word and letter if she would come to Ty-llwyd, Cwmystwyth, to work and in 1938, she agreed. She remained with this family till her death on November 17th 1989 aged 89 years. She was presented with a long service medal by Prince Charles at the Royal Welsh Show in 1988. Marged Jane's role in life was one of caring, and she had seen many changes in her life, always appreciating many of the modern facilities which came her way. Towards the end of her life she said she missed many of the characters of Cwmystwyth and surrounding areas, and although she made friends with most of the incomers, she felt the depth of conversation was not the same. At her funeral there were two people who I thought spoke a lot for her life, to both of whom she had been a nanny and a friend – one was past his seventieth birthday (Mr Steven Griffiths, Braich-y-fedw, Staylittle, born in 1918) and the other, a teenager (James Raw, Ty-llwyd, Cwmystwyth, born in 1976). People meant a great deal to her and she knew them well (and their ancestry) from Oswestry to Lampeter, and I often jestingly say that those she did not know, weren't worth knowing!

■ Margaret Jane Rees with her long service medal.

One of the highlights of Marged's year was the May Fair held at Rhaeadr, where she would meet umpteen friends, and catch up with the happenings in that area. She would work herself up before going, to ensure that she had not forgotten anything, and that everything would be all right at Ty-llwyd till she came back. Off they went once, with James Raw (1893–1957) driving, and when they were near Pen-rhiw-wen, Marged shouted, 'Boss, boss, I've still got my slippers on!'. It was a point of no return, so the first task Marged Jane had to do in Rhaeadr was buy a new pair of shoes!

She had, like a lot of people born in the hill-shepherding areas, a fantastic memory, and exceptional sense of observation. She was like a time machine, able to take you back to the events in the last century in a twinkling, because of what she remembered her grandmother talking about.

Her father, during the course of his work sometimes went to the outlying farm of Claerddu, in the Ffair Rhos area, to fetch sheep back or whatever, and was always given material to take home to make a frock for Marged Jane. Marged remembered the religious revival of 1904/05 at Blaencwm Chapel and Miss Jones, Claerddu, under the emotion of revival was singing and rejoicing to the extent that Marged (who would have been about four years old at the time) asked her mother 'Why is Miss Jones making such a lot of noise today?', to which her mother replied, 'Be quiet, or you might not get another frock from her'. Blaen-cwm chapel was demolished in 1971. A bungalow called Y Gorlan (the fold) was built on the site, and it was here that Marged Jane and Mrs Raw spent the twilight of their many years together.

There were at Ty-llwyd maybe a dozen to eighteen hens when I was there and Marged had a name for each one and such was her power of observation, that she recognised the egg of each one! She often recollected the times when she and a gang of locals used to walk from Ty-llwyd to be joined by the family of Tymawr and others to go to concerts or services at the Chapel or the church of Eglwys Newydd in Cwmystwyth. The miles or cold weather were shed off by the warmth of this communal spirit. She told me once that she had met Jim Lewis, Tymawr on a Wednesday, and part of their conversation went like this;

> *'Did you see that car that went up last Sunday?'*

which proved how infrequently cars passed years ago, compared with today when dozens, if not hundreds per day go that way. She told me an old weather related saying which is almost one hundred per cent true, which I had not heard previously – '*O farrug i wynt, o wynt i law*' – which, translated means 'From frost to wind, from wind to rain'. At the same time she also said that her father, when going about his work in the springtime, would see the black buds of the first stages of the cotton grass (*penllwydiaid*), which is one of the first plants to grow after the winter. He would pick one and put it in his hat as an indicator that spring was not too far away. Since that time, I have every year religiously done the same thing – not only to preserve the tradition, but to bring to mind a truly wonderful person. It was believed by the old people that this stage of cotton grass was as good for the sheep as oats is to a horse.

Marged Jane was laid to rest beside her parents and sister in Llangurig cemetery, to the left of the gate as you enter. I wonder if Prince Charles realised how great a hand he shook in July 1988 – a hand that notched 74 years of loyal service.

Edward Bonner Rees

Marged's brother, Edward Bonner Rees, of Pengarreg, Elan Valley, who was born at Blaen-cwm and baptised in the chapel there, moved when he was four and a half years old to Blaen Hafren, in the upper reaches of Llanidloes, where his father shepherded for the Evans family of Glyn-hafren. His older brothers and sister had a basic schooling, but because of his age, and moving to an isolated area, he had very little, if any, formal education, but developed into a sound personality, on who's opinion you could depend. His observation was second to none, and if, when gathering he saw an un-earmarked lamb (*oen gwyn*) with a stray ewe, he would pick it out hours later from among hundreds of similar lambs. Men like that are rare. Education is not a substitute for intelligence.

Ned, as he was familiarly known, went to work at Eisteddfa-fach, Ponterwyd at £15 for the first year, £20 for the second and £26 thereafter for about four and a half years, but came back to help his father after the death of his sister Mattie (1932) and worked at various places including Hengwm-annedd where Richard Morgan and his wife Sarah Jane lived. They had lost their adopted son a few years previously. Ned gave them a hand with the harvest and peat-cutting as well as carrying meal and provisions from Nant-y-moch – their nearest neighbours three miles away. He also fondly remembered the potato cake Mrs Morgan had waiting for them after a hard day of cutting peat.

Peat-cutting was a very important job on all upland farms, as this was sometimes their only fuel. This work was usually done in May or June, depending on the weather, so that it was allowed to dry over shearing. The peats were turned, one would be laid flat, with two on top so that they were diagonal to the ground. In a few days' time, four would be raised (so that they formed a pyramid-like structure) with one laid flat on top, always allowing about eighteen inches between each stack (*crugiau*) for sheep to pass without knocking them over. Peat varied a lot in quality – some with a lot of fibre to it, while another was very solid and became rock hard. The fibrous ones were handy if you wanted a quick flame to bring a kettle, or pot, to the boil. Sometimes the peat was a long way from the house and had to be hauled by a rough sleigh, occasionally down very steep gradients. Tracks often had to be made to ease the job of hauling. Prime examples are to be seen at Blaen-myherin – one of which is still known as '*ffordd fawn Jim*' (Jim's peat track), cut by a James Powell who lived there around 1900. Another is to be seen above Gelli Uchaf (commonly known as 'Quick') Ponterwyd where my great grandfather Thomas Howells carried peat from the top of a steep hill, and it took several of his numerous children to hold the sledge back on the downward trip. Somebody once asked how he coped with all his children, to which he replied 'We nurse a bit of the younger ones and the rest look after themselves'. Once the peat had formed a crust, it would repel a lot of rain.

■ Ned Rees and his family taken at Tyrpeg-y-mynydd c.1949. Left to Right: Ned Rees, Bessie Rogers, Blodwen Rees with Bonnie, Mrs Alice Evans (Blodwen's mother), Front: Pat Rees, Margaret Rees.

Many of the peat cuttings are still known by the names of the farms that used them years ago. For example, on the land of Lle'r-neuaddau there is a *Ceulan fawn Siop Ceiro* (peat cuttings of Siop Ceiro) – a small farm three miles nearer Ponterwyd.

Returning to Ned Rees, in 1935 he helped to move Richard Morgan and his wife to a farm called Cae'r Arglwyddes near Talybont. It was with Richard Morgan that Ned saw his first Border Collie, or 'Scotch' dogs as they were known – a bitch called Queen. He worked afterwards at Glyn-hafren (his sister Marged being there at the same time) moved with the family to Oswestry in about 1938 and then moved back to the hills at Claerwen in the Elan Valley to shepherd for his brother Richard (Dick). He then moved to a farm called Lluest-aber-caethion in 1942 because they had to evacuate Claerwen due to army training manoeuvres, and was there for four years, still shepherding for his brother. He then moved again to Tyrpeg-y-mynydd or 'Hill-gate' as it is sometimes called as there used to be a tollgate there at one time. It is also known locally as 'Trympeg'. One of the gate keepers many years ago was a Thomas Hughes, great grandfather to Tommy Hughes Aber-glan-hirin. Thomas Hughes used to walk with the takings of the tollgate to Presteigne, the main town of Radnorshire (a distance of about 30 miles).

The Rees family were there in the violent storm of 1947 and their son Bonnie was born in January 1947 and it was such a task to keep the family warm that Ned had to burn a lot of the interior wood from the outbuildings. Simon Jones in his book *Straeon Cwm Cynllwyd* relates how he had to burn the piano for the same purpose. The daily trek to Claerwen in all weathers to tend his brother's flock must have been quite a trying one at times.

Old Lewis Rees, when he was living at Lluest-las, Llangurig would ride up to 'Trympeg', stay the night, and then set off next morning to attend the shearing at Claerwen, and see his other son Dick and his family. One can only imagine the total pleasure this old shepherd had over these few days, seeing his family, and a host of old friends.

In May 1954, Ned moved to Pengarreg, where he stayed till his death on the 16th of July 1994, aged 80. His wife, Blodwen, died the previous October, aged 86. She was the daughter of Tom and Alice Evans Aber-gwngu. She was born at Aber-glan-hirin, as was her sister Ethel, the family then moved to Pengarreg (so Blodwen had lived there twice) and then to Rhaeadr. Blodwen was in London for twenty two years. Her other sister Mary (Polly) who was born at Dôlfeiniog, now beneath the waters of Elan Valley, became the wife of Bill Pugh, Bodtalog.

It is difficult for us today, with all the injections and doses available to us for various ailments and conditions, to imagine the trial-and-error medicines of yesteryear and it is thanks to the memory of people like Ned Rees that we are able to hear about them. A great loss that worried shepherds of old was the losing of ewe lambs that were to be the replacements of the following year, and these were some of the 'cures' that he told me about. One was that the ewe lambs were given a drench of pig manure and water, and another was that a spoonful of turpentine was put on the loins, and also that the tip of the tail was cut. Another person who believed in cutting off the tip of the tail was Tom Morgan, Nant-cae-rhedyn, Ponterwyd, to get rid of the watery end of the tail. Long tails can cause a lot of grief, if not death to sheep when there is snow on the ground. The bit dangling in the snow gathers a ball which grows bigger and heavier, and can sometimes, when the ewe lies down to rest, actually freeze to the ground, rendering her unable to move, and therefore without nutrition and at the mercy of the elements.

In mentioning diseases, a 'new' illness in sheep came into Cardiganshire in 1902. It was caused by the 'Bot' or 'nostril' fly. The local name for it was 'snuff', because the larvae blocked up the sheep's nose.

Ned used to take ewe lambs to 'tack' (over-winter) to Llanfair-caereinion, the charge then being 7/6 per head. Blodwen Rees well remembered a lady, who I believe was called Jeanie, who worked at Claerwen. She had come there from the homes, salting not only bacon, but mutton as well. Another item which was bought by most people in winter was salt herrings (*sgadarn coch*) which Ned remembers being a half-penny each. These came in wooden boxes or sometimes small casks, and were a great asset to vary a bit of the diet which was rather repetitive, yet mananged to make many people healthy, and live to a ripe old age.

Frank Pugh

Another character that lived at Tyrpeg-y-mynydd was called Frank Pugh, who was well known for his craftsmanship in making handles for all sorts of tools. Most of his raw material was carried on his back from the Wye Valley, as precious little wood grew in his home area. He was known to be careful of his pennies, as he obviously had to be in bringing up a family of 8 children, and I was told by Bill Pugh, Bodtalog that at the end of his life he had quite a sum of money by comparison to his circumstances. Unfortunately I do not remember the amount, but a lot of effort had been made to make ends meet. It was Frank Pugh who told Ned Rees the way to Claerwen, taking note of every hillock, dip, rocks etc. and as Ned said, you would have to be very dull not to find the place after such a detailed outline, such was the familiarity of the hill people with their surroundings.

In mentioning the scarcity of trees in the uplands, most hill shepherds would, during the winter months, allocate a day to go down-country into the valleys to cut sticks, and as some areas were better than others, there was a bit of secrecy as to where you went.

■ Mr Frank Pugh, Tyrpeg-y-mynydd in 1933, with a shed full of peat in the background.

In the Tregaron area, when questioned as to where you had cut a good stick, the evasive answer 'In Nant-y-Maen woods' (*Allt Nant-y-maen*) was given – Nant-y-maen was a hill farm where hardly any trees grew! A good ash stick with a root that formed a head was much sought after, as well as mottled hazel to make shafts for horn crooks. Rams' and cows' horns were not wasted but used in the making of shepherds' crooks, buttons, whistles and handles for knives and tools. Cow horns especially were used as hand grips for peat irons, as containers for lard and sand when scytheing, as shoe horns, and as funnels for liquid. It was very often a case of 'waste not, want not'. A passable whip was made out of a bull's penis. It was hung to dry with weights attached and could inflict quite a painful blow. Small gorse bushes were used to clean chimneys. A piece of string with a stone attached was dropped down, and the gorse pulled through. These gorse bushes were brought near the house and used to brush mud from boots. Flour sacks were washed and used to make aprons, and the soft cotton ones were used to make undergarments. Unfortunately, the maker's name was difficult to remove and many an apron had inscribed across the front the brand name 'As you like it'!

■ Mr and Mrs Frank Pugh, Tyrpeg-y-mynydd in 1933.

Richard Rees

Richard (Dick) Rees was born at Penbryn, near Blaen-cwm and went to school at Cwmystwyth for a period before the family moved to Blaen-hafren. He went to work in Glyn-hafren and then came back to Ty-llwyd to work for five or six years. While employed here he attended a shearing at Aber-gwngu, and there met Winnifred Ann Lewis (familiarly known as Winn) his future wife, and probably because of this attraction, went to work for her father William Lewis at Claerwen.

Annie Lewis, born on the 23rd of March 1873, was Winn's mother and a sister to David Evans, Aber-gwngu, who's children and grandchildren still farm there today. David Evans, Aber-gwngu, became the official sheep counter with the Birmingham Corporation. The Evans family came to Aber-gwngu in about 1875. William Lewis' father Thomas was shepherding at Claerwen for the Lloyd family of Nant-gwyllt, and had been asked to do something with the sheep to which he could not agree, and therefore left to live at a place called Blaen-methen on the land of Henfron, Elan Valley. The family were there for a short time only (probably 2 years) but it was here that William was born, and they returned to Claerwen when he was still a baby.

William and his brother Edward were outstanding runners, and this was told to me by the late William Owen, Ty'n Ddôl, Ffair Rhos, a friend I miss very much because of his vast knowledge of the history of the hills above Pont-rhyd-fendigaid, and his knowledge of ear marks especially. There was a genial welcome at Ty'n Ddôl with Mrs Mary Owen enriching the conversation, because she also came from hill stock. The Lewis brothers used to go to the hill armed with only a head collar, and after spying a group of wild ponies, and probably getting them into a position from which they had to run through boggy land, they ran them down, caught one, and were able to ride it home. William Lewis, for all his athletic prowess when he was young, became seriously crippled by arthritis as an old man. Claerwen was very much a half-way house to shepherds and farmers going about their business, and there was hardly a day without there being somebody extra for meals. During the season, night lines were put in the river ensuring fresh fish next morning, to vary the healthy if rather mundane diet.

William's and Edward's sister Sarah married a Roberts of Frongoch. The Roberts family, I believe, came from North Wales and were in Frongoch in the early 1700s, if not before. They were referred to in one funeral report as 'the respected clan of Roberts'. Many of their descendants are still around today. When Sarah's husband died, Edward moved to Fron-goch. Other siblings of William and Edward were Mrs Margaret Parry, Dre-isaf, Ystrad Meurig; Thomas Lewis, Bridgend, South Wales; and Winnifred, who died during the massive snow-storm of 1895, which involved taking the coffin to be buried at Strata Florida, where several generations of the Lewis family are buried.

There was also another brother called Dafydd, and a sister who became Mrs Ann Oliver of Pengraig, Cwmystwyth, and her great-grandchildren still shepherd the hills around Cwmystwyth, giving people like myself the confidence that this way of life will continue for many years to come.

In mentioning Winnifred Lewis' funeral I should have said that the family had tried once unsuccessfully to take her body towards Strata Florida, but were beaten by the weather. Funerals from these outlying hill farms during the winter caused tremendous problems. The funeral of Evan Price (aged 80 years) from Nant-y-beddau which took place on the 8th of February 1902 was one that stayed in the memory of the local people for a long time. They started from Nant-y-beddau in the morning on the seven mile journey to Llanwrthwl under atrocious conditions, and it was dark that night when he was finally laid to rest at Penuel Chapel, Llanwrthwl.

Country funerals, then and now, bring whole communities together, as in the funeral of Daniel Price, Nant-y-beddau (Evan's son) who died on the 8th of August 1928 aged 65. There were one hundred and ten horses following the coffin from the house to the Claerddu ford, where some of them turned back for various reasons, and from there on towards Strata Florida, there were 87 mounted mourners.

In 1942, Dick and Ned and their families (both were living at Claerwen) had to move down to Lluest-aber-caethon with very little notice, because of the military training. Shells were being fired from Beulah to Pen-rhiw-wen, and some fell short, actually damaging Claerwen house. The present house of Claerwen was built in 1922. Dick was always renown to be at the right place at the right time during a gathering. Most hills have certain points where you can see either a good distance, or into hollows where it is very easy to miss a bunch of sheep. A solid piece of advice I was given years ago was to always look back every now and then as you go along. In May 1947 Dick and his family moved to Lan-fadog, to work for the War Agricultural Committee, still shepherding Claerwen, and about two years later he was given the tenancy of Lower Lanfadog. With the death of Mrs Winn Rees in 1963 the tenancy of Claerwen came to an end, therefore cutting the long Lewis connection. (Incidentally, Claerwen is the nearest point of Radnorshire to the sea.) The Rees family have made a valuable contribution to the shepherding community – their stable, solid way of living and their fantastic ability to memorise and re-tell their tales make many people, who are considered clever, look very insignificant, considering the many disadvantages they had. A gentleman, for whom I have great respect, said of the Rees family, 'They couldn't think crooked, even if they wanted to' – which is as great a compliment as can ever be paid to any family.

Dafydd Evans, Esgair Wen

Across the river Ystwyth from Blaen-cwm there is a cottage called Esgair-wen which was the home of our next shepherd. He was called David (Dafydd) Evans. Surnames did not count for a lot, and he was known to all as Dafydd Esgair-wen. He was born lower down the valley at a house called Aber-nant. He was a tall long-striding man who, when ordering his boots from the cobbler, said 'I want large elevens, with small nails'.

His wife Ann was a sister to the Reverend Michael Williams of Cilfynydd, South Wales. Dafydd had been shepherding for Mr J.E. Raw (1862–1940), Ty-llwyd for over 39 years and, as written in his obituary, 'faithfull and true, he well earned the title of the good shepherd'. He was much beloved by everyone who came in contact with him. He had spent much of his youth in Radnorshire. Dafydd was a shepherd at Gwern-arglwydd, Pen-y-bont by the Radnor forest, and probably lived at the Shepherds' Cottages in Cwm-bylchau. A great pity that his recollections of this era were not recorded. At the time of his funeral (he died on the 6th of May 1934 aged 76) Mr Moses Griffith – who had shortly before taken up his position as Land Director with the Cahn Hill Improvement Scheme at Pwllpeiran – asked a local wag and character called Dick Howells, Ty'n Rhos (1866–1941), 'Who is that man that is being buried today?' and was told 'That is not a man. That is a Christian! And they are as scarce in this area as apples on Pumlumon!' Dick Howells in his last years, told Morgan Griffiths, Nanty, 'Old age is a funny thing, when I was young, I used to put my hand on a gate and jump over it, now I couldn't jump over a hen's egg!' Dafydd was a faithful member of Blaen-cwm chapel, which was situated just across the road from Esgair-wen. It was built in 1857 and was demolished to build a bungalow in 1971. Dafydd's dogs on hot summer Sundays would creep into the chapel for shade, and he could be heard to mutter under his breath 'Get out dog' during the sermon.

A book written by the Dean of Edinburgh, Edward Bannerman Ramsay called *Reminiscences of Scottish Life and Character*, published in 1865, states 'In districts of scanty population, the congregation was made up of one half dogs, as each individual had a canine companion – as they had followed their masters through the labours of the week, they (the dogs) did not see why they should not share their Sunday observances'. In many churches years ago they kept 'dog tongs' which were used by the church warden to evict unruly dogs who did not respect the sanctity of their surroundings. Over 200 years ago in the Church of Llanddewi Abergwesyn, there were wooden dog tongs used by the bell-ringer to drag fighting dogs outside (*Cymru* 66).

Across the stream from Esgair Wen was a house, now in ruins, called Troed-rhiw, where Ann Evans (Dafydd's wife) had once lived, and another house further on, on the banks of the river Ystwyth called Glan-yr-afon. From the census of 1861, a Richard and

33

■ Left to Right: Dafydd Evans, Esgair-wen; Walter?; Richard (Dick) Rees, Claerwen and Lan Fadog. Photo taken near Ty-llwyd farm.

Mary Prosser lived at Troed-rhiw and again in the 1871 census it shows them to have six children with an age range from 4 to 19. Richard died in 1871, aged 44, from the effects of working in the lead mines. Mary (1823–1916) had to struggle to make ends meet and the late Mr J.E. Raw from Ty-llwyd stated that she never asked anybody for a ha'penny. Three of her sons went to America. One, Azariah (1857–1915) became a preacher. He emigrated when he was 24 years old and amongst other places was taught at the Moody Bible Institute of Chicago and was minister with the Calvinistic Methodist in Ethel, Montana. In 1905 he returned to Wales, and to Llanilar to look after his aged mother, who ironically out-lived him by a year. It is stated that one son became a doctor, but I have no proof of that. From hardship and humble beginnings many have made good of their lives, proving that cream always rises to the surface.

One of their children, Margaret Prosser, married a Thomas Parker on the 6th of February 1885 and lived at Shrewsbury. I wonder if there are any descendants still around? The fields around Troed-y-rhiw are still known as *Caeau Mari* – Mary's fields.

Moving down from Esgair Wen, we come to Ty-llwyd where Alfred Edwards had served three generations of the Raw family – Mr J.E. Raw, James Raw, his son and the recently deceased Jim Raw. The Raw family had come from Yorkshire to the Devil's Bridge area. They were living at a farm called Ty'n-rhyd at one time and there is a record of a Mr James Raw marrying a Miss Owen from Ystumtuen in 1827. In 1830 a James Raw was recorded as shopkeeper at Smelting House and later as Innkeeper at the same place, although it had changed its name to 'King William IV'. (It is known today as Rheidol House). He left to farm at Ty-llwyd circa 1833 and also to keep the inn there which was called 'The Lisburn Arms'. He was the grandfather of Mr J.E. Raw. According to one report there were no taverns in Cwmystwyth after 1849, due to the pressure of the staunch Methodists of the area.

Alfred was the son of Richard and Winnifred (nee Hopkins) Edwards. Richard Edwards had been a shepherd for Mr Waddingham of the Hafod Estate circa 1900 and it is with regret that I know very little about him, yet having been in a position to know almost everything, had I but asked.

Richard Edwards was given a medal by the RSPCA in 1938, when he was 66 years old, for rescuing a sheep from a cliff in the area (*Welsh Gazette*, 28th March 1938). He died on the 18th of March 1945 aged 73. Winifred (or Winnie, as she was known) used to smoke a clay pipe in her old age, and her favourite meal for supper was a thick porridge that was then put in the frying pan and heated. She died on the 27th of January, 1963 aged 89.

Alfred had worked at Botgoll, near Devil's Bridge for seven years. He was put before a tribunal for exemption purposes in 1917 (1st world war) and was described as a 'skilful shepherd of 700 sheep'. He spent one year at Dolfor near Trawscoed, which held the sheepwalk of Dôl-wen, above Devil's Bridge from the early years of this century, if not before, till 1928 when it was put up to let by the Hafod Estate. Dôl-wen grazed 1,387 sheep at the time. There is on Dôl-wen Hill a very rough piece of land, with a southerly aspect, facing the hill of Ty-Gwyn, where my father said that they were always able to find a fat wether, even in winter. This was most important to a family who were virtually self-sufficient. One record shows that in 1928, the family of Nant-y-maen, Tregaron, killed 12 wethers in a year for their own consumption. These, during the summer months especially, would be shared as the meat did not keep, and they in turn would get fresh meat when neighbours were killing. In very hot weather the meat was sometimes put in cold water for short periods, in an attempt to keep away the blowflies. Meat for the dogs was also kept in this manner.

Alfred then moved to Ty-llwyd where he worked and lived till his death in 1979 aged 80. He was there when I worked there in the late sixties, and I will not pretend that he was God's

■ Mr James Raw, Ty-llwyd, with his wife Annie in front of him, Margaret Jane Rees to his left and his son Jim in front of her. Ifor Edwards is on the right of the picture and Alfred Edwards on the left.

gift to new blood working there, but he had been there for such a long time that he probably found it difficult to accept others infringing on 'his' territory. He had a lifetime of experience and often said of Ty-llwyd, a hill farm with many steep slopes, that you were always 'pulling on your collar or holding on your breeching' – that is to say going up or down, and comparing this to work-horse traces. Another thing he said was 'Give the Welsh sheep plenty of time, and you can do what you want with them', and very often when I am working sheep in difficult places, and feel that they could move a little faster, these words come echoing back to my mind. It was Alfred who pointed out to me that sheep have a social order on the hills, inasmuch as they live in groups, or families in the same area. These would be in numbers of 15 to 25, and having got into the habit of counting these 'families' I was surprised to see that the numbers fluctuated only by a few each time I went round. It was at this time that the importance of observation was drilled into me, and I was often rebuked for any lapses. Many people, as Sherlock Holmes said to Dr Watson, 'see but do not observe'. These lessons were not easily forgotten, and have stood me in good stead many years later.

It is interesting to see in different people the degree of observation present in their characters, and many of these are descended from shepherding forefathers, some not

■ Group taken near the lead mines of Cwmystwyth. From the left: Byron Howells, London; Richard Edwards, Nant-Watkin (Alfred's father); Dick Evans, Ty Capel; Dei Evans, Esgair Wen.

even remotely connected with agriculture today, yet have a keen sense of observation. Many country characters I have known would have made better detectives than those employed by many police authorities, had they been channelled in that direction. Alfred, like many shepherds, was called upon for several years to kill about 5 wethers for the Evans family at Pwllpeirian (1947–1955) for their shearing food. He also killed pigs, but I was told that he became very nervous before the act of sticking the pig! He was blessed with a strong baritone voice, and called upon to sing at local concerts, and with his brother Ifor, and Tom Emanuel and his wife Dorothy of Lluest-dôl-gwiail formed an entertaining group called 'Parti Blaencwm' who were often asked to sing in social evenings, and especially at the 'welcome home' concerts for soldiers on leave or home at the end of the War (1939–45). This singing talent was probably derived from his mother's (Hopkins) side of the family, of which, many descendants have an interest in music. His voice was a benefit to the singing at his local church at Eglwys Newydd, and at the graveside singing of hymns at the many funerals he attended.

He also gave me another piece of advice which can be a life saver, inasmuch as when crossing slopes, which are frozen or partly so, wearing oilskin clothes can be a recipe for disaster, because if you lose your footing, these act as a sleigh, and could be dangerous, if not fatal. Before the time of being able to buy ready made waterproofs, or because they could not afford them, many of the shepherds' and farmers' wives made them from calico treated with linseed oil. Two of the last to be remembered to make these were Mrs Lois Jones from Blaen-myherin and Mrs Edith Morgan, Eisteddfa fach, Ponterwyd. My father had a pair of leggings made by Mrs Jones, and a row of buttons were provided to open and close them. My mother remembers making a pair for my grandfather in the mid forties.

I well remember how Alfred and I used to go over to Rhaeadr in my Morris 1000 (Alfred did not drive), and it was he who introduced me to most of the farmers and shepherds of that area, and as he was quite fond of his whisky, he was very jovial and talked incessantly on the way home. He went fairly regularly on a Saturday night to the pub at Devil's Bridge and very often would be the last in at Ty-llwyd, and automatically

■ Alfred Edwards. Photo by Norman Roderick Jones.

locked the door. However, on one occasion, I came home an hour later and found the door locked and despite shouting and knocking, could not get an answer. That night was the first time I slept in a very cold car, with only a box of *After Eight* mints for comfort!

One of the most unusual things that Alfred saw during his career were sheep being lassoed. A man, quite famous in the area, David Rhys Jones of Pont-rhyd-y-groes, had been born in Patagonia (there is a colony of Welsh settlers there). He was born on the 10th of June 1877 and died on the 9th of January 1946. He came from Patagonia when he was 14 years old, and could speak only Welsh and Spanish, but quickly learned English and became a qualified tutor in that language. He was an accomplished musician as well, and spent many years as headmaster at Pont-rhyd-y-groes. He was known generally because of his Patagonian connection as 'Jones Pat'. When on a visit to Ty-llwyd, Jones Pat walked down to the yard, which was full of sheep, and entertained the shepherds by getting them to point out a sheep in turn, and he would then throw a lasso around its neck with great accuracy – probably the first and last time such an act took place in Ty-llwyd.

He remembered being in queues extending way above Bodcoll when people from the Cwmystwyth area used to walk their sheep to the market at Devil's Bridge.

Some people at times would be surprised to see Alfred performing a hand-stand against a wall (this was in his younger days), but the explanation was that he suffered from a hernia, and this was his method of getting relief from it.

A minor triumph I had over Alf during my time at Ty-llwyd was that one day I had been on the hill, and came back and said that I had seen some black heath berries (*grug-lys*), or crowberries as they are often known. Alfred insisted that I must have seen winberries, and the argument got quite heated, till I stated that I would bring some back the next day. I did so, to prove my point, at which stage he had to admit that even after a lifetime traipsing the hills, he had not seen that particular berry before.

There was at one time a spade in Ty-llwyd, with a hole in it, and the explanantion for this was that Alfred and a neighbour were digging after a fox, which had been killing lambs, and David Evans, Esgair-wen, being a good shot, was waiting for it to bolt, but Alfred, seeing the fox coming out could not resist taking a swipe at it – at the same time as the gun went off!

Alfred had been a devoted shepherd throughout his life, and very true to the Raw family. They, in turn, gave him a good home, indeed, as part of the family, and looked after him in the twilight of his life, as was befitting to a 'good and faithful servant'.

In talking about Ty-llwyd, it would seem appropriate to record the untimely death of on the 25th of September 2001 of James Edward Raw (Jim) Ty-llwyd, Cwmystwyth, who died after a four year battle with cancer, aged 59. As was mentioned earlier, his family had been in the same farm since about 1835. I once asked Jim if he would note down on a map of the area, the names of various places, brooks, hillocks, rocks etc. on Ty-llwyd and Blaen-cwm land, as he was the only one working the area who knew of them, and thankfully he did, so these names are now preserved for the future, as many of them had never been written down, only handed down by word of mouth, and in serious danger of being lost. *Diolch yn fawr Jim.*

Within three months, another untimely death occurred on Sunday the 30th of December 2001 – that of Bonny Rees, Pen-garreg, Elan Valley, aged 54, and he was buried at St. Brides Church, Cwm-dauddwr on the following Wednesday under his 'proper' name (which many people did not know existed, as he was always called Bonny) – Edward Thomas Lewis Rees.

Bonny was one of the invaluable people involved in the gathering of sheep from many thousands of acres in his area, involving many farms. His knowledge of where the boundaries were, and where different lots of sheep were cut was second to none. His work, and his sense of humour will be greatly missed. People of his calibre are not taught in colleges, but in the College of Life, and a thorough college it is. I quote from his memorial card:

> *You left us quietly, your thoughts unknown*
> *You left us a memory we are proud to own*
> *Treasure him Lord, in your Garden of Rest*
> *For when on earth, he was one of the best.*

Predators

Foxes have been a thorn in the side of farmers and shepherds alike for a long time, especially at around lambing time. According to evidence I have heard from Miss Margaret Rees and Mr Jim Lewis, Tymawr, the fox population on the hill were not many, and they said that the news of somebody having caught a fox or indeed a litter of cubs, made news that was talked about for quite a while in years gone by. The damage they can cause can be quite disturbing, when one hears of farmers losing a third of their lambs, which was the case of a Cwmsymlog smallholder years ago who expected to have around 100 lambs yet 30 were killed in one year by foxes. There were probably two litters of foxes in the nearby woods. Foxes, badgers, crows and dogs cause a tremendous loss to the sheep industry every year. They all kill very differently. Crows, very cunning and wary birds, most often start with the eyes and tongue. In fact, some of the worst culprits I have seen, actually peck out the eyes and tongue before the lamb is fully born, rendering it helpless for them to finish off their dastardly deed. Even if the lamb has a protective mother, it is unable to suckle and therefore falls easy prey to marauding crows. They are probably the predators which cause most suffering in terms of the time it takes for lambs to die. Foxes are usually the cleanest killers. They usually go for the throat and suck the blood, which is then regurgitated to the cubs when they are a certain age. The tell tale signs of a fox kill is that the head is cut off, as is the tail. One pattern that they often use is to kill (sucking the blood), decapitate the body, and leave the lamb where it is, or partially bury it, and collect it the following night. Killing every other night is a pattern that denotes that the killer is a fox. Rhys Goch of Eryri (who died about 1420) composed a poem full of satire and derision at a fox which killed his favourite peacock.

A report in the *Welsh Gazette* in 1903 states that in 1788 in the Llanbadarn Fawr Vestry books – 'To Morris Evan Owen for killing an old dog fox and bitch fox with four cubs £1–2–6', which in those days was a princely sum. Another entry is in 1760 – '1/6 for killing a fox' and again in 1788, 'To the Miller of Wallog [near Clarach] for killing a bitch fox and three cubs 15/–'. The coming of the Forestry Commision to the area, led to an increase in the number of foxes. In the *Welsh Gazette* 1943 it states that there is an accumulating number of complaints about foxes harboured by the Forestry Commision, and in the same year a report says that 53 foxes were caught in one week by a hunt in Glamorgan. A white fox was seen in Cwm Rheidol in 1931. Ponterwyd farmers used electric lights (flashing) in 1938 to ward off foxes, but according to a local paper 'it was to no avail'.

Small-holdings used to, in a bid to keep off foxes, store human urine, and pour it over young lambs to safeguard them.

The Ponterwyd Fox Destruction Society records show that they caught 380 foxes in the area between 1946 (the year it started) and 1953.

Mr David Thomas, Eisteddfa and Mr Tom Howells, Gelli-isaf, Ponterwyd, many years ago caught a vixen and cubs near Dyffryn Castell and there were 23 lamb carcases in and around the lair. I once saw 13 carcases by Nant Llyn at a spot called Fainc Ddu while I was still in school, in the company of Mr David Thomas, Eisteddfa, and my father. The earliest cubs I have seen on Pumlumon were ones caught by my father and myself at a place called Craig-y-wledd (the rock of the feast) above Nant-y-moch on the 28th of March 1968, and they were about five days old at the time.

My father, having spent many years as trapper and shepherd for the Forestry Commision had had a great deal of experience in the ways of foxes, and his words were often, when having caught some magnificent down-country fox whose coat was in a glossy condition, and almost the colour of a Golden Labrador, 'It's a pity that they do harm.' These splendid specimens were a great contrast to the dark wiry little fox of the uplands. The biggest litter he saw was one of eight in the Machynlleth area, in the company of his brother-in-law Richard Jones, Cefn-maes-mawr, Derwenlas. A litter of nine were caught by John Jones from Talybont, a very experienced trapper, and Meuryn Davies of Devil's Bridge at a place called Nant-carreuau in the Myherin Valley. From this spot, many years later, a dog fox used to come and kill lambs every other night, regular as clockwork, in the Dyffryn Castell area.

My father's uncle, Edwin Howells, followed a fox from the very front of Dyffryn Castell Hotel to Craig yr Eglwys rocks in Hengwm-annedd after a fall of snow, a distance of five miles. We have been blighted by foxes coming from greater distances during the last decade, that is, that they have been carried from urban areas and let go in the country by people who, although well meaning, had no idea about nature and its intricate ways. These urban foxes were very dull compared to the indigenous population of foxes and were soon caught, because they had no fear of man, which was proven several times when they actually walked towards their hunters, and were shot. Their knowledge of their new terrain was nil, which tipped the balance of their getting away very much against them. One can but marvel how some of the experienced foxes, often an old dog fox, will shoot out of a plantation, even before the hounds have been released. They probably have had a close call before, and don't want a repetition. These country packs of hounds are very necessary to find foxes in the thousands of acres of blanket afforestation that we have in Mid-Wales, which afford more than ample cover for 'Reynard' and his family. To the majority of country people, keeping the fox population under control is a business and not a sport, an ingrained part of their nature to protect their flocks against predators. Many have little or no time for the 'tally-ho brigade' dressed in their finery and galloping roughshod over good agricultural land.

Another aspect of the damage foxes do is the fact that they used to kill sheep which were fully grown, for example lambs that had been left to winter on the hill, or weak yearlings. All the examples that I have seen took place in early January when these sheep were often at their weakest, and may coincide with the fact that the foxes were heading for the mating season, as all the culprits I have heard about were old vixens, with their hormones probably working overtime, and it may be significant that two of them had lost parts of their legs. Lambs left to winter on the hills are now few and far between.

One thing that is happening at present which is of great concern to me is that foxes and an increasing number of badgers are devouring the eggs and young of ground-nesting birds. There has been a significant decrease of red grouse in the area as well as curlews and lapwings, which were such a familiar sight years ago. The last black game I saw was on Bwlch-styllen land in 1973. Badgers seem to be encroaching on hill land, and in some places where they have not been seen within living memory. Because of their systematic way of finding food, badgers present a bigger danger to ground-nesting birds than the fox. I have a pet theory that badgers should be discouraged from inhabiting land more than 800 feet above sea level. To be quite fair to the badger, they are not as big a danger to lambs as foxes, but some rogue specimens have been known to kill quite a number of lambs. In my experience I have only come across three instances of badgers killing lambs, but have heard of a number of other cases. Their way of killing usually is to crush the skull of the lamb, and then, grabbing hold of the middle of the backbone till it is severed, they start to eat through that break. They usually take very young or newly born lambs. Badger cubs have not the aggressive attitude of fox cubs. The fox will often live in a badger earth and the badger, being a very clean animal, clears out his home every now and then, and fox droppings and hairs can be seen amongst the debris. Badgers often defecate near their kill.

Dogs killing sheep are another kettle of fish in as much as that they can kill any age range of sheep. Some go to kill and then may be harmless for a period and start again. Very often these are bitches who experience hormonal changes about a fortnight or so before coming on heat, and their normal behaviour changes if they are studied closely. Others may not get a chance to go free except every now and then, and unless caught on the job, may carry this pattern over a long period as in one instance where 25 to 30 lambs have been killed or maimed over a long period on about five different farms. One victim was left so badly maimed, with its intestines hanging out, that I had to shoot it to put an end to its suffering. One such example appeared in the *Welsh Gazette* in 1924 where dogs had been killing sheep in Ysbyty Ystwyth for the past 3 years.

Another aspect of killer dogs is the size of the attacker, which can vary a lot, or the number of dogs involved, making it difficult to put a pattern to these gruesome acts. One attack I came across a few years ago involving a terrier and lurcher had resulted in them running their victim into a swampy area, worried it quite a bit, and then proceeded to eat the entire shoulder down to the bone, while the sheep was still alive. In the hills above Tal-y-bont (North Cardiganshire) in October 1967 a strong alsatian bitch started killing sheep with a vengeance. In two separate incidents she tore the lower jaw from a potential victim and in another case yanked the foot and shoulder clean away from a sheep. Her reign of terror came to an end when the Llanwnen pack of foxhounds were brought into the area and she was shot by Mr Ieuan Jones, then of Ynyshir Farm, Eglwys Fach. He had started from home with only one cartridge, and had borrowed one from a friend! According to the *Welsh Gazette* (a paper which has proved to be a mine of information to me) in the autumn of 1899, a killer dog in the Llanilar area (south of Aberystwyth) killed two calves, sixty sheep and a number of chickens. He was shot by a

Mr Hiller at Cefngraigwen farm in October of that year, when a bitch in heat had been used as a lure. Several other cases spring to mind including the Afghan hound in the Tregaron area circa 1970 when I was a shepherd at Abercoed, Tregaron. Much time was spent in hunting and in meetings. She was eventually enticed into a cage and put down, much to everyone's relief. In Ysbyty Ystwyth in the spring of 1937 lambs were taken from certain fields and in one incident eight lambs were taken from one field overnight and found buried nearby. Was this the work of a dog? One killer bitch in the Talybont area, in 1909 moved a local poet to write about her deeds and predictable end. A dog killing sheep in Llanfihangel, Meirioneth which was shot on the 21st of December 1933, was reputed to have killed 150 sheep.

Predators have varied from times gone by, as can be seen from the following extract form Robert Burton's *Wales* p. 166: 'King Edgar, surnamed the Peaceable, imposed a yearly tribute of 300 wolves' heads upon Tudwal, Prince of Wales, and now the hills are covered with flocks of sheep, which are the only riches of this County' [Merioneth].

Thomas Emanuel, Lluest-dôl-gwiail (1904–1968)

This shepherd, already mentioned as a member of 'Parti Blaencwm', was a cousin to Alfred Edwards (both mothers being sisters). His parents married at Eglwys Newydd, Cwmystwyth on the first of November 1899, his father decribed as 'coachman' to the Hafod Estate. Many people with unusual surnames came into North Cardiganshire, either with the various mansions that housed the landlords of vast acreages, or as workers or managers in the local lead mines, e.g. Ball, Bennet, Barclay, Blackwell, Bonner,

■ Cutting peat on Captain Bennett Evans' land C.1951. Left to right: Gerald Davies, Arthur Evans and Tom Emanuel. Photo by Dr T. Ifor Rees, Bron-ceiro, Bow Street.

Bonsall, Dudlyke, Little, Lowe, Lumley, Mason, Oliver, Ferant, Wigley and Valentine. From 1800 onward other names came into the area such as Bray, Burbeck, Collins, Gill, Goldsworthy, Gray, Mitchell, Paul, Pickering, Pascoe, Raw, Rowe, Scott, Taylor and Vigis. Many of these married and integrated into the local Welsh community. There must have been a lot of fun in the communications as many of the locals had no English at all!

I had heard of Tom as a talented, colourful character, and of his wife Dorothy, who had such a powerful voice, that it was stated she could have sung alto for a whole choir if necessary. During the storm of 1947 Mrs Emanuel hardly saw anybody, other than immediate family, for about six weeks, and Tom said as a joke that he might have to put a halter on her in case she got frightened in fresh company! I asked their daughter, Mrs Elin Davies of Llangurig to make a summary of her parents' life, which is as follows:

Tom was born at Dólogau, Pontrhydygroes to David and Mary Ann Emanuel, later of Crugiau on the Hafod Estate. His father was head gardener at the mansion and his mother was a former parlour maid at Hafod. He was one of seven children.

In 1925, he married Dorothy Jenkins. She worked as a nanny to Mr Morris Davies' son Teddy at Pwllpeirian where Tom Emanuel also worked as a foreman for eleven years on the Cahn Hill improvement scheme under Sir George Stapleton.

In 1936, he moved to Prignant, Devil's Bridge. It was in that year that Llewelyn Phillips took over at Pwllpeirian from Moses Gruffydd. Mrs Emanuel was well known for her contralto voice. She had attended college under Sir Walford Davies.

Tom Emanuel had five children, two sons and three daughters. He was also well known for his brown dogs. During the 1947 snow-storm when he was a shepherd for Gareth Raw-Rees at Lluest-dôl-gwiail, his old dog Bob used to lead him home safe after walking down to Pwllpeirian for the groceries, arriving home about 12.30 at night. During that storm Bob also 'marked' a ewe under snow twelve feet down. She had been there from the beginning and had grazed all the ivy and moss around the little rock where she had sheltered.

His two youngest daughters were home from school from Christmas until Easter. That year he raised only fifty lambs on the hill.

In those days, the hills were all open, rivers and brooks being the only boundaries separating the different hill farms.

In 1950 he moved to Llangurig, where he managed a farm for old Jack Stirk. He then went as a farm manager for Mr William Davies, Pentre Farm, Capel Bangor. He worked for him at Henfaes Uchaf, and then at Tynllwyn, Devil's Bridge. His motto was 'a rolling stone gathers no moss, but you gain experience'.

His greatest challenge was to go somewhere where a flock of sheep had been run down, then he would build that flock up to a high standard. Then, once he had done this, he was ready to move on again.

Whilst at Lluest-dôl-gwiail he received the British Empire Medal, but at the time of the presentation, he was in bed with rheumatic fever.

The late Llewelyn Phillips (1914–1981) started his job as farm manager at Pwllpeirian, where he remained for twelve years, on the 5th of February 1937, being, by his own admission, a genuine 'low-lander'. He had his first contact with a hill shepherd, namely Tom Emanuel, and was given a proper baptism of fire by a severe snow-storm (at the end of February 1937). The storm came from an unusual direction, and the snow was wet and heavy, leading to thousands of sheep being buried and killed in Mid-Wales. He recalled how Tom, himself, and a black and white Welsh sheepdog called Turk went to the hills to look for buried sheep. Turk was a very plain working dog, and not without his shortcomings, but when it came to finding sheep buried under feet of snow he was worth more than his weight in gold. Some of these dogs who would be marking sheep under drifts for days on end, if not of the right temperament, would resort to their natural instincts and kill sheep if they were left to their own designs.

On one occasion, Pwllpeirian took sheep to the market at Devil's Bridge on a Wednesday, but failed to sell, and Tom was given the task of walking them to Rhaeadr on the Thursday, to be sold on Friday. When he worked for Captain G.L. Bennett Evans (from 1953 to 1963), he was the subject of an article in the *Farmers Weekly* (10th of February 1956) and was referred to there as 'the laughing shepherd'.

■ Lluest-dôl-gwiail.

Thomas Rhuddnant Morgan

He was born the son of David and Anne Morgan (nee Jonathan) who lived at Nant-rhys (1,273 acres in 1840). They were married at Eglwys Newydd in 1860, David aged 20 and Anne aged 24. Anne's father John Jonathan worked as a shepherd to Captain James Raw of Ty-llwyd, Cwmystwyth.

Tom had very little formal education. He attended Llangurig school, which was then held at Capel Uchaf. He was of a very intelligent nature, and in a short time became quite a scholar, but as circumstances dictated to him, as to many others of his era, he was called upon to work at home. Who knows what heights he would have reached had he had a fuller education? The Morgan family at Nant-rhys were shepherds to Thomas James Waddingham, who was the Squire of the Hafod Estate near Pont-rhyd-y-groes. Tom had a charismatic nature, was lean and long-striding with an imposing carriage as befitted a hill shepherd. He was very much a ladies' man, and in his youth would be absent from home for days when the mood took him on some romantic adventure. He was an accomplished poet and won at least two bardic chairs for work submitted to local Eisteddfodau. He also wrote articles to the periodicals of his time.

■ Tom Morgan, his wife Alice on the right, and Edith Clarke. Taken at Parc, Henllan, near Llandysul. The ladies are sitting in two bardic chairs that Tom had won.

■ My father, John Byron Howells, dipping sheep at Gelmast, Cwmystwyth.

About 1923 he married an Alice Price, from Gwar-coed in Lampeter, of whom I know very little other than the fact that she had strong religious inclinations. She also had a 'companion' called Edith Clarke, who probably had come from the 'homes', and was profoundly deaf. Edith lived with Tom and Alice Morgan throughout her life.

It was about this time that Tom had the job of Patrol Shepherd. This work was directly involved with the control and eradication of sheep 'scab' – a very contagious disease caused by a small mite, hardly visible to the naked eye, which lives on the skin surface, and causes intense irritation, which in turn leads to serious loss of condition, and often death. This disease is often prevalent during cold weather, and many times I have heard of sheep being 'compulsory-dipped' during the winter and actually freezing to each other in the draining pen. With scab being a notifiable disease, the dipping was supervised by the police, who, often with a watch in hand, made sure that the sheep stayed in the bath for the required minute. Many an officer was 'accidentally' splashed or given a severe soaking in order that they might leave, so that the work could be done at a faster rate! According to the rules of the Cardiganshire Agricultural Committee in 1936, 'the Patrol Shepherd should patrol the hills to look for stray sheep while dipping is in progress.'

There often would be a systematic gathering of several farms bordering each other so that the dipping would have the maximum effect. The job Tom Morgan did had its unenviable aspects inasmuch as he sometimes had to take farmers to task for not dipping, or reporting that they had affected sheep in their holdings, which sometimes made it necessary to take them to court to answer for their deeds. Tom lived at a house in Talybont called Craig-y-delyn (Harp's rock) and a local farmer, who had been summoned to court for a scab problem, said that the house name should be changed to 'Craig-y-diawl' (The devil's rock)! Thanks to the sovereign work of Tom and his contemporary John Erwyd James (the son of David James, Hirnant, Ponterwyd), who was appointed to the job of Patrol Shepherd in July 1910 at a meeting of the Cardiganshire Public Health Committee, the county was free of scab in any epidemic incidence during the late twenties and early thirties, with several years being noted as totally free of scab. The Patrol Shepherds of the time had to be very vigilant of sheep coming into the county, especially those being over-wintered. There was a report in October 1901 of a David Powell, Aber-sefin, Brecon, bringing into Cardiganshire 2000 sheep without the proper documentation under the Scab Order Act.

It was stated in 1910 at an agricultural meeting concerned with scab that it was important to have Welsh-speaking inspectors, as evidence was often given in cases solely in Welsh which was the first, and only, language of witnesses.

A Mr D.C. Roberts asked – 'Does the inspector understand Welsh?'.

Mr Llywelyn – 'No'.

Mr Roberts – 'That is a great misfortune.'

Mr J.T. Morgan said he did not think a single soul at Bwlch-styllen understood English!

(I believe that the last person who spoke nothing but Welsh died on the Lleyn Peninsula circa 1950.)

In 1902 the cases of scab ranged, in decreasing figures, from Meironeth – 127 cases – to none in Radnorshire and Pembrokeshire.

The early method of transport for the Patrol Shepherds was on horseback, and as many shepherds will testify, that is the most satisfactory method of covering vast acreages of hill land; especially when the weather is fine, one feels very close to nature. A shepherding horse was deemed best if it had a good stride, and a good splay of hoof, which was a great asset in boggy conditions. Many hill people used to abide by the old adage, 'No feet, no horse'. There are many stories of shepherds on horseback in misty conditions, virtually letting the horse take them home. It was good to find a stream, and then follow the flow of the water. Even so, in very thick mist or darkness, it was sometimes necessary to put a hand in the water to see which way the water was flowing. John Erwyd James was given a motor cycle to go on his rounds (1926). I was shown his diary for 1926/7 by his nephew Gomer Teifi James, Bont Farm, Ponterwyd, from which I take this extract:

> *Monday 24th of January 1927*
> *Visited and examined 122 sheep, property of William Morgans, Goginan-fawr Farm. Mr William Morgans was ill in bed. I was accompanied by his daughter Miss Morgans to the fields to examine the sheep, and in my opinion there were 12 of them affected with scab. They were not very bad, but could easily be detected. Miss Morgan said that all the sheep had been dipped twice last November. They intended to report them to me on Saturday, as they were suspicious about some of them, as they were rubbing themselves last few days.*

> *27th of January 1927*
> *Visited and examined 200 sheep the property of Mrs Morgan, Nant-cae-rhedyn, Ponterwyd – found everything satisfactory.*

Almost nightly he met and made a report to PC 32, D.J. Davies at Goginan.

In 1944, the Patrol Shepherd in Meirioneth was paid £4 a week, with £60 a year for travelling expenses. At this time the three trade-names associated with dip in this area were Coopers, McDougalls and Hewthorns. Prior to this, circa 1910, there were home-made recipes, of which, the following were the most popular:

■ Dipping box used at Cefn-gweiriog, Tre'r ddôl c.1901.

The twin dipping baths at Eisteddfa Gurig. Emyr Thomas and myself holding the protective covers which also acted as sides when dipping was in progress. Photo by Ian Sant, Goginan 1998.

    1) Quicklime and sulphur
    2) Carbolic acid and soft soap
    3) Tobacco and sulphur

I cannot vouch for the effectiveness of these concoctions, but they were ousted by the proprietary brands before very long. Columella, of old, wrote about washing sheep in a solution containing 'soap wort'.

The dipping baths deserve a little attention, and there were many variations on that theme as well. One of the oldest types I have seen were wooden boxes measuring 3 feet by 4 feet, and 2½ feet deep. Working with these was a strenuous and messy business, where the sheep had to be lifted into the bath, held in, and then lifted out onto a sloping draining area. Anybody who has handled wet sheep will know how heavy they can be; no wonder there were strong men around years ago. My father last used one of these dipping boxes at Blaen-myherin in 1938. There were two noted swim baths of concrete (built in the early 1920s) at Nant-llyn and Lluest-y-rhos. The bath at Nant-llyn measures 20 feet, and the sheep, by their swimming action, had a thorough dipping. The stone-walled yards (there long before the dipping bath) were built, according to John James, Nant-y-moch, by a man who walked up from Ponterwyd, five miles away, for a shilling (5p) a day. Although Father Time has taken his toll on many of them, others remain in good order, much to the credit of this unknown man's skills.

The best dipping bath I have used is at a place called Bwlch-y-garreg, near the Esgair Hir lead mine above Talybont. It is of an oval design, capable of holding 600 gallons of water, and about a dozen Welsh sheep at a time. A Mr Hugh Baker and his sister who lived in Wiltshire, bought a farm called Blaen-einion, above the village of Furnace, and it was Mr Baker, along with his shepherd (a Mr Charles Cooper who had worked on the Barcaldine Estate, about 12 miles from Oban in Scotland) that were responsible for building this bath in around 1923. It is still in use today, and probably will be for a long time to come because of its solid structure. It had for many years been the communal bath for many of the flocks grazing the hills above Talybont.

Probably the most efficient dipping system built in this area, was instigated by the Abermad Estate (near Llanilar, south of Aberystwyth). This was built at Eisteddfa Gurig, Ponterwyd, probably around the late 1880s. This system originally consisted of three baths, side by side, with the entire floor of the shearing shed, covered in blue flagstones, acting as a draining area. The Abermad Estate owned vast tracts of hill land (bought in 1886, when the farms were sold as part of the dispersal of the Gogerddan Estate, which belonged to the Pryce family), and therefore needed a system with a big throughput, and this they certainly achieved. The bath at Eisteddfa was modified from three baths to two many years ago, and thankfully, although the actual building above it has been demolished, the baths and draining pen are still there, and are used when the need arises

■ My parents and myself at Nant-rhys on the 2nd May 2004. Thanks to the Thomas family of Eisteddfa for the transport there and the photograph. This was virtually our last trip together, as my father needed residential care from June onwards. He passed away on Sunday, 19th December 2004, aged 82.

by the Thomas family, whose forefathers were employed as shepherds to the Abermad Estate.

The cost of installing a dipping bath (including drainage system and haulage) plus a sheep fold at Bwlch-styllen in 1939 came to £65.

I would like to return briefly to the Morgan family of Nant-rhys. They had a line of big strong sheepdogs, coloured in big black and white patches (*cwn brith*) which had originally come from Scotland, bought by Mr Waddingham, who then owned Nant-rhys. They worked in a plain manner without any 'eye', and were considered to be intelligent dogs. Lewis Morgan, Lluest-dôl-gwiail had one of this breed when my father was working there circa 1940, and he would say to the dog when they were seated around the fire at night, 'Bob, go and fetch a peat' and he dutifully fetched a peat for the fire. Around this time, Lewis Morgan fed white corn to his sheep on the hill (it was about £4 a ton at this time), and Bob would pick out and drive away any strange sheep that came in to feed on the corn.

Tom Morgan (the Patrol Shepherd) had a wonderful way with animals as the following tales will reveal. One day he was on his way to Aber-gwngu, where they were dipping, and the farm dogs ran out at the sight of a strange dog approaching, and Tom's dog got stuck into them, felling them left and right. Tom came onto the scene of the battle, and spoke to his dog, 'Well, well, you've come all the way to Aber-gwngu, and the first thing you do is quarrel with these little dogs', and his dog sank lower and lower with each word as if in shame. 'Now then, to show that you are sorry, jump up into that cart and sing for the people' – and jump up into the cart he did and started howling in earnest!

Tom was invited in for a meal, and his horse was put in the stable. After the meal, Tom was ready to set off, and asked a nearby lad to open the stable door, but not to touch the horse. The door duly opened, Tom gave a whistle, and the horse made a bee-line for him. On another occasion, he had asked the dog to sing for the old Mr J.E. Raw at Ty-llwyd (Jim's grandfather) and the dog duly set about his piece with gusto, but Tom told him, 'Mr Raw doesn't like loud singing – a little quieter please', and the dog obliged – in a lower tone!

Tom, as already mentioned, lived at Craig-y-delyn, Talybont, where incidentally he taught many youngsters to recite. He then moved to a place called Parc, in Henllan, near Llandysul, and afterwards moved to retire at a house called Bryn-tegwel at New Quay. Mrs Alice Morgan died on the 11th of February 1956 aged 74. Tom died in July 1962 aged 86. Both were buried by the west door of the church at Lampeter. Of Tom's literary and poetical works, I shudder to think what has happened to them. Rumour has it that Miss Clark's relatives came down to New Quay, and that there was a massive bonfire. In all probability, pages of history and local interest went up in smoke. As for his bardic chairs?

Ifor Edwards

Ifor, a brother to Alfred Edwards, on leaving school, went to work at Tymawr, Cwmystwyth, for a few years. He then moved up the valley to work at Ty-llwyd. This was originally only a temporary job, as he intended to learn a trade, namely carpentry, but as many know 'the best laid plans of mice and men' don't always get carried out.

Soon after he started in Ty-llwyd, Mr Raw sent Ifor up Llechwedd-isaf, the steep bank facing Ty-llwyd house, and Ifor set off at quite a pace. When he eventually came back Mr Raw asked him if everything was alright, to which Ifor answered in the affirmative. Mr Raw then remarked 'I don't know how you can say that, because you didn't stop to look!'

He was paid £11.00 a year for the first few years. In later years he became shepherd on Blaen-cwm, across the river Ystwyth from Ty-llwyd land. Ifor was passionately fond of singing, and as mentioned earlier, a member of 'Parti Blaencwm'. He stayed with the Raw family for 32 years, and afterwards went to work as head shepherd for the Pwllpeirian Experimental Husbandry Farm. He was there for 19 years until his retirement in December 1976. Being a car driver, his horizons were a bit wider then Alfred's, and he did quite a lot of travelling with his wife, Nancy (my father's cousin) whom he married in 1957. Ifor liked to change his car regularly. One of his early driving lessons was rather dramatic, and could have had serious consequences. Mr James Raw, Ifor, Tommy Hughes, Aber-glan-hirin and John Lewis, Ty-mawr, had gone over in 1952 to a shearing at Troed-rhiw-drain, Elan Valley. On the way back, Mr Raw asked Ifor to drive, and all was well until they were on the hill and nasty bends by Pont-ar-Elan, when something went radically wrong with the car, and it started going back, out of control. Tommy and Ifor jumped out, and the car turned on its side, with James Raw, who was sitting in the front, ending up in the back seat with John. None of the men were seriously injured, but it was a narrow escape.

I remember Ifor telling me how he nearly fell foul of one of Dafydd Lewis' (of Glan-hirin) jokes. He had gone to fetch some stray sheep (about 25 of them) from Bodtalog, and amongst them was a black wether, who was to say the least a handful to handle. It was common practice to keep one of these on a hill, and they were known as markers – easy to see in snow, and born as near as possible to the sheep boundary so that you knew when gathering that if you had got the 'marker' in, you could be fairly confident of a clean gather. These strong old wethers (apart from being the 'markers') kept a guard on the boundaries, keeping neighbouring sheep away, therefore giving the ewes their fair share of allocated land, which led to the old saying, 'It's the wethers that rear good lambs'. Dafydd had gone to help Ifor start on his way home, and had one of his dogs ahead of the sheep, in full control of them, despite the black wether's continued attempts to break away. When Dafydd thought the time was right, he started back

■ **Monarch of the Elan**. A black/grey marker wether from Aber-glan-hirin. About twenty years ago there were about 300 wethers kept on this upland farm, whereby today (2005) only about a dozen remain. This wether will stay on the hill for the length of his natural life. Photo by Seiriol Dafydd.

towards Bodtalog, and whistled his dog so that it came slap bang through the middle of the sheep, scattering them in all directions. Ifor had a terrible tussle trying to get them together, but did manage without having to call for assistance, which would have added extra mirth from Dafydd's point of view.

With the road passing through Ty-llwyd and Blaen-cwm, the dogs' work on the slopes was very often in the view of the passing motorist, which drew favourable comments and admiration, although unfortunately they also came when a dog was doing its worst, and there was a lot to live down after that.

Ifor had a very good dog at one time, and a farmer who was driving past, had seen the dog work, and taken a fancy to it. He offered Ifor £12. That was a lot of money in those days, and Alfred was advising him to sell, but to Ifor, the dog was a very valuable commodity, and he would be at a loss without it, and another of that calibre might not come along for a long time. The farmer left without the dog, and Alfred kept harping on that Ifor had made a mistake, but Ifor told him in the end – it loses in the translation – 'What's the benefit of selling my arse-hole, and having to shit through my side!'

I heard Alfred and Ifor recounting several times how, during some severe weather at lambing time, they took many lambs from their mothers in the in-by fields, put them into a building overnight, gave them a good feed of warm milk spiked with a little gin, and returned each one to its mother the next morning, having made a mental note of which ewe had which lamb. These lambs would most probably have perished, but were given a second chance thanks to their keen observation. By today things have changed dramatically in many aspects. I well recall a story about a farmer from the Cwmystwyth area, Tom Evans, (his hill called Ty-gwyn was a good distance from his home) actually having to drown orphan or ill-thriving lambs because he had nothing to give them. This was done for humane reasons, as opposed to hours or days of dying from hunger. It was noted that Tom Evans had an excellent type of speckled hill sheep on Ty-gwyn.

Ifor always told his under-shepherds or students going to the hill, 'Remember to take some string with you to tie the gates'. Sometimes they would come back saying that the *LandRover* had got bogged down, and his reaction would always be the same, 'If you buggers walked a bit more, you wouldn't get stuck!'

Ifor Edwards died on the 7th of November 1988 aged 80.

John Lewis, Tymawr

John Lewis, Ty-mawr was a jovial personality, with a booming voice and a hearty laugh that could be heard above any crowd, who, like his forefathers, had spent a lifetime in the hills of Cwmystwyth. He, like the Pughs of Bodtalog, showed me kindness and gave me encouragement as a youngster, with timely advice. It was the days of catching sheep to sort them, and often re-catching the same ones many times in the same day – not only tiring for the men, but also, I would imagine, stressful for the sheep. It would be easy for people like John to say 'catch that one' or 'that one' to youngsters, but that wasn't his style. John would merely nod his head in the direction of the ewe to be caught, and you got on with the job of catching without any pressure. They do say that it is the small deeds in life that show how big a man is. John was also very human, and when the veins on his temple started sticking out, it was time to hold your peace. There is a notion that a stout man is less taxing for a horse to carry than a lighter lankier person, and John fitted this picture to perfection. Most of his shepherding was done from the back of his strong cob-type horse 'Dick', and the image I still have when I think of John, is of the surefooted Dick and himself going over the rough terrain of Ty-mawr, with his two strong Welsh sheepdogs – Roy, a blue merle heading dog, and Lad, a driving/barking dog he bought from the Tregaron area. They made up a wonderful team for a hill gathering.

When I exchanged labour on behalf of Ty-llwyd at Ty-mawr, I was asked to stay on a particular part of the hill until John had covered the far end, and the horizons I could see from that point were Cadair Idris to the north and Y Drygarn Fawr, near Abergwesyn, to the south – a distance of nearly 40 miles as the crow flies. I have not been to that spot for over 30 years, but hope to go there in the near future – a journey that will surely bring back a lot of memories of happy days. Not far from this spot is a lake called Llyn Wngu, where John told me that geese from Ty-mawr and Ty-newydd used to be sent up over the summer to feed on the abundance of vegetation there in peace and quiet, before being brought home in the autumn to be fattened for Christmas. The keeping of geese was a sideline many upland farms dealt in to bring in a little extra revenue, at a time when things were lean, to put it mildly. They had their annual customers, but further back in time, there were dealers and drovers of geese, who bought them, walked them through warm tar, and then through sand to 'shoe' their feet for the long journey ahead.

The last drover of geese in this area was a William Davies of Aberbotgoll, Devil's Bridge, and he, like another old geese drover called Sion Gruffydd of Dinas Mawddwy, who used to drive 150 geese at a time to England, many times saw their charges take to the air, causing a lot of bother to chase after them and getting back onto the road they should have taken. Incidentally, geese used to be marked by making a hole in the web of their feet, at different points, to identify them from neighbours' geese.

John's main helper was his brother Jim, who farmed independently at Ysbyty Ystwyth. He and his wife Annie, were a great backup to John, who was a bachelor. I well remember Jim, after we had been gathering, coming from the back of the buildings and saying to me, 'Well Erwyd, I've just been doing something which I don't think you've ever done'. To my 'What was that?', he replied, 'Milking a mare', at which I had to confess that I hadn't. It was obviously a practice after riding or working a mare that was suckling a foal, to drain most of the milk which had been in her udders, as it was believed that this overheated milk made the foal scour.

It was very seldom you would pass Ty-mawr without there being sheep in the yard. The old house of Ty-mawr was where the present stable is today. John and Jim's father, Richard Morgan Lewis (1883–1946) was well known for his physical strength, and many people have I heard saying that he would put his arms on either side of an unbroken horse's neck, cupping his hands above its mane, and holding it there until it was totally subdued. He also used his strength to good effect when dealing with the gypsies and horse dealers that came to the famous fairs that were held at Ffair Rhos, where arguments broke out regularly. Some of Richard's contemporaries used to cut fresh sticks before going to these fairs, because they were better than seasoned sticks – inasmuch as they didn't bounce when they landed! What would Richard say if he knew that his great-grandchildren, Simon and Richard Emms, both strongly built, use their physical strength to play rugby?

John's mother Elizabeth (nee Williams, of Ty Canol, Pont-rhyd-fendigaid) had been home to Ty Canol to visit one day, and drove home in a pony and trap with a very young John as companion on a very dark evening. Coming along the road by Eglwys Newydd – an eerie place at the best of times – the horse stopped and positively refused to move on. John recalled that his mother, despite being obviously frightened, in an era when there was so much talk of ghosts, had found some reserve of strength to call out, 'Who's there?', and lo and behold, a feeble voice said 'It's only me'. It transpired that an old lady living at Pant-y-mawn nearby was on her way home, and hearing a horse coming had moved behind a tree to hide, but had not considered that horses have keen senses. John told me this tale about 60 years after the event, and still marvelled at his mother's pluck that night.

Shearing day at Ty-mawr was, as in most places, a big event, but there was a little extra at this shearing, because the children from the local school were invited to tea, and were also given a gift of money from the big-hearted owner.

There was an outside toilet at Ty-mawr with two seats. A lady, obviously from an urban area, who had moved to live at Cwmystwyth, came to help with the shearing food, and wanting to answer a call of nature during the day, went to the toilet, came out again, and asked one of the ladies 'Which one am I supposed to use?'.

John related many tales about the taking and bringing home of ponies from 'tack' in the lowlands. They sometimes took off along narrow country roads, and had to be pursued for a long time (on horse-back) before they could be turned back.

Ty-mawr was, and still is, owned by the Birmingham Corporation, because part of the watershed for the Elan Valley is on Ty-mawr land – as indeed is the source of the river

■ John Lewis, Ty-mawr, Cwmystwyth with 'Roy' on his right. Roy was the son of 'Bell', a notable blue/grey bitch that belonged to Richard Edwards, Argoed, Talybont. Photo by Edgar Smith.

Elan, which has the beautiful Welsh name 'Byrlymau Elan' (the bubblings of the Elan). The pitch mark for the farm was a square. Richard, John's father, bought a neighbouring hill called Dôl-twlc in the mid 1920s. Dôl-twlc had its own earmark, and a pitch-mark of 'H' after the family of Howells who had lived there for a long time. Across the river Ystwyth from Dôl-twlc there is a smallholding called Ty'n-ddôl, where in the early 1970s, a family came to live who had been involved with missionary work overseas, and John, passing by Ty'n Ddôl on his way to Dôl-twlc on a Sunday morning, heard hymns being sung there. In about 1750, Methodism started coming into the Cwmystwyth area, and under a lot of persecution, they had to meet in secret, and had worked out a code that a certain coloured garment was put on a certain bush on the day when a meeting would be held that evening. The venue for these meetings for a very long while was Ty'n-ddôl. They say that history repeats itself, and this is a typical example, even after 220 years.

John, in his youth, had gone down to Cwmystwyth to attend a social function, and one of his dogs had decided to follow him, which was not an unusual occurrence. Later on that evening, John had the company of a young lady whom he took to a secluded spot, but the dog, seeing his master going through unusual motions, started barking, which well and truly put a tin hat on that evening's romance!

I have been told that John only spent one night not sleeping at home in Ty-mawr, and that night (during the war years) was spent at Llaeth-dy, near Pant-y-dwr. He had some ponies on tack in that area, and had gone there the night before to stay with his cousin, Albert Edwards. Albert's mother was a daughter of Ty-mawr. John must have been like-minded to the person who wrote:

When I was young, I had no care
I never used to roam
I thought that beauty only dwelt
Amidst my highland home.

John's widowed sister, Lal (Mary Elizabeth Emms), came to live at Ty-mawr for a period, and made life a lot easier for him, not only to help with culinary matters, but also to provide a special companionship. I have been enriched by the many happy evenings I spent in their company. Mrs Emms later re-married and moved away to live in Deganwy, North Wales. John's other sister, Ellen Ann (known as Nell) married Mr Tommy Hughes of Aber-glan-hirin – a first class shepherd – to be mentioned again later. They had another sister called Gwyneth, who died as a baby, and was buried at Eglwys Newydd on the 10th of April 1923.

Jim Lewis died in May 1985 aged 68, and as a close friend said, John was not the same after that, after losing a brother, a friend and a workmate. In May 1986, after an angry and relentless spring, many minor problems seemed to accumulate on the shoulders of the ageing John, and he chose to leave this world by his own hand, within days of his 74th birthday.

Tom Williams (1916–1989)

Tom Williams was of a humorous nature and was very quick to see the funny side of a situation. His quiet spoken manner seemed to accentuate the hilarity, and had his friends in stitches. He worked in his early years at Llwynglas in Talybont, and possibly at Pen-cefn, Capel Seion, but soon headed back to the hills of Cwmystwyth, where he was born, and spent the rest of his working life there. He was at Lluest-dôl-gwiail in 1932 and possibly afterwards at Ty-llwyd. A period was spent in the company of his brother David John driving sheep for two local dealers – Richard Lewis of Erwbarfau, Ponterwyd and Richard Morris, Rhos-y-rhiw, Pont-rhyd-y-groes. They bought sheep from the markets at Tregaron and Devil's Bridge, and these would be driven to a holding field at Cwmystwyth, and then driven on a Thursday to be re-sold at Rhaeadr on Friday. Tom had, as I remember, some very good dogs, and had, as do most hill shepherds, some heading dogs and always one that would 'course' (drive) the sheep away, hence Tom's well known saying that he had 'a dog for every occasion'. He used to enjoy competing at local sheepdog trials, especially the one at New Row, Pont-rhyd-y-groes – how successful he was, I can't remember. His great side-kick, and friend, as far as dogs and trials were concerned, was Mr Richard John Howells (known locally as Non Howells), who had worked as a banker in Cheshire, but came to retire at Pant-llidiart, Bryn-afan, where he and his wife had local connections. He used to visit Pwll-peirian regularly to give the dogs a workout, with Tom as coach, and they would go of an evening to the 'Miners' in Pont-rhyd-y-groes, where they would do total justice to *John Barley*, and have a great time. New Row Sheepdog Trial started in 1933, lapsed in the war years, but was re-started in the late fifties and is still going strong.

Tom's father, David Williams, coming towards the end of his days, was quite ill in bed. The local preacher, Rev. D.H. Lloyd came to visit him, and after a while asked him if he would like something, thinking perhaps of something spiritual, but the answer he got was, 'I would like to see a good dog!' The reverend D.H. Lloyd was preacher at Cwmystwyth from 1903 to 1947.

Tom had been a keen jockey in his youth, and entered the many races for ponies that were held at sporting events in the locality and neighbouring areas. One of his rivals was Alfred Edwards, who rode for many years an exceptionally good pony called 'Charlie' (whom I rode as a very old horse) and who, if my memory serves me right, died aged 29 at Ty-llwyd in around 1968. Charlie's favourite race, which could be revived to encourage practical horses, was one which involved walking a lap, trotting a lap, and then galloping a lap. It should be remembered that they were ridden quite good distances to reach these venues prior to competing, and sometimes had to carry an extra rider, who had over-indulged, on the way home. One of their favourite venues was

Llangurig, and I was told recently by Mr Alun Jones, Ystrad-olwyn that even though they won many a competition, they steadfastly refused to take any prize money, and gave it back to the organisers.

Tom started work at Pwllpeirian farm (which was run by the Cahn Hill Improvement Scheme) in 1939 and saw many changes in methods of agriculture and staff before his retirement in 1981. It was during this time that he was involved in the rescue of a lamb from the Rhuddnant gorge. A letter from the RSPCA (shown to me by his sister, Mrs Elizabeth Allen, Devil's Bridge) dated 14th of April 1961 reads as follows, 'Due to your co-operation and assistance with the handling of the ropes, it was possible for P.C. Owen to persuade the lamb to move off the ledge, and rejoin its mother, unharmed by its experience.'

Tom differed from all the other shepherds that I mention inasmuch as he was mostly bare-headed, unless the weather was extremely severe. At one time, Tom had a bitch called 'Wendy', and while helping to gather at Ty-llwyd on a rough day, with Bill Pugh, Bodtalog next in line to him, Tom had shouted, 'Wendy here' several times, and Bill shouted back (obviously having made an earlier remark that Tom hadn't heard) 'By damn, I've already told you its windy once!'

Tom and several others had gone to a whist-drive at Llanfihangel-y-creuddyn, and Alfred Edwards had bought three or four flagons of Brown Ale, but his so-called friends found where he had hidden them, drank them dry, and re-filled them from a nearby tap. A week or so later, there was a gathering at Ty-llwyd, and at dinner time Alfred told Mrs Raw not to put water out for the helpers, as he had a treat for them of Brown Ale. The rest of the story is better imagined than told!

Possibly at a shearing at Lluest-dôl-gwiail, Tom and Ivor Edwards (Alfred's brother) slept overnight there, and two girls who were there helping, took away their clothes and boots and hid them, so they both spent a lot of time in bed the next morning not being able to get up!

Another aspect of Tom's life was that he had a store of local knowledge, and stories galore about life in Cwmystwyth when he was a youngster. On days when the weather was extrememly wet or there was drifting snow, the staff at Pwllpeirian would be in one of the sheds and Llewelyn Phillips would turn to Tom and say 'What was the story about so and

■ Tom Williams, Pwll-peirian.

so?' and that would ensure a couple of hours of entertainment. I am still living in the hope that Llew Phillips might have recorded these stories on paper somewhere (he wrote reams of material on agricultural matters) but alas, to date, nothing has come to hand. One of the things that rubbed Tom up the wrong way, when he was driving sheep along the road, especially in summer when traffic was heaviest, was the stream of cars that were behind the drove, and he was known once to ask a driver 'Is your journey really necessary?'.

On a personal note, having driven sheep along all sorts of roads for many years, I can truthfully say that only two motorists have given me any sort of aggravation – one in July 1968 and the other in January 1995, so I am able to thank thousands of motorists for their patience. In fact, many of them thought it was great to see the sheep, and the dogs working hard to control them. I was driving sheep up the hill towards Lovesgrove farm in the mid-seventies, and there were seven or eight cars behind me. The car immediately behind me contained a family, the youngest of whom was an adorable little angel, five to six years of age, blonde haired, with a big gap where some of her teeth were missing, possibly giving her a bit of a lisp. She was completely enraptured by the sheep and lambs, and the dogs darting back and forth to keep the flock moving. Then suddenly came the unexpected comment, in a strong Midlands accent, 'Hathn't 'e got big bootth'!

When we were sorting young lambs for ear-marking at Ty-llwyd one spring, a group of children who were camping with their parents in one of the fields, took a delight in identifying the sex of the lambs as they were caught, and there were cries of 'Boy', 'Girl' as the lambs came out. Tom, seeing a chance to create some fun, caught a male lamb, held his hand over its scrotum, exposing two teats, and the gleeful cries came forth, 'It's a girl!', at which point he withdrew his hand to cries of 'Oh no, it's a boy!'. Harmless, impromptu fun that was a key factor in boosting morale when the work was often arduous and repetitive.

A lot of Tom's work involved helping the resident shepherd of Nant-rhys, which was the sheepwalk of Pwllpeirian. The first shepherd he worked with was William Griffiths (to be mentioned later) and he was succeeded by John Davies (1913–1992) who came there in the early forties. During the storm of 1947, hay bales, tied with wire, were taken to Blaen-cwm, and Tom tried, often without success, to take the bales, one on either side of his gray horse to Nant-rhys. It was a token gesture to try to stem the effect of nature's great catastrophe. At another point during the storm, John Davies and Tom had been to Cwmystwyth shop to get much needed supplies, calling on the way home at Ty-mawr, where both, according to John Lewis (of Ty-mawr), stayed for longer than they ought to have done, and were caught in severe drifting, whereby they had a terrible time reaching Nant-rhys, where John's wife Maggie was almost beside herself with worry.

The house door at Nant-rhys had blown open one night and the family were faced the next morning with a drift that reached half-way up the stairs. They had almost run out of hay at one stage, and John walked down to Nanty, Llangurig, to get some hay from Morgan Griffiths. He had with him a large sack that had once had bran in it. This sack he stuffed as tight as he could with hay, stuck a pitchfork in it, and carried it the two miles back to Nant-rhys. The Davies family saw great hardship during that storm, and left before the onset of another winter. When driving sheep from Nant-rhys to Pwllpeirian, Tom would always try to take the first drove, as they were the strongest sheep, and therefore able to go at a good rate. Canny sheep psychology?

Tom died on the 7th of December 1989 aged 73.

The weather, which is the opener to most country conversations, can make or break a day's work, especially with sheep, and more so in upland areas. Mist and rain can delay gathering for days, if not weeks, in areas that exchange labour, because each place has its allocated days, and if you miss out, you finish up at the tail end of the queue. This can be most frustrating, especially at shearing time, as so much labour is involved, and doubly so for the wives because of the mammoth task of preparing food, and the thought of having to start from scratch again is a daunting one. The real problems came, as touched upon in the last chapter, when snow fell, making it difficult to get to the stock and making access virtually impossible at times. Real storms of snow and ice, thankfully, come only every now and then – in fact, with an average gap of ten to twenty years in between. We are now experiencing a mild spell, with winters with very little snow.

The period from 1500 to 1850 was one that was very cold with many storms of ice and snow, and it was stated that the Thames froze over 15 times during this period, with fairs being held on the river. The last fair was held on the Thames in 1814. According to a report in *Cymru Coch* the winter of 1814 caused severe hardship, with one example of a pig killed in Maes-yr-onn, Llangammarch, remaining frozen solid for 13 weeks, and loaves of bread froze in Dôl-goch, Cwm Tywi to the extent that they had to be cut with an axe next morning for breakfast. Many farmers lost two-thirds of their sheep, and had very few lambs from what stock that was left. One farmer, David Pritchard of Dôl-gaer, Llangammarch, owning a vast number of sheep, had only five lambs to ear-mark that spring. Another hill farmer, Peter Jones, of Llwyn Derw, Abergwesyn, whose flock of several thousand was severely affected, was reputed to have sold over 2,500 sheep skins, plus hides from mountain ponies. A thaw came at the end of April, itself causing widespread losses, with ice blocking the bridge at Gwarafog near Garth, until it finally gave way under the tremendous pressure. The effect on bird life at that time was horrendous, and it took many years to build up their numbers again.

This severe winter of 1814 was followed two years later by another, with snow falling regularly throughout the February and March of 1816. As if this was not enough, it was followed by the wettest summer for a hundred years, and was known as 'the year without a summer'.

In the Tregaron area, there was a gentleman called William Williams of Dôlgoch, who was obviously the owner of a vast tract of land, for it was stated that he owned 20,000 sheep. He had heard however, that a lady in Scotland owned 24,000 sheep, and it was his ambition in life to beat her record, but Mother Nature had other plans, and a horrific snow-storm in 1772/3 brought his flock down to half its number. He died in 1773, and was buried at Llanddewi-brefi churchyard.

Severe snowstorms are etched on the memory of many hill shepherds because of the devastating effect they had on them, their families and their flocks. Writers and poets have seen fit to record such extremities of weather. Huw Morris, a poet, records in a poem the 13 weeks of freezing conditions in 1683 in which oak trees snapped under the weight of the ice. Rees Jones, Pwll-ffein, Llandysul, mentions the snowstorms of 1823. It was in this year that a hill farm called Cae Coch, Llanuwchllyn, which had a flock of 1,200 ewes prior to the storm, was left with 500 after its rages.William Saunders writes of a severe winter in 1828. One of the earliest falls of snow of substantial amount recorded, as far as I know, was on Pumlumon on the 28th of September 1835, where there was in some places a covering of three feet.

Caledfryn, the bard, mentions in one of his poems, the snow-storm in February 1853, and Trebor Mai, another poet, records in verse the snows of January 1863. The year 1881 saw a great snow-storm which severely affected the numbers of sheep in the uplands of mid-Wales. The grand-father of Hugh Jones, Pant-y-craf, Tregaron (also called Hugh Jones, born 1809) had moved to Dôl-goch, an upland farm 10 miles from Tregaron in the Tywi Valley, a year or so previous to this storm, and as a consequence of severe drifting lost hundreds of his sheep, and was able to pay only part of his rent to the Lisburn family of Trawscoed from the money he got from the skins that he sold. During that storm one of the servants at Dôl-goch had started to cut down a tree near the house for firewood, but Hugh Jones stopped him and the tree is still there today. His son, John Jones of Dôl-goch was a mine of information on the history of the uplands of the Tregaron and Abergwesyn areas, and it is one of my great regrets in life that I did not meet him, but I've been able to glean a lot of knowledge from his son, Hugh, of Pant-y-craf. (Pant-y-craf means the dingle of wild garlic.) The long connection that the Jones family had with Dôl-goch came to an end on the 20th of October 2000 when Mr Hugh Jones relinquished his connection with the holding, and sold the last sheep of Dôl-goch.

The next serious snow-storm came in 1895. This was one of the severest winters. The Hughes family of Ceiro, Ponterwyd were able to walk in a straight line to the Chapel without seeing a fence, gate, or hedge. My great-grandfather's brother, John Howells owned Cwmergyr, Ponterwyd and a lot of the surrounding hills, and had a large flock of sheep, plus about a thousand wethers, and the losses and hardship was such that only one lamb was reared that year. John Howells, probably because of experiences like this, would not allow his shepherds to go out when the storm was raging, reasoning that human life was more valuable than sheep. Since storms of this magnitude come infrequently, many people have no experience of how helpless a human being can be in severe drifting, when you can't see, are hardly able to breathe, and virtually unable to stand – it is only then that it is realised how puny a man's strength is compared to a howling blizzard, and how easy it is to lose one's life under such circumstances.

In 1895, the temperature fell as much as 34 degrees below freezing and on a hill farm called Dôl-wen, near Devil's Bridge, 1600 sheep were skinned and it is reckoned many others were swept away by streams. Prior to, and during this time, it was a practice on many hills to cut hay (mostly molinia) on the open hill and make it into a stack. The initial work of making this stack was to drive posts into the ground, and pile the hay around them. This was to safeguard the hay from being blown away. Molinia hay, called

■ Photograph showing the arctic-like conditions of the weather on the summit of Pumlumon, 5th of February 1966. Photo by Dave and Jenny Dee, Erwyd Garage.

'*gwair cwta*' in Welsh or '*rhôs* hay' in semi-Welsh areas, because of its make-up, could be cut one day and carried the following day, providing the weather was right. This would heat in the stack and it smelled like brandy. Hay of this nature was cut at Hirnant in Ponterwyd in the mid-seventies, and it was possible to smell it down-wind half a mile away. Wonderful stuff.

   Such stacks were on the hill of Glan-hirin in 1895, and despite the severe winter the sheep fared well while the hay lasted, but alas the supply ran out, and the sheep died in their hundreds. This tale has been handed down through the late Harold Hughes, father of Tommy Hughes, Aber-glan-hirin. The sheep total on Glan-hirin at shearing in 1893 was 2,371; in 1894 it was 2,673; at shearing in 1895, they were down to 1,958 with only 328 lambs reared. A fair proportion of wethers (castrated males) were kept on all hills, where, as old stags, they would keep the sheep boundaries, and if there was a fall of snow and drifting, these strong animals would be able to fight their way out of the drifts, therefore enabling the weaker ewes to follow. On many hill farms very few, if any, lambs were sold, because ewe lambs were at a premium for flock replacements, and almost all strong males were kept as wethers. These wethers, when sold at about four years old, contributed much to the farm's income. It was of paramount importance that they were sold off as soon as possible after gathering, because when kept under fence, all they did was pace the fences day and night in a bid for freedom, thereby losing condition. The last lot of wethers I saw going through these motions were with John Lewis at Tymawr, Cwmystwyth, with a brown trail around the perimeter fence. Mutton, the meat from these aged animals, when well hung, and cooked slowly, is in my mind as good as any meat you can get, with a full flavour. The family living at Ty'n-y-maes, not far from Devil's Bridge, would have welcomed a bit of this mutton as they had hardly anything but swedes to eat for the best part of a week during this storm. The thaw came on the 5th of March 1895.

   The next severe snow-storm came in 1917, plus freezing conditions, affecting the whole country. One bout of snow was like a fine powder, finding its way into every nook and cranny, making life difficult in houses, as well as out-houses.

A cracker of a storm came in 1929 causing a lot of havoc. This storm started in earnest on about the 15th of February, with temperatures plummeting hour by hour. It is stated that in Ross-on-Wye, there was 40 degrees of frost, with drifts of 12 to 15 feet, which were frozen rock-solid. The late Mr W.D. Owen, Ty'n-ddôl, Ffair rhos, came across a tramp who had died in the snow, near one of the Teifi Pools, towards the end of February 1929, and he was buried in Strata Florida cemetery.

This snow-storm was followed soon after by one in 1933. This started towards the end of January, building up towards the middle of February. Storms like these tested the people living in isolated places to the utmost, and put a great strain on their resources of food and fuel, but, as the old adage goes, 'When the going gets tough, the tough get going'. I have been told that there was a farm sale in the Rhaeadr area (possibly on the 23rd of February) and only one man attended! According to the *Welsh Gazette* (23rd of March 1933) Captain Bennett Evans lost 300 sheep during this storm. For the first time, hay was dropped from an aeroplane to sheep in the Brecon area in 1933. The following June there was a terrific storm of thunder and lightning with lumps of ice two inches in diameter falling. There had been a similar storm of hail in June 1835. Whitsun 1933 was one of the hottest possible. No wonder the weather is such a talking point with its variation of extremes.

Another storm of severe proportions came four years later in 1937. A group of Ponterwyd farmers had gone, on the last Saturday in February, to the funeral of Mr John Griffiths, Troed-rhiw-goch, Ponterwyd. Not being a native of the area, the funeral was held in Machynlleth, and the day was described to me as 'fine, with sun'. On the same day Richard Morgan, living at Cae'r Arglwyddes, Talybont (formerly of Hengwm-annedd) had come up through Ponterwyd to visit his sister, Mary Ann Thomas, at Eisteddfa Gurig and several people have said that he was in his shirt-sleeves, proving that the weather was fairly kind. During that night and the next day, a howling blizzard came, with the wind coming from the South West. As this was an unusual direction from which to have snow, sheep were being buried in places where no-one remembered severe drifts before. To make matters worse, the snow was very wet and heavy, and the dead sheep under some of the worst drifts were pressed flat like pancakes.

Richard Morgan had to stay in Eisteddfa for a week before he could return to Talybont. At Gelli-isaf, Ponterwyd, 60 sheep died under drifts within 150 yards of the house, to pinpoint just one local catastrophe.

Another type of storm came in the end of January 1940 – freezing rain, of a severe degree. Everything was covered in a sheet of ice, and if it wasn't for the hardship it caused, it could have been described as a fairyland, with a local correspondent (*Welsh Gazette* 8th of February 1940) comparing the area of Cwmystwyth to Finland or Norway. The temperature fell to 18 and 20 degrees below. Trees were cracking under the weight of the ice, 'till in afforested areas, it sounded like artillery fire. The oldest person in Cwmystwyth, a Mrs Mary Morgan, Ty'n-rhyd (aged 91), compared it as being worse that 1895, but this bout lasted only a week. It was sheer starvation as far as sheep were concerned. I often think that if such a storm came again, with all the phone and electricity wires we have around, it would cause unimaginable chaos, without even thinking about road conditions.

There was a comparative respite from heavy snow after 1937 till nature took its course again in 1947. This one was a corker. There are many people alive today in whose memory every hour of this storm is painfully etched, because of its severity and hardship. The wet summer of 1946 meant many farms had not had enough fodder – not even for a mild winter – and much of what they had was of very inferior quality. Upland farms had not been able to get much hay of any description till October when a strong, but drying, wind came. The semi-drying of an already poor quality crop meant that a lot of hay actually rotted even after harvesting.

There had been a keen northerly wind and frost, as though preparing a bed for the snow when it came. The first snow started in the Pumlumon area on the 24th of January and the freezing conditions kept every grain of it, accumulating all the while, with further heavy falls in February, and conditions for both humans and animals getting worse and worse. The late John James of Nant-y-moch, had said several times 'I've seen it worse than this' – that is, referring to the storm of 1895. Although conditions were critical by the end of February, Mother Nature still had her finale up her sleeve and this was played out with a vengeance on the night of Tuesday the 4th and the whole of Wednesday the 5th of March, which left even John James with nothing to say. This onslaught left whole farms buried, whole valleys filled from side to side – in other words, a total disaster. Such was the fury of that Wednesday, that many hardened people could not go out at all. The days following were spent in digging tunnels to reach stock in out-houses, where even they, in many cases, were buried under snow. Two cows and a mare perished in the buildings of Nant-y-moch. Getting water for the animals was virtually a full-time job, even finding a stream was difficult, with paths closing as well as any open water freezing. The main road (A44) past Eisteddfa Gurig was closed for three weeks and three days. As someone once said 'Winter destroys the romance of shepherding'.

■ An all too familiar scene in 1947. Mr Abraham Morgan (1873–1949), Ty Newydd, Cwmystwyth at a mass grave. Photo by Mrs Edith Morgan, Eisteddfa fach.

The sheep losses were horrendous, with many flocks annihilated. Skinning dead sheep was the order of the day, with a view of salvaging something. John Owen, a shepherd at Lovesgrove, was working with Captain Bennett Evans at Llangurig at the time, and stated that 1,700 skins had gone off on one load. Fuchesgau in Ponterwyd had only 7 sheep left from their flock, and the fence from the house to the road, was covered with skins. Only three lambs were reared at Ceiro, Ponterwyd. Nant-cae-rhedyn lost all their sheep on their side of the Rheidol, except for 2 rams which Miss Sarah Morgan kept alive somehow in one of the buildings, even giving them aspirins in a bid to keep them going. Some of their sheep that had crossed the river Rheidol onto Dinas land survived, as there was not the same thickness of snow there.

On a happier note, a sheep from the Tywi (Tregaron) area had wandered down to Pont-rhyd-fendigaid, and adopted, or was adopted by, a local lady who carried the post. She fed her on tit-bits and ivy. This ewe became quite tame, and followed at her heels through the village,which reminds me of Robert Burns' lament, *Poor Mailie's Elegy*:

> *Through a' the toun she trotted by him;*
> *A lang half mile she could descry him;*
> *Wi' kindly bleat when she did spy him,*
> *She ran wi' speed;*
> *A friend mair faithfu' ne'er came nigh him.*

Mr Dewi Roberts of Lle'r-neuaddau had gone up to Nant-y-moch, and was surprised to see virtually the whole place covered in snow, except for the house chimney and the ridge tiles of the chapel. In the Cwmystwyth area, a house called Tai-newyddion was completely covered. A neighbour's son, Edgar Morgan, on his way to school, had to shout down the chimney to see if the occupants – a brother and a sister – were all right.

David Evans, Abergwngu, told Tommy Hughes, 'I don't know what you will see [in your life], but you can tell everybody you've witnessed the worst storm in history' and maybe he wasn't far from the mark. Every able-bodied person was out clearing the roads, with gangs of men walking many miles to get essential supplies from town. Many of the sheep at this time were not used to being fed, and one old character in the Ponterwyd area – William Henry Hope, of Llywernog (an old carrier, with his faithful horses) – actually let what sheep he had left into the hay-rick, and he couldn't understand why they died there! But it was too little, too late. There were so many stories of hardship in different areas, that they would easily fill the next Bible.

The thaw came on the 16th March and with it another cruel blow. As if to add insult to injury, seriously strong winds came that blew hundreds of sheep, almost too weak to stand, into the swollen rivers. John Lewis, Ty-mawr reckoned that this wind killed more of his sheep than the storm itself. A shepherd, out at the height of this wind, saw his dogs, howling with fright, being blown like leaves across a field. One report I have seen estimated that 3,000,000 sheep had perished and a disaster fund was set up, which in May 1947 stood at £240,000. Money, however, would not bring people like David William Harries of Nant-gwernog, Llanddewi Brefi back. He had committed suicide – allegedly because of the calamity the weather had caused to his livelihood.

The losses at Bwlch-styllen, Ponterwyd were as follows – 311 ewes; 80 shearlings; 14

rams; 65 ewe lambs; 15 wether lambs; 10 wethers; 2 cows and an estimated 350 less lambs in the spring.

In the middle of the storm, a hill farmer from the Llanidloes area (David Lloyd, Gorn Farm) went into the town, and during his visit went to the cafe kept by a Dick Jervis, who had a few sheep of his own on the outskirts of town. Dei Lloyd was bemoaning his losses, and told Dick, 'You are lucky, you've only got a few sheep to worry about' and got the reply, 'If this weather carries on, you might be as lucky as I am!' Two old friends, and no hard feelings. As a matter of interest, Dick Jervis (1886–1965), when he lived at Cefn-brwyn, attended Pennant school, near Llanbrynmair.

My father-in-law, John Griffiths was ploughing (with horses) at Cefn Gwyn Hall, Pennant, near Cross Inn, on May 28th (1947), almost within sight of the sea, but was not able to plough a part of the headland because of drifts still left. He was walking to his home in Bethania with telephone lines at ankle height in some places.

Building up a flock after such a storm, some virtually from scratch, took a long time. It was around this time that the hill subsidies started, giving people a better living.

In June 1946 a Mr and Mrs Hurford had moved from Stone, in Staffordshire to live in Dôl-wen, but the lorry carrying their furniture got bogged down, and they unloaded everything into the barn at Blaen-myherin, where they had to live over the weekend, as there was nobody to help, cooking on an open fire in the yard. On Monday the Forestry lorry moved their belongings to Nant-syddion (where my grand-parents lived) and Mr David Davies from Ty-mawr moved everything in his horse and cart to Dôl-wen, while my grand-mother helped them with meals etc. Jim Hurford worked for the Forestry Commission, while Betty his wife looked after the smallholding and their five children. During the snowstorm the young men of Ponterwyd had walked down to Goginan to get bread for the villagers, and Betty Hurford had walked an eight mile round trip from Dôl-wen to meet them on their return, taking 12 loaves home with her. Quite an experience for anybody, let alone someone newly moved from Staffordshire to the Welsh hills. They moved from Dôl-wen in October 1947 to a house called Erwyd View in Ponterwyd, where their youngest son (Stephen Erwyd) was born and thankfully, he still retains a strong affiliation for the area of his birth. Many of the family live now in the Brecon area.

A gap of 15 years ensued before the severe winter of 1962/63. This storm involved there being a hard frost virtually from before Christmas till March – a total of 13 weeks. This winter was similar to the storm of 1929, although the temperatures did not plummet as low. Great piles of snow formed deep drifts and caused many losses as far as sheep were concerned. Roads opened were closed again within hours in places. I believe the road to Ystumtuen was opened five times. A lot of manpower was used at this time, and after having opened a road a few times the height of the sides made it difficult to get rid of the snow, which was cut in blocks. Lots of jokes are made about council workers, but at times like this they pulled all the stops out, and gave an exceptional service to their communities. The snow-plough went through Ponterwyd up to Eisteddfa Gurig every day for eleven weeks. Three, if not four, funerals had to be undertaken in the remote hamlet of Ystumtuen during this time. Difficult occasions, made even more so by hampering weather. I well remember helping to load sheep belonging to Mr Emlyn Thomas, Talwrn farm, Ponterwyd, in the lane by the chapel.

These sheep had been on his sheepwalk of Blaen-peithnant, and their backs were covered with small blocks of ice which, whenever the sheep moved, made a jingling noise. They were loaded in a lorry driven by Ceredig Howells, and were taken down to Aber-cwm-dôlau in Capel Bangor. (They had an agreement that their sheep went up over the summer, and Emlyn Thomas' sheep spent some time on the lowland during the winter months.) He probably moved around 400 sheep down-country – quite a change from their snow-bound terrain at Blaen-peithnant.

Helicopters were used to carry hay to outlying farms such as Aber-glan-hirin. They carried 20 bales at a time, and a round trip from the Elan Valley Hotel took 11 minutes. Hay at that time was around £20.00 a ton.

The thaw came around the 5th of March, with an early spring to follow. It is surprising how long the remnants of these drifts last in cold, back-sided pockets. There is a report in the Western Mail (4th of June 1963) of snow still left in Cwm Gerwyn, Bleddfa, Radnorshire in June that year. Around this time, my father and I were in the valley above Ceiro, Ponterwyd, where we found the the very last piece of snow in the area. I was about 18 inches in diameter and almost black in colour. I regret that I did not take note of the exact date.

There was a sudden fall of snow on the 17th of April 1967. This had a devastating effect in hill areas as many young lambs were around at that time. It was a sorry sight, that is still in my mind, to see them dead in groups of five or six at a time – having gone, in their minds, to a sheltered spot, but alas, it is in these places that drifting takes place, and it turns out to be their last resting place.

■ John Owen (on post) and Fred Lewis of Lovesgrove near Hirnant in the severe weather of 1963.

1981/82

Following a short sharp storm at the end of April 1981, which played havoc with the hill lamb crop, there came a severe fall of snow, with a lot of drifting on Sunday 13th of December (1981). Being out that day was no laughing matter. There were times when you were completely blinded by drifting, and sinking in soft snow up to your thighs at every step, making progress very slow. This was fine powdery snow that penetrated into every nook and cranny, similar to the snow of 1917. I believe the Indians of America have a saying, as we have in Welsh, 'fine snow, big snow' (*eira mân, eira mawr*).

This was followed by a violent snowstorm, plus high wind on Friday the 8th of January. A day to remember. From where I live, I could see hundreds of acres of clear ground, but the lanes in the valleys and sheltered places were full to capacity. I well remember having a pig at the time, and not being able to get food to it, and having to throw half a bucket-full of potatoes, one by one, through a small hole, so that he would not go hungry till I had time to dig a tunnel. This was the last time that I saw sheep buried under the drifts. A neighbour, John Watkin, had sheep buried in the shelter of a hedge, and a while later I found a ewe on Lluest-y-rhos land that had been under a drift for 18 days. She had eaten the grass and lichen around her to the roots, and also a bit of the wool from her sides. Apart from being a bit thin, she was perky, and ran away to join her mates. Ironically, sheep that have been imprisoned thus for a while, after being rescued and let out of what was a warm place, are sometimes susceptible to pneumonia, and can die as a result.

Strong sticks, 6 feet in length (*pastwrn lluwch*) are used to try to detect sheep buried under drifts, and these sticks are invaluable when having to go across soft drifts, on your hands and knees, to prevent sinking. Sheep that have been in drifts (not too deep) for a while, can be detected because of a tell-tale hole in the drift, caused by their breathing and body heat.

I was not able to move my car from the house till the 18th of January. This storm, made worse by a personal tragedy at the time, will be one that I won't forget in a hurry. Modern, warmer clothing would have made life a lot easier for the people of yesteryear in their comings and goings through blizzards. The old tweed great-coats were warm, but took in a lot of moisture, and under freezing conditions, you sometimes had to wait for them to thaw a bit before you could take them off, and even then they would stand up on their own!

Hugh Edward Griffiths (1884–1960)

A man who saw his fair share of snowstorms is my next shepherd, Hugh Griffiths. He was the son of Evan Griffiths (1837–1906) and Mary (nee Rowlands) of Lluest-dôl-gwiail (known locally as Lluest). Evan Griffiths' landlord could have been the owner of the Clochfaen Estate, Llangurig. Evan Griffiths had taken the tenancy of Dôlogau, a farm in the ownership of the Hafod Estate (just across the river Ystwyth from Hafod). This was a low-lying farm intended to better the management of Lluest-dôl-gwiail, but alas, all the crops sown were mostly eaten by the game and rabbits of Hafod, and to shoot them was frowned upon by the landlord, so after a few years the tenancy was given up. It was during this stay at Dôlogau, that Hugh was born, with the family then moving back to Lluest.

Hugh was one of 14 children – 7 girls and 7 boys. I was told that their father, Evan, being eager to know what was going on in neighbouring villages, would send two of his eldest boys – one down to Llangurig, and the other down to Cwmystwyth – to find what news they could glean, and then report back to HQ!

Hugh's first job was to open the flood-gate of the leat (*rhewyn dwr*) that carries the water to the Cwmystwyth lead mine. The feeder dam is on the River Ystwyth by Blaen-cwm land, and the spot is called Pant-yr-argae (the hollow of the reservoir). This had to be done very early in the morning, so that the water reached the mine before the workmen arrived. He then had to walk along the leat to make sure that there were no obstructions. I have often looked at this leat, and thought it a wonderful feat of engineering, as it wends its way down behind Ty-llwyd farmhouse, collecting water from various sources en route. The amount of labour involved must have been tremendous.

A notice was put in a local paper (*Welsh Gazette*, 1st of December, 1904):

> *To shepherds – A waterman is required to turn water for Cwmystwyth mine early every morning. Pay: 21/– per week for 8 summer months and 24/– for 4 winter months.*

Hugh later worked for Dr John Morgan of Pont-rhyd-y-groes, an exceptional country doctor, with a massive area to cover. Somebody should have written a book about his selfless service to the community. After this Hugh worked for Mr Tom Vaughan Lewis, of Nant-arthur, Devil's Bridge – work which involved a lot of hauling of timber.

He then worked at Ty-llwyd for several years, and it was from Ty-llwyd that he married. His wife, Elizabeth Davies, was born at Ty-newydd, Cwmystwyth. She was the daughter of William Solomon Davies who married Elizabeth Morgan of Ty-newydd, on the 29th of October 1886. It was unfortunate that her mother died when she was born and Elizabeth was therefore baptised on her mother's coffin – an event that was all too common many years ago.

Elizabeth, or Leis, as she was locally known, had gone, prior to getting married, to help her aunt Mrs Jane Oliver, who was then living at Rhydôldog, near Rhaeadr, during a confinement. Hugh, obviously eager to see his girlfriend, actually 'borrowed' a fast pony after dark from Blaen-cwm at one time, and was back at Blaen-cwm before the family got up the next day. Because of the caked mud on the pony, they pointed a finger of suspicion at him, but had no proof. All's fair in love and war.

After their marriage Hugh and Leis Griffiths went to live at Chatham, Cwmystwyth (there must be a maritime connection with a name like that) and then they moved a fairly long way to a farm called Cymerau, near Glandyfi, Machynlleth. Hugh worked as a shepherd for a Mrs Pugh, and then moved as a shepherd to Nant-llyn, Ponterwyd under the same ownership. This was about 1909–11. Their children, as listed in the Nant-y-moch chapel book (Capel Blaen-Rheidol) in 1910 were: Willie Hugh, Mary Lizzie (Polly), Evan Rowland, and Ann Jane. They had 13 children, of whom 11 survived. Hugh jokingly said to someone, 'I've only got to put my trousers on the bed in May, and Leis gets pregnant!'

Feeding and clothing a large family like theirs must have been a big problem, on what was a small wage, and living for most of their time in isolated surroundings. They were fairly self sufficient in milk, eggs, butter and bacon. They grew as many vegetables as they could at a high altitude. Their diet, however mundane or basic it may seem to

■ Nant-llyn as it was in 1977.

today's people, was wholesome and nutritious. I have always maintained that boiled food, especially meats, when put into '*cawl*' or '*potes*' (two Welsh names for broth) with whatever vegetables are available, is as good and healthy a way of feeding the human body as possible. Herbs and young nettles were also put in to enhance the taste. This *cawl* was even better when it was re-heated the next day. Many of the healthiest people that I know, and have known, who have lived to a good age, hale and hearty, were brought up on this diet, along with home cured bacon, much of which was fatty, but this was absorbed by the fact that most of their work was physical, and a lot of walking was done to get anywhere. Much was made of oatmeal for various foods as well.

I am reminded of the words of *God speed the plough*:

> *Let the wealthy and great*
> *Rule in splendour and state*
> *I envy them not, I declare it*
> *I eat my own lamb*
> *My chickens and ham*
> *I shear my own fleece and wear it*
> *I have lawns, I have bowers*
> *I have fruit I have flowers*
> *And the lark is my morning alarm...*

■ Hugh Griffiths, Ysgubor fach, Cwmystwyth on his 70th birthday. Photo by Mrs Dicks, Cwmystwyth.

Hugh and Elizabeth's family are a very good advert for this diet and way of life. At the time of writing (23rd of February 2001), six of their children are still alive and cheerful – Morgan, aged 87; Margaret (Maggie), aged 84; Christmas, aged 81; Blodwen, aged 76; Ceinwen, aged 74, and Thomas (Tom), the youngest, aged 70. William died on 14th of March 1991, aged 84 and a sister, Mrs Mary Elizabeth Lewis (Polly), herself with a family of 10 children, died on the 6th of January 1994, aged 86.

The family moved c1912 to Ty-nant in Ponterwyd. This small-holding was owned by David Tannet of Pompren-llwyd in the Llangurig area. Hugh had gone over Pumlumon from Nant-llyn to ask for the tenancy, arriving there at 11 o'clock in the morning, only to find that the owner was away from home, and would not be back till late. The boss came home, Hugh put his case before him, got the tenancy, and stayed there till 11 o'clock that night, and it was noted by the family that he did not once go out for a pee. He must have had a strong bladder! This story was told to me by Marged Jane Rees many years ago.

During this time Hugh worked for a while at Cripiau Bach lead mine, near Dyffryn Castell, and then, in the company of my great uncle, Isaac Richard Howells, went down to work in the coal mines of South Wales. He then had the idea of joining the army, as the pay was much better than anything else. He passed his physical with flying colours, and then somebody asked him how many children he had, to which he said eight, and was told it would cost more to keep him than a General, so that was the end of that!

If Hugh was more famous for one thing than the other, it was talking. He was a story-teller of note. His children told me once, 'If Dada was short of a story, he would make them up!', and he often did, adding at the end of a dubious story '...and they tell me that's true'! Had he been born several centuries ago during the time of the Princes, he would have been a court entertainer of the highest order. He would visit neighbours and friends of an evening and would talk incessantly till 2 to 3 o'clock in the morning, and then walk home a good distance.

The late Llew Phillips, whilst at Pwllpeirian, set up a discussion group called *Cymdeithas yr Hafod* which was held once a month, with a guest speaker. They had a break for a cup and something to eat half-way through, so that the speaker would not be overtaxed before the second half of his talk, but the poor fellow had not a snowball's chance in hell. Hugh would virtually take over the meeting and keep everybody amused, and educated, by his stories. A true master at his art.

In 1914, my great-grandfather's brother, John Howells, owned and farmed Cwmergyr in Ponterwyd. The weather that year was not special around shearing time, and although the sheep were gathered and dry, a heavy shower came at daybreak, but the whole gang of shearers and helpers were there, waiting for them to dry out in a few hours. While they were waiting, they set up an impromptu Eisteddfod (a competitive meeting) with the old John Howells as adjudicator. There was singing, and reciting, with everybody joining in, showing how cultured these country people were. There was one competition as to who was best at telling a true story, and Hugh told the story of his life whilst shepherding at Nant-llyn. What a gem that must have been, and to think that that has gone into oblivion makes me sad.

One of the great loves of Hugh's life was horses, and during the season, he would spend some time taking the stallions of a Richard Morgan, Lluest-y-broga, Penuwch, to different parts of the country. This was while at Tynant. Richard Morgan had connections with the Cwmystwyth area, and was famous for his Welsh cobs. He owned, amongst others, 'Welsh Comet' (*Cel du bach*) and 'Welsh Model', and also a strong cob called 'Garibaldi'. Hugh travelled a lot during this time, and got to know a lot of places and people, especially around the Gower, and the Swansea valleys in South Wales.

During the late summer and autumn, he would drive sheep for Mr John George, Garth, Lledrod from Tregaron to Brecon to be sold. He had a partner on these long arduous drives called Evan, known as Evan Bach (Little Evan), whose surname I don't know. Often they had a drove numbering 1,100, and on one occasion, when there was a big flood in the river Irfon by Llannerch-arfan, they had to take these sheep across a footbridge. This took four hours. After the sheep were sold, Hugh often had to drive them a short spell for the convenience of the new owner and then make his way back to Aberystwyth by train, where he stayed overnight with his brother Dafydd, and then off to Talybont on a Saturday morning to fetch some more sheep, and drive them to Lledrod. He then made for his home at Ty-nant, and yet would be punctual for the church service at Ysbyty Cynfyn on the Sunday morning. Fitness and dedication combined.

This driving took a big toll on the dogs as well. He used to say that in a particular pub in Brecon, the landlady would not only prepare food for them, but also for the dogs, and that the dogs were, at times, almost too tired to eat. Another tale that one of his children told me, was that after coming home from one of these drives, one of the dogs, called Fly (a favourite with the children), would be virtually out for the count, since she was so tired, and that they once ran into the house crying, because they thought she had died, due to the fact they could not wake her up!

In 1923, Hugh's family moved to Nant-rhys to shepherd for John George, and the day they chose to move was the wettest imaginable. Christmas Griffiths, aged about 4, spent most of the time under a big washing tub. William, who had just started working at Erwbarfe, Ponterwyd, had taken a day off to help his parents to move. Such delays took place because of the weather that he stayed the night at Nant-rhys, and went back to work the next day rather late, and was given such a severe row for being late, that William ran off, straight back to Nant-rhys, and never went back.

In 1943 Hugh and family moved to Bryn-peirian (from where he went to work at Pwllpeirian), and later to Prignant, a wonderful spot to live, and then a final move to Ysgubor-fach, Cwmystwyth. The fences of Ysgubor-fach, as many places were then, were not up to scratch, and many of Pentre farm sheep came in from time to time, and Hugh then asked an exceptionally good bitch called Fly, to go down to the field, and she would sort them out of her own accord, and drive the Pentre sheep down the road towards their home. Hugh Griffiths, on a Wednesday, would tie Fly in a shed, and start on his journey to Devil's Bridge mart, only to find that Fly would be there before him. When he went to Aberystwyth on a Monday, she wouldn't leave home, but the excitement of Devil's Bridge mart on a Wednesday was too much to miss!

A few stories that I have heard about Hugh might help to build up a picture of him. When he was single, he worked or helped out on a farm, and one of the cows was bulling. Hugh's term for any animal in heat was to say that she was 'happy' (*'yn sionc'*).

He and a servant girl, (I have no name, but will call her Jane) were to take the cow to the bull on a nearby farm, and were given 2/– to pay for the service, but somehow things didn't work out, and the cow was brought home. The boss was told the story, and he asked for the 2/–, and Hugh told him, 'I gave it to Jane, she was 'happy' on the way home'!

While at Ty-nant, Hugh was faithful to the church services at Ysbyty Cynfyn. He was a church warden, and used to take the collection plate around. One Sunday, before the service, local children had gone to the nearby field to see the new bull Erwbarfe had bought, and in scrambling back through the hedge, Haydn Jones, of Bryn-chwith, who had been given a penny for the collection, lost it. When Hugh came around to Haydn, rather than do nothing, Haydn went through the motions of putting something in the box, but the keen eyed Hugh saw this, gave a chuckle, but said nothing. His heart was obviously in the right place.

A shepherd's son, Charles Evans of Dôl-wen, Devil's Bridge, aged about 13, had a dog that he found difficult to stop, and asked Hugh Griffiths for advice. Hugh asked him what acerage Dôl-wen was, and Charles answered. Then he asked him how many sheep there were, and again Charles told him (probably 2,000 mid-summer), and Hugh said to him, 'Well, the best thing to do with the dog, is to run him till his arse is round his neck!'

Hugh, on one of his visits to Rhaeadr, met up with Dafydd Evans, Esgair Wen, and set to to celebrate. Both came home to Esgair Wen fairly oiled, and Ann, Dafydd's wife came out to meet them, and said, 'I know you've had a drink, because your eyes look like kipper's eyes!'

His funeral report states 'Deceased had a most varied and romantic career' and no words could be truer. People from far and near came to form a large funeral at Eglwys Newydd on the 25th of February 1960 to bid their last farewell to a truly great character. His wife, Elizabeth died on the 8th of October 1952, aged 65.

William Hugh Griffiths

William was the son of Hugh and Elizabeth, and he stayed on as shepherd at Nant-rhys when his parents moved from there. He started his working life with Thomas Morgan at Ty'n-ffordd, Ponterwyd, which was the 'agricultural college' of the area. Many youngsters started off here before moving on to other farms. Thomas Morgan was an educated man, a good farmer, but was of a strong willed nature that made him difficult to get on with at times.

I well remember William, or Will, as he was called, telling me one tale of his time at Ty'n-ffordd. They had been washing sheep, and had taken a number of tools with them to help dam the stream. That night, when Will was fast asleep, Thomas Morgan woke him up and asked, 'Billy, did you bring the new spade back with you', to which he had to confess that he hadn't, and the reply came, 'Well, you'd better go out and get it then'. He had to get up in the early hours, and walk half a mile to the washpool to get the spade. He said it was a lesson for life, and that he never forgot anything afterwards!

He spent a very short while at Erwbarfe, and then co-shepherded with his father at Nant-rhys. I have heard that they were paid £10·00 a year between them. That could have been in the early years, with probably a rise as time went by.

Many of the sheep went down to over-winter in Garth Fawr, Lledrod, owned by the George family, and Will went with them to stay in Garth for about two months. Will proved himself to be an excellent shepherd with the minimum of losses according to his employers, and was an extremely keen horseman as well. It is suprising how these traits run in families, generation after generation.

After lambing, he used to walk the sheep back to Nant-rhys. The old lady from Cae'r-meirch (Mrs Edwards) would hear them coming, and she would make them a cup of tea with something to eat, and bring it down to the road to meet them. It must have been a genuine treat after a long trek, with several miles still to go. Many of these people were not well off, yet their generosity and neighbourliness knew no bounds. When the old lady died, Rhys George (the son of John George, Garth Fawr, Lledrod) and Will's companion in droving, said he must go to her funeral out of respect for her kind deeds over many years.

John George took over the farm of Nanty in Llangurig, but the two ladies who lived there continued to do so. Will moved in to live with them when he was given the job of shepherding Nanty.

On the 8th of August 1936, Will married Margaret Rogers at Carmel Baptist chapel, Pont-rhyd-fendigaid. She came from Dyffryn, Ffair Rhos. Her mother, Elizabeth (nee Thomas), came from Cwmystwyth. They started their married life in Nant-rhys, and made the best of their circumstances. A grocer's van used to come from Aberystwyth to Blaen-cwm chapel, and Will would come down to get their weekly groceries. It was mostly, if not all, barter for butter, or eggs, and he very often had not only his groceries, but a little cash as well to take home.

Their only means of travel was by horses. At one time, Will and Maggie had gone to Llanidloes and were on their way home, when a thick mist closed in on them. Maggie was on the oldest and most knowing pony, so Will suggested that he rode that one, and gave her her head, and she took them home safely.

In 1937, a little girl called Betty came to enrich their world, but unfortunately she died in March 1938, aged 8 months. Another daughter – Megan – was born in 1938. In late 1939 Maggie again became pregnant, but in late January 1940 she suffered a miscarriage, and if that was not enough of a problem in such an isolated place, it coincided with a storm of freezing rain, the like of which has not been seen since. Everything was covered in a sheet of ice which made even walking a most serious business.

I have often thought of the terrible predicament Will was in at the time, with Maggie very ill in bed, in urgent need of a doctor, with the nearest one at Pont-rhyd-y-groes. Another problem was 1½ year-old Megan. She was tied in her pram, and the pram tied to the dresser. William set off to Lluest-dôl-gwiail, and somebody from there went down to Ty-llwyd. Ifor Edwards went down to the shop at Cwmystwyth where thankfully, there was a telephone to communicate with the doctor at Pont-rhyd-y-groes. Dr Anderson, the resident doctor, had broken his arm, and a locum had to come instead. He came up to Ty-llwyd, and was escorted by Dei Evans, Esgair-wen, up to Nant-rhys under atrocious conditions. All this took a long time, and the locum made up a tonic for

■ William Griffiths at Nant-rhys in 1940. The wether that he is holding was buried in a snowdrift for three weeks during the storm of 1937.

Maggie, but did not have iodine and there was none in Nant-rhys. However, there was some at Lluest, two miles away, so my father, who was working there at the time, took some up, and Maggie thanked him, saying, 'When you get married, I'll give you a present', and indeed, when my parents married seven years later, she kept her promise, and gave them a teapot.

Marged Jane Rees went up from Ty-llwyd to help Will and Maggie through their ordeal, and they could have no better soul around at such a time. This complete covering of ice may be difficult to imagine, but it was total starvation for the sheep, and Will went to one part of the hill, and thought that there were less sheep than there should be, and was at a loss to know where they had gone. Suddenly a ewe appeared from a hole in the ground, and all became clear. The ice had formed a layer over a large patch of thick rushes, and the sheep somehow had managed to get under this layer, eating the roots of these rushes as they went, making what seemed like an underground shed. How good for the sheep these roots were, I don't know, but it kept them alive, and I remember William saying that not a rush grew in that particular spot for many years afterwards. Several people have told me that so treacherous was this covering of ice, that the dogs could not be coaxed to come out of their sheds at times.

During their stay at Nant-rhys Will and Maggie were very careful of their pennies, and were able to start farming on their own account at Ty'n ffordd, Ponterwyd, in 1942, renting the farm to start with at £40 a year, from Miss Mary Morgan (who moved to Rheidol View, Ponterwyd). In 1943, a son called Hughie was born, and in October 1948, they bought the place for £1650.

William was deemed always to have good dogs, and he used to walk sheep regularly to the local market at Devil's Bridge, and back again if he was not satisfied with the price. He might sometimes have a swift glass at the Hafod Arms Hotel on the way back, and many remember him leaving the dog in charge of the sheep, while he went in for a drink. He was a dab hand at pulling lambs when the ewe was having difficulty in giving birth. He had long lean hands that seemed to have been made for the job of working in confined spaces. Many of the descendants of the Griffiths family seem to have inherited this type of hand.

In 1945 Will and Maggie became foster parents to twelve year old Ronnie Hope. Ronnie had to stay with Maggie's sister in Penparcau for almost two weeks because of a very heavy fall of snow. He came up to Ponterwyd on the first available bus, and was the only passenger from Aberystwyth to Ponterwyd. Will came to meet him, and on their way home Ronnie remarked on how small the telephone poles were (because of the snow) and Will with his typical humour told him, 'You wait until summer, and you will see them grow'! Ronnie testifies that he had an excellent home with them, and has a wealth of stories about his time at Ty'n Ffordd.

On the 16th of June 1974, Maggie passed away, and in 1975 Will moved to a farm called Pendre, in Llanbadarn, which was very convenient in many respects, especially as he did not drive. He became very interested in sheepdog trials, and he and his friend/co-competitor/chauffeur, Ken Jones, from Ty'n-llechwedd, Llandre, clocked up many miles travelling to local trials. This period of his life gave him much satisfaction and enjoyment, and he made many new friends, and he always had a good tale to tell to acquaintances old and new.

William died on 14th of March 1991 aged 84.

Morgan Griffiths (1913–2003)

Born at Ty-nant, Ponterwyd, Morgan Griffiths was another son of Hugh and Leis Griffiths. He gave his whole life to shepherding, and I, as well as others are indebted to him for his many words of timely advice.

He started school in Ponterwyd, but left when the family moved to Nant-rhys. He told his best friend at school, Tom Morgan, Nant-cae-rhedyn that he was going to Nant-rhys to keep ponies. It is surprising how some things seem to be in the very soul of some individuals. His working career started when he was around twelve years old, when he went for a summer to work for Morgan and Lois Jones, of Blaen-myherin. Lois Jones (nee Thomas) was the daughter of Eisteddfa Gurig, Ponterwyd. Blaen-myherin was attached to Maen-arthur farm, Pont-rhyd-y-groes, and he well remembers himself and Lois Jones, carrying large sacks of chaff for the horses at Blaen-myherin from there.

Morgan then moved to Glan-gwy in Llangurig when he was thirteen. Being young and small, he recalls how he had a job to put the collars on the big work-horses at the time, often having to go up in the manger to do the job properly. He was there for eleven months, and then went to work at Ty-llwyd, Cwmystwyth. His main work (in the summer) was to drive the sheep up to the top of the hill. This was common practice in order to keep the lower slopes for the autumn and winter. Having been at the same job myself, there was quite a lot of walking to do from Aber-nant up to the Cardiganshire boundary at Pen-rhiw-lwyd.

There were eight cows there and he was taught to milk them by Elinor Raw, the daughter of Ty-llwyd.

Ty-llwyd was a busy place at the time, because they kept visitors as well, and produced a lot of their own food. A lot of country people lived off their farms, whereas today most live mainly from shops. Alfred and Ifor Edwards were there at the time. Morgan was there for 9 years and 5 months.

His next place of work was at Ty'n-bryn, in the same area, where he remained for 5 years. The owner was Morgan Howells who lived there with his two nieces Margaretta (Getta) and Elizabeth (Lizzie) Jones. Morgan Howells was not given the name to be a dog man, but he was a most astute person in the yards when it came to sorting out sheep. A lot can be learned from such people when you keep your eyes open, and mouth shut.

Morgan Howells believed in giving young lambs that were un-thrifty, or feeling the cold, a little gin, and he would give the shepherd a little to take with him to dish out to the needy ones. A shepherd he had in later years took the bottle round the corner of the rickyard and downed the contents, saying he needed it more that the lambs did!

Many years later than this, one of the nieces, a spinster, used to go and visit the Davies family who lived at nearby Bryn-peirian, and perhaps sometimes outstayed her welcome.

■ Morgan Griffiths, Nanty. Photo taken at Ty-llwyd in 1935.

The eldest son then made as if he was going to have a bath, bringing the cottage bath out, and placing it in front of the fire. She soon made her excuses and left. When the Devil drives...

Morgan Griffiths then married Eirwen Ann Jenkins, Ty'n-rhos, Cwmystwyth in November 1941, and they started their married life at Nanty, Llangurig, working for John George of Penwern, New Cross (1866–1946). All Eirwen had to start her married life with, was a clock presented to her by her employers (the Tarrant family of Hafod) and £1! Morgan was known from then on as 'Moc Nanty', and there are very few people who do not know him as such. They had five children – four boys and one girl. Eirwen and Moc made up a wonderful team. There was always a mountain of food there for anybody that called at their home, and I dearly treasure the visits I made there over the years. I took them once to the May Fair in Rhaeadr (while at Ty-llwyd). Morgan and I went for a drink in one of the pubs there, and I asked him what he would like, and he looked at a row of bottles, and saw one called *Forest Brown* and said 'I'll take that one, I live in the damn thing, I might as well drink it!' Nanty is surrounded by forest. I believe the first trees were planted there in 1929. Hours seemed to fly when in their company – the stories, leg pulling, recollections, and genuine hospitality. No matter how hard you tried to get away, it was always late when you left.

Morgan's employers spent a lot of their lives buying and selling livestock, and Lloyd George (1912–1994), John's son, took, over the years, thousands upon thousands of sheep to be sold at Brecon market, with Morgan as his right hand man. There was a need

■ Blaen-myherin in 1966. It is shameful that this beautiful, very typical hill farmhouse has been left to go, to what is today, a virtual ruin.

for good dogs to handle the sheep amidst the melee that was there on market day. Morgan had one dog who, when the sheep went down a certain street, shot off down some back alley and came out in front of them. He said he could never fathom how the dog had worked out which route to take, but he always got there in time.

Driving sheep from Nanty to Penwern, New Cross, formed part of his life for many years. There was less traffic at that time, but there were also less fences, which meant he had to be extra vigilant to keep the sheep on track. There were some steep slopes on either side, and if the sheep went down these slopes, it took a while to get them back up again.

At the time Morgan moved to Nanty, David George, Brenan, New Cross (1894–1981, also a son of John George) took over the hill of Blaen-myherin – a neighbouring sheepwalk of 1,200 acres – which was also looked after by Morgan.

Blaen-myherin had been home to the Evans family (who moved from there to Lluest-newydd, Ponterwyd), then to the Powell family, who later moved to Brynbrâs, Ponterwyd. The family consisted of Mrs Margaret Powell, her son Jim and three grand-children by her daughter, who had died young. They were called David James Jones, his brother Richard Gilbert and sister, Maggie May. Where did they go? Any descendants? Lots of questions, but few answers. Mrs Powell had a daughter Edith, who died in Tunnelton, West Virginia on the 20th of November 1910, aged 24. She had gone to the USA in 1907, and is buried at Camp Meeting Cemetery. I don't know what her cicumstances were when she died, but it was a long, long way from the peaceful valley of Blaen-myherin, to die so young, and so far from home.

Jim Powell had made a track to bring peat down from the top of the hill at Blaen-myherin, which is still called *ffordd fawn Jim* (Jim's peat track). I was fortunate, many years ago, to come across Jim Powell's account book, from which I took the following extracts. I believe this book may have been burned when its owner died.

Blaen-myherin was divided into 5 lots, (these figures from 1909)
Banc Mawr, 304 ewes
Y Groes, 352 ewes
Ffrwd, 128 ewes
Bistell, 226 ewes
Banc-isaf, 58 ewes,
with an extra 83 ewes appearing after shearing bringing the total count to 1,151. Lambing figures for this year show 46.9%.
Total ewes in 1905 = 1,445.
Total ewes in 1913 = 1,535
Prices of sheep in 1913, ewes at 19 shillings and 9 pence
Wool prices: 1913 = 11d per pound
                    1914 = 10 ¾d per pound
                    1916 = 11 ½d per pound
For sheep on 'tack' over summer the price was 2/– per ewe, and 1/6 per lamb. About 400 sheep were kept for summer grazing.

Jim Powell retired to a private house called Green Villa in Ponterwyd around 1931, and died on the 7th of January 1933, aged 61. His mother Margaret Powell died on the 24th of July 1928, aged 76, and the family graves are at Ysbyty Cynfyn Church.

After them came Morgan Jones, to shepherd Blaen-myherin, which was the hill attached to his family farm of Maen-arthur, Pont-rhyd-y-groes. He married Lois Thomas, from the old shepherding family of Eisteddfa Gurig, in Ponterwyd, and they had one daughter, Mair, born in 1926. When she started school, her father used to take her on a pony down to the next farm, Nant-syddion, where she would join my father, and his brother for the three mile walk to Ponterwyd school.

■ Children, attending the school at Ponterwyd in 1935, who had to walk over three miles to get there. L to R: Mair Jones, Blaen-myherin; Ritchie Howells, Nant Syddion; Tom Roberts, Lle'r neuaddau; Curigwen Morgan, Eisteddfa fach; John Byron Howells, Nant-Syddion (my father); Mair Roberts, Lle'r neuaddau; May Thomas, Eisteddfa Gurig. Photo by Miss Maggie Davies.

They as a family would walk the steep uphill and downhill to Cwmergyr Chapel, where Morgan Jones was precentor. Morgan Jones' brother Dan was a very capable engineer, and he rigged up a water-driven system to produce electricity which put them, in some respects, well ahead of many people, considering they lived in such an isolated situation. He was also the instigator of such a scheme in Pont-rhyd-y-groes and Ysbyty Ystwyth. He had also designed a small binder, when cutting corn. Obviously an ingenious man in his era. They also had a wireless there with head-phones, and M.J., when listening to it, had to make a simultaneous translation of what went on.

85

Morgan, Lois and Mair moved from Blaen-myherin in 1939 to Rheidol View in Ponterwyd, and then to Werndeg for a short spell, before going back to Maen-arthur in Pont-rhyd-y-groes. Mair married Richard Lloyd Hopkins in 1948, and their two daughters, Delyth and Gwyneth, have distinguished themselves on the cultural scene.

Blaen-myherin, like many of the surrounding sheepwalks, came under the ownership of the Forestry Commission, but the farmhouses and immediate fields, were let to tenants. My facts here are a bit fuzzy, but I believe a Major Lloyd came next to Blaen-myherin. (Was he the one who had a motor-bike and side-car selling cosmetics?) He had built himself a trailer, within the comfort of the parlour in the house, but found out when he had finished it, that he could not take it out! He recruited the help of the passing Morgan Griffiths, but in vain, and he had to dismantle the whole thing. Another time he asked Morgan to ring a pig for him, and when Morgan saw the pig, it was the thinnest he had ever seen. When he remarked upon his condition, the Major said, 'I can't understand him not doing well, because he gets all the straw he can eat!'

Morgan Griffiths and his brother Dan were handling sheep in the yards of Blaen-myherin, and the Major kindly brought them out some tea, with two big wedges of cake, which he told Morgan he had made himself. Dan not having caught this, asked Morgan what he had said, so Morgan enlightened him, and Dan, who was quite hungry said, 'I don't care if he's mixed it with his feet, I'll eat every crumb of it!'

During a very cold spell, the Major had put up a bed near to the fire, and he spent a lot of time in it to keep warm, and every now and then he would rush out, bring in some stakes from an old fence, jump into bed, and saw them up from there to feed the fire.

He was succeeded at Blaen-myherin by a Mr Hinds and his family. Had he connections with Poland? During his time there he had the misfortune of losing a mare, and he recruited the help of a gang of local forestry workers to help bury her. This was quite a task, and all done by hand at that time, after a day's work. They surely deserved the meal he gave them afterwards.

Next came Fred Jones, with his wife Daisy and son Alan. They had come there from Staffordshire in 1954. Fred worked for the Forestry Commission, as well as working the smallholding. It was with Fred that I saw my first Border Collie, called Nip, with my father explaining to me how they used their eye to control sheep. Morgan Griffiths was driving sheep up from down-country, and there was a big flood in the river, so the only way to get them over was on a narrow foot-bridge. Daisy Jones came down to investigate, and although she was heavily pregnant, helped to get the sheep onto, and over the bridge, and also pulled many out of the river if they fell in. Their daughter Delyth was born at Blaen-myherin in May 1956, and indeed was the last baby to be born there.

Alan and I, being of the same age, were school pals, and I well remember going up there, and riding on their pony 'Dolly'. Having my photo taken on her back was a big bonus, as we never had a camera at home. Happy, blissful days.

Fred and his family moved from there in 1958, to a farm called Nant-yr-arian (silver-brook) in Goginan. Very soon after they had moved, Nip had been tied in an out-building, but unfortunately jumped through an opening, and hung himself. That incident has never left my mind, and I always try to ensure, whenever I tie a dog, that it is not in a position to commit such an act. The Jones family were the last to live at Blaen-myherin full-time.

Morgan Griffiths spent a lot of his time in later years at Nanty helping neighbours, especially at Hendre, Llangurig, at Lluest-dôl-gwiail, and with Captain Bennett Evans in Bont-rhyd-galed. He was a strong advocate of the Welsh sheepdogs. He bought his first bitch from Lewis Morgan, Lluest, when about 12 years old for six shillings, and was quite proud of her, but said he was running almost as much as her, in order to get the work done. Years later he bought a strong Welsh, slate grey dog from Cwm Dewi, in Brecon for £1, and thankfully that dog's lineage is still around.

After a gathering, when the sheep were in the yards, you would see him sending his heading dogs away a good distance, and telling them to lie down there. The object of this was two-fold – firstly, so that they would not be rattling around in the yards, therefore spoiling their heading instincts, and secondly, to make sure that they were rested and fresh for the next gather.

It was Morgan who drove his brother Will's cattle from Nant-rhys when he left, to Ty'n-ffordd, and he also drove John Davies' cattle from Nant-rhys to Waun-fyddau, Llanfihangel-y-creuddyn, in 1947. John Davies and his wife lost a little girl called Elen, when she was about a year old, while at Nant-rhys. They were the last family to live there, and their daughter Olwen, born in 1945, was the last baby to be born in this isolated hill farm, all under afforestation by now.

Morgan farmed the in-by land of Nanty himself, with a full and quality stock, but on the 25th of April 1991, he lost Eirwen, who had been his main-stay for fifty years. She was 70 years old, and was buried at Cwmystwyth chapel. He moved later to a small holding near by called Bron-gwy, with his son Ronnie taking over at Nanty. His other son Gareth is a shepherd at Nant-yr-Hafod, Staylittle, and you'd never guess, but he is interested in horses, and Welsh sheepdogs!

Morgan passed away on the 30th of August 2003, aged 90. His funeral at Siloam Chapel, Cwmystwyth, was a massive one, with family and friends from near and far coming to bid him their last farewell and respects. The volume of people in attendance meant that the quality of the singing was something that will be remembered for a long time, as a truly meaningful way of saying goodbye to a man who had seen so many changes during his lifetime, and yet kept young in spirit. I will always be grateful for the many reminiscences he shared with me over the years, and many are recorded here for posterity.

Pigs

These animals were very important in the society of yesteryear, as they provided meat in abundance, which was preserved by salting. Pigs also served to use up all sorts of scraps and vegetable waste, and there is not an animal on the farm that utilises its food to better advantage. I heard one old boy from the Welshpool area say 'A farm ain't a farm without a pig and a missus' and indeed the pig was thought of as a very valuable member of the family. In many cases it was a custom to keep two pigs, one to kill and one to sell, which was alluded to as 'the gent that pays the rent'!

I came across the following poem which was pubilshed in the *Cambrian News* in 1882, but is probably a lot older than that:

> *Ye pigge he is a pretty fowl*
> *And wond-rous good to eat*
> *Hys ham is good, lykewise his jowl*
> *And eke hys little feete.*
> *But if you try a thousand years*
> *I trow you still will fayle*
> *To make a silk purse of his eare*
> *Or a wissel of his tayle.*

It is often stated that you could use everything from a pig except its squeak.

Pig killing day was an important one, the cumulation of a year's careful feeding, and some pigs grew to monstrous sizes, with strong neighbours coming to help haul the beast to hang. Most of the hill people would be able to kill a pig, and if not, a neighbour would be at hand. Many people made a side-line of the job, and went around many farms in the area, and were indeed very clean and skilful butchers. The squealing which was associated with the job was due to the pig being restrained, and not with any act on the butcher's behalf. The knives used were absolutely razor sharp, and the incision made to cut the main arteries was made in a twinkling. A perfect stab meant that the knife came out without a trace of blood on it.

The timing of the killing was important when you intended to salt the meat. The cooler the weather the better, and it was deemed best if there was an 'R' in the name of the month. Sows had to be not in heat at the time, as it was said the meat would not keep. Women who were pregnant were not allowed to salt the pig. How much credence to the ill effect this would have I do not know, but anything which might have an adverse effect on a whole year's supply of food was shunned.

The blood was collected to make one of two dishes. One was the well-known blood pudding, and the other a much less known sweet dish also called blood pudding or blood cake. It was also made out of goose blood. The blood when caught was stirred vigorously to keep it from clotting. When it had cooled it was boiled and continuously stirred, and then brown sugar and treacle and currants or sultanas were added, and the whole put in an oven. Waste not, want not.

The next job was to clean the pig of its hairs, and the outer layer of skin. This was done by scalding. Boiling water was poured onto the pig, and special scrapers were then used to remove the hairs plus excess skin. In a hard water area washing soda was sometimes added to the water.

The pig would then be hung up and washed thoroughly. Then came the disembowelling stage. The first item to be taken from inside was the caul, and this would be draped over the pig's hind legs to dry out. It would be used later for covering faggots. The bladder was then taken out, and this would be blown up and used as a football by the children. Alternatively, it would be filled with lard after it had been melted down, and hung under the loft. From this came the saying about a bald man – that he was 'as bald as a lard ball'. The gall bladder was taken off the liver and hung to dry. This would be used as a poultice, especially good for thorns embedded in flesh.

The innards would then be put in a large clean receptacle, and later they would be 'picked'. When I was working with Charles Evans in Glaspwll, Machynlleth, in 1970, a man called Mr David Lloyd from Staylittle (Dei Gronwen) came to kill the pig there, and proved himself to be a tidy and competent butcher. In a chat afterwards he said that one of the most interesting things he had experienced was his mother teaching him to 'pick' the pig's intestines. I was fascinated by this, and wished to see the job being done. I, however, moved to work in the Tregaron area, and our getting together did not materialize, and eventually I heard that he had passed away. I felt really bad about this, as I had lost a chance at a craft of which I had heard nobody else mention. However, all was not lost. By chance a David Jones from Llanidloes was delivering coal to Gelli-Isaf, Ponterwyd, and it turned out he was a nephew to Dei Lloyd, and having told my tale, he said his mother Nancy (Dei's sister) knew about the picking. So, at the first opportunity, I shot off to see her, laden with a pig's insides, and the art was demonstrated to me – about 25 years since I had first heard about it. The pickings were then put in an oven with a bit of seasoning, and after a while the excess fat was poured off, and the remaining bits cooked till they became similar to crackling. Pure satisfaction at having experienced something I thought I had lost forever, and it was she who also taught me about the sweet blood pudding. To all this came the bonus of a friendship with a truly remarkable lady. Nancy Jones had been disabled from birth, but possessed a kind, bubbling personality, and a heart of gold that encompassed everybody she met. Her energy, and the kindness she showed to so many would be difficult to measure. She passed away on the 13th of May 2001 aged 89 years. My gratitude for having met her will remain while my memory lasts. Rest in Peace, Nancy for you did a very good day's work.

The next day, the pig would be cut up. First the head was taken off, and then the carcass was marked with a knife along both sides of the backbone. The carcass was then cut along these marks, producing three lengthwise sections. The middle piece (containing the backbone) was then cut up into blocks, and this was shared with neighbours, who would return the favour when their pig was killed. The two sides were then lowered onto benches, and the fat was taken off, likewise the ribs (spare rib) and the prized fillet of pork (*golwyth melys*). After this the sides were cut into three big pieces – the ham, the flitch (in the middle), and the shoulder. At the top of the flitches was a thick piece of lean meat, and a lot of this would be eaten by the salt so it was cut with a sharp knife in long thin strips. This would be material for a fry-up for the family and workers, and food truly fit for a king.

The hip-bone part of the ham (*asgwrn y bwmbel*) was then taken away, leaving the hip joint exposed, and then the meat was ready for salting. The salt was rubbed into the meat and a lot of rubbing was done on the outer (skin) side. Some people put the salt in the cut-off ears of the pig and used them to rub instead of their hands. A bed of salt was then laid on stone slabs, and the meat laid upon it, skin-side down, and the whole covered with salt.

After 3 to 5 days this salt would begin to 'weep' (get wet, *wylo* in Welsh) and it was thrown out and the re-salting took place. This time the pieces were put back meat-side down. After a week from the re-salting the cheeks or jowl cut from the head were taken out to be hung, and after another week the flitches were taken out, and then in another week or fortnight, depending on their size, the hams were ready. Salt is a very penetrative agent and many old farmhouses still bear the trade mark of these saltings in the walls near the salting slabs. The modern plastic baths make a far better place for salting, without the unwelcome side effects.

Some people put saltpetre or pepper around the bone area as an extra precaution. Others would rub brown sugar into the meat-side a few days before it was taken from the salt. This served to give the meat a more moist texture, as well as added taste.

The head, after it had been cut up, was allowed to soak in saltwater for 24 hours and was boiled to make brawn, with the trotters thrown in to produce the gelatine which helped bind the meat together. Brawn varied from cook to cook. Sometimes it was an unappetising wobbly jelly mass, while others produced a delicious solid and sliceable product. A recipe which my late wife got from Miss Mair Jones, Tan-yr-allt, Capel Bangor, involved a pound of pig's liver and a pound of shin beef. All this would simmer for at least 4 hours. Seasoning would be added to taste. This would be put in basins with enough liquid to bind the meat together, left to cool, turned out and sliced.

Over-night Houses (Tai Unos)

These sprang up on Common land in a desperate bid to thwart poverty by smallholders, and especially landless villagers, after the coming of the Tithe Commutation Act in 1839. Many villagers were able to keep a cow or two, and perhaps a few ponies, by turning them out to graze on the common, where they would also cut rushes for bedding, and for thatching their cottages. They were often totally dependent on this common for their peat, which was vital for their heating, and more often than not their only source of warmth.

After the passing of the Act, farmers and landowners took this Common land to be part of their domains, and so the long-standing practice of turning cows out, peat cutting etc. was denied to the villagers, causing great hardship as a result. For some, the only way out was to build a house, and fight their corner to try and keep the land they were able to enclose.

The way they set about it was, that they first of all had to decide where to build, then get as many friends and neighbours as they could (20 to 35 people, armed with various tools) in on this closely guarded secret. Many of these were craftsmen of one sort or another, many picked for their physical strength to manhandle timber and stones. On a given night, everybody was called together, and a rough house was erected. What was important was that smoke had to appear from the chimney at dawn next day. The then new owner could throw an axe in every direction from the house, and enclose the land within that boundary. Within a year they would add another field to their holding.

The preferred time for this work was in late spring/early summer, so that a better house could be built before the onset of winter. This undertaking called for a stout heart, as farmers and landowners made life as unpleasant as possible for these squatters, often employing drunken blackguards to destroy their crops, and kill or injure animals, in a bid to oust them.

This practice of building over-night houses may have been an old conception, as many places still hold the name *unos* (one-night) – for example, Hafod Unos Hall in Conwy, North Wales. I know of two places that are known locally as 'Quick' – one is Gelli-uchaf in Ponterwyd (incidentally where my father was born on 14th of November 1922), and the other is Gwar-ffynnon on the land of Mynachdy in Ystrad Meurig – perhaps alluding that the original houses were *tai unos,* that is, built suddenly.

Postmen

In mentioning these isolated farmsteads that are indeed 'far from the madding crowd', there was one person who was very important to one and all of them, and that was the local postman. There was many a week that passed, and he was the only person that the occupants saw. His role in delivering letters was a small one compared to being the bringer of good and bad news, gossip, and the carrier of messages by word of mouth from one family to another. He also brought small items and medicines from the villages they dealt with.

Alfred Morgan (Alf the Post) Lan-fawr, Cwmystwyth, was such a man. His daily round was 17 miles covering some bleak and rough ground, although, if the truth was told, he had been in worse places. While serving with the South Wales Borderers during the First World War, he was one of the few that came out alive from Mametz Wood. 12,000 troops entered the Woods on the 7th of July 1916, and five days later, after experiencing a true hell upon earth, there were 4,000 dead, wounded, or missing.

Alfred, like many who had had such dreadful, almost indescribable, experiences, especially from the First World War, seldom spoke about the carnage they had witnessed, but he once told me that it was no good making friends at this time, because they were there one moment, and the next, all you would see was a pile of rags. I shudder to think of people today, who have actually *volunteered* to go into various Services, knowing full well that they might see something gruesome, then claiming post-traumatic stress, and actually being given compensation of thousands of pounds. People like Alf were rail-roaded into a situation that was the furthest thing from their minds, and having witnessed the slaughter of the cream of our society, did not get any compensation.

His post round, when Nant-rhys and Tyrpeg-y-mynydd were populated, must have been quite a trek. Needless to say he did not go to these places every day. He left his bike on the Blaen-cwm side of the young Ystwyth river, and crossed over onto Lluest-dôl-gwiail land, and followed the river Diluw up past Lluest, and on to Nant-rhys. From the time he left his bike, to the time he returned, it was 10 minutes short of two hours, just to deliver mail to two houses.

There was a move at one time to have the post to Bodtalog and Tyrpeg-y-mynydd delivered from the Elan Valley side, but Bill Pugh opposed this quite strongly, as it would mean he would miss his friend Alf, and of course the news of Cwmystwyth, and the advance warning of imminent gatherings, stray sheep etc. that Alf relayed between one farm and another, which were more important sometimes than the letters he delivered.

Alfred and Bill, as can be imagined, were good friends over many years, and Alfred, being fairly tied to his post round, had asked Bill to go and buy a pig for him, and the pig was duly delivered after dark one evening. Next morning Alfred was aghast to find that the pig was a black one (they don't come up as clean as a white pig after scraping, because of the pigmentation) and one of the local wags, who was also a bit of a poet, made up some poems for the occasion. That episode took a lot of living down!

He retired in 1964 on his 65th birthday. I believe he had the opportunity, if he wished, to go on until 70, but he declined, saying 'I want to finish with the job, before the job finishes me'. He said he would miss seeing his friends on the round, because he had seen most of them daily since 1929, when he started on the post.

Alf was a very genial person, full of compassion when needed, and yet a leg-puller of the highest degree at other times. I will always treasure the times I visited him and his wife Annie (both were relatives of mine). All visitors were given a warm welcome, and after Alf's death on the 7th of July 1972 aged 73, I would like to praise the modern postmen, who afterwards called with her every day for a cup of tea, and to make sure she was all right, regardless of whether there were any letters or not. Postmen, thankfully, if unofficially, still play this vital role in our society, especially amongst the elderly. Annie died on 9th of July 1983 aged 70.

My father had an aunt (Mrs Mary Rees) living at Rhos-yr-hydd, in Trisant, and we had gone there one day, which happened to be about a fortnight after the local postman, Mr Evan Davies, Ty'n-Lon, Devil's Bridge had retired, and Aunt Mary was bemoaning

■ The local postman with a group of shepherds. L to R: Alfred Morgan, Lanfawr; Ifor Edwards, Pwll peirian; Christmas Griffiths, Nant-rhys; William Griffiths, Nant-rhys; Tom Emanuel, Lluest-dol-gwiail; Alfred Edwards,Ty-llwyd. Every chance was taken to create humour as can be seen by Ifor wearing the postman's hat.

his loss, and said: 'This new postman is good for nothing except delivering letters!', which in itself says reams about the value of people in public service with local knowledge. The letters they received were not so important, but the news they gleaned from Evan Davies meant a lot to them.

I relate the following story to prove, if at all it is needed, how astute and studious these people were. John (Mary's son) – a cool, fairly non-descript individual – would go to the market in Devil's Bridge on a Wednesday, and he would memorize who had sold, how many sheep were in the lot, who was bidding, who bought them, and for how much. He would return home that evening, relate all this to his mother, and if somebody happened to call on the Thursday, and have a chat with her, you could swear she had been at the market herself, so detailed was her account.

Another old country postman had at one time been given a young lad to help him out. He handed the youngster the mail to deliver, and gave him another package tied with string. Then he told the young man 'When you get to [such-and-such a] quarry, burn this package'. The young postman, on reaching the quarry, was afraid to tamper with the mail, as it might affect his job if he were caught, so he delivered all the contents of this package to an isolated community. In about a fortnight's time, a lot of parcels arrived at the local Post Office, and the old postman turned on the youngster, and said 'You little bugger, didn't I tell you to burn that package'. The package had contained mail-order catalogues, and he had worked out that if they weren't delivered, there would not be the follow up of large parcels to carry a long distance!

Such mail order was a great boon to some of these cut-off communities, as they could get new and fashionable goods without leaving their homes, and delivered to their door.

My paternal great-uncle, the late I.R. Howells, Ponterwyd, took on a job as postman when he was a youngster, and used to have a cup of tea every morning with a lady who was kind-hearted, but a little half-baked. She used to talk to herself a lot. One day he was having his cuppa, and she was in the pantry talking to herself, and saying 'The stranger doesn't know a little mouse drowned in the milk last night!'

From 1902, the mail to Ponterwyd used to come via the narrow-gauge train to Devil's Bridge, but in 1925 that changed, so that it came direct from Aberystwyth. The out-lying farms of Nant-syddion and Blaen-myherin used to be served by postmen from Ponterwyd, but in later years their postal address was changed to Devil's Bridge, which made more geographical sense. Mail to the upper Cwmystwyth area was at one time delivered to Ty-llwyd, and then via their shepherds to the out-lying farms. The letters to Aber-gwngu were taken by the shepherd of Blaen-cwm who, on his rounds, would be certain to meet the shepherd of Aber-gwngu at his duties. How things have changed.

A historic note in passing, while mentioning Nant-syddion. It was here that the first quads recorded in the area were born, three girls, Catherine, Elizabeth, and Margaret, and one boy, Isaac. They were the children of Isaac and Margaret Hughes. Alas, their fate was sealed because of circumstances of poverty and typhus, and they all died between their fourth and tenth day. That, unfortunately, was not all that fate threw at the family, another son, Hugh, 5 years old, died, as did his sister Hannah aged 3, and their father Isaac, aged 31. All this happened between the 23rd of February 1856 and the 12th of March 1856. A sorry tale which is recorded on a headstone, not far from the door of Ysbyty Cynfyn Church near Ponterwyd.

■ My grandparents, John Rowland and Margaretta (Getta) Howells at Nant Syddion. Getta was a sister to I.R. Howells. They lived there from 1932 to 1954.

Nobody knows what happened to Margaret (the mother), the only one of the family to survive, but a Margaret Hughes from nearby Parkgwyn was buried on the 6th of April, 1871 aged 46 at Ysbyty Cynfyn. Could she have been the mother? The age fits, so another mystery to solve.

Another postman in the Ponterwyd area was Edgar Jones (1904–1984). He was, as a young man, on the Nant-y-moch/Hengwm round, and at one time, during a heavy snowstorm, he had to stay overnight at Nant-y-moch, because he could not get back to Ponterwyd.

Edgar was of a light physical build, and used to go to help his relatives at Eisteddfa Gurig to catch sheep at shearing time. His co-catcher was Baldwin Jones, from Llanbadarn, a shorter but stronger man (who worked for Lovesgrove Estate) and Edgar said jokingly to him 'Let's get one thing clear before we start – you catch the big ones, I'll catch the little ones!'

Edgar Jones had some land in Ponterwyd, with a few sheep grazing there, but he lived in Penparcau, on the outskirts of Aberystwyth. If one of the sheep had anything wrong with it, and needed special attention, he would liaise with another postman (well known for his exploits in carrying anything and everything in his van – once bringing a washing machine for a country friend from Aberystwyth) and the ewe was taken in his van to Edgar's shed. A friend in need …

Another postman story was related to me by my father-in-law, John Griffiths, Llangeitho. The postman in question was delivering to an isolated farm, and the occupant, interested in horses, asked him daily whether a certain mare at a farm lower down the valley had foaled. One day he had the satisfaction of being told that she had. But that alone did not satisfy his curiosity, he wanted to know of what sex the foal was. The postman went up in a few days' time, and as it happened the farmer was out at the time, so he left him a note:

There's no portmanteau hanging
Nor yard beneath is showing
I'm positive it is a She
I saw her pee this morning!

Just in case anybody thinks the post delivery job is male dominated, there were many women who did this work with great dedication, and I can think of two, still around, who took letters to the widely-spread community, they being Mrs May Morgan (nee Jenkins) Ochor Rhos, and Mrs Elizabeth Allen, The Vicarage, both of Devil's Bridge. Mrs Allen is a sister to Tom Williams, the shepherd already mentioned.

Isaac Richard Howells

Since mention was made of I.R. Howells, here follows a short account of his life and achievements. The following is a record of his working life in his own words, probably written around 1968:

> *My parents were Richard and Anne (nee Thomas) Howells, and I was born at Ochor-glog, Cwmystwyth in May 1892. My first job after leaving school at the age of 14 was shepherding on common land – here it was everybody for himself working with good dogs to try and keep within the boundaries. After a while I left this work and returned home to work in the lead mines for 10d per day. At that time my father earned 18s per week with five to provide for.*
>
> *After this I took up employment at the shop and Post Office at Ponterwyd. The work included delivering post twice a week to Nantymoch, Hengwm and Camdwr Mawr Lead Mine. At that time there were about 200 or more miners working there and, riding a pony, it was 4pm by the time I returned. During the rest of the week I had four horses to look after – without any help – and all the chaffing and feeding was done by hand. I also had to make visits to Aberystwyth with a cart drawn by two horses to meet the steamboat that was delivering goods to Aberystwyth harbour. In those days we were hauling basic slag from the harbour to local farms. The roads at that time were in a very bad state and heavily rutted.*
>
> *At this period of time there were three shops in the Ponterwyd district and four lead mines. Everything had to be carried by road and one would often see up to 14 horse-drawn carts – there were no motor vehicles. In fact one could sleep on top of the load for miles!*
>
> *I later left the Post Office to work in South Wales. When the Great War broke out I had to return to work in the lead mines once more. In 1916 I was married but there was no honeymoon. At the cessation of hostilities we went back to South Wales. During 1921 there was a strike which lasted six months, after which I returned to South Wales where I suffered an accident, after which I could no longer do heavy work.*
>
> *After this I decided to buy a fourteen-seater bus to run to Aberystwyth. At that time I was living at Mount, Ponterwyd, and I took over 15 acres of rough land. I had an idea that if I threw acorns and put four pigs on it they would cut up the ground – but this idea didn't work. Neither did the attempt to plough with horses. I bought one of the first Ferguson tractors from a man called Tom Norton but this again did not work. Sir George Stapleton, who came to*

Aberystwyth in 1912, was in charge of the Cahn Hill Improvement Scheme at Pwllpeirian and offered me a Caterpillar and driver. Sir George was a pioneer in reseeding, and I also had the help of Mr Moses Griffiths and Mr Llew Phillips. They introduced me to better seeds, and taught local people to take advantage of their sterling work, and it worked very well.

As we were so pleased with the first seeding, it was decided to buy two more tractors to continue the reseeding which had improved the whole district. As pioneers in the district we had about a 15 mile radius of ploughing at different farms, where we continued our successful reseeding. We, ourselves, reseeded somewhere around 220 acres of fields and rough ground, scuffling with about four tons of lime and one ton of slag per acre and, of course, the best seeds. The first sowings of 33 years ago are still good. It is important to get the suitable grass and clover balance to stand grazing for 20 years, and no less important to have a guarantee on all seeds. Also planted were twelve shelter belts, and these became very useful for hurdles and gates, and, at the present time we are preparing for next year, planting 38,000 trees. Grants for building came from the Aberystwyth R.D.C. for six houses. Agricultural grants were also obtained for outbuildings, sheep bath and drainage scheme.

My sons and I were pioneers for collecting milk under Cow & Gate for North Cardiganshire, and also pioneers in collecting refuse for the R.D.C. Meat was hauled from Aberystwyth slaughterhouse to Smithfield, London four times a week, other haulage and garage work was also carried out for 35 years. An added calling was taxi work as very few people owned cars at this time.

[The mention of reseeding reminds me of a paragraph I read, probably written almost 300 years ago: 'Whoever can make two ears of corn, or two blades of grass to grow upon a spot of ground where only one grew before, will deserve better of mankind, and do more essential service to his country than the whole race of Politicians put together'. How very true, then and now.]

He was a self-made man, beginning with very little, but had a strong business acumen, and a lot of foresight. His farming and environmental contributions still hold good today, and others still benefit from them, as will probably other generations.

One not-so-good thing that he did, was to pull down the large water-wheel at Llywernog Mine (*Gwaith Poole*) – possibly to get the pitch-pine beams in its structure. This wheel measured 50 feet in diameter, by 3 feet 6 inches wide. This happened in January 1953. The metal parts realised £50 scrap value. For the story of the demolition, see the *Welsh Gazette*, 29th of January 1953. It states that £3 worth of gunpowder was used to blow up what would cost today £50,000 to replace!

He worked hard, but also knew how to enjoy himself, and at various functions connected with public life, he would impress the ladies with his dancing, and his charismatic nature made him popular in many circles of life.

One of his strong loves in life were sheepdogs, and he had a wonderful way with them. His father (my great-grandfather) was reputed to take in a new dog, and within a week he would have got him to do most of what he wanted, just by understanding the nature of the dog. I.R.H. had definitely inherited this talent from his father. I remember

■ Mr I.R. Howells with his dogs, taken in 1953 near the garage he established in Ponterwyd.

his old dog Jock who almost understood all that was said to him. Even the household cat, at his '*hyssgit*' would go like a bat out of hell for the nearest opening, and yet at his '*pws fach*', would turn on the window sill and come back to nestle in his lap.

Mr and Mrs Howells would enjoy going to some of the major sheepdog trials, especially in the company of their daughter Beryl, and son-in-law, Norman Smith (he worked in the Rheola Forestry, near Resolven, South Wales). I can picture them now, each one sat in a folding chair by a picnic table that was loaded with every conceivable kind of food, and anybody they knew who passed by was invited to have a bite to eat. How Beryl managed to create such a feast, let alone stuff it all in a car, I could never fathom. This scene conjured up a vision of totally content country folk, after a lifetime of hard work.

I.R.H. and a helper were at one time moving sheep in the village of Ponterwyd, and a passing lorry meant that they had to move the sheep to the side of the road, and this happened to be near a house called Trinity (in a row of three houses, now no longer there). The door of the house unfortunately was open, and a ram, not only went in, but went up the stairs, followed by about a dozen of his wives! They went up in about half a minute, but it took a lot longer to get then down. A shepherd's lot can, sometimes, not be a happy one!

Isaac Richard Howells died in 1972 aged 79 and Mary Jane, his wife, died in 1973 aged 80.

Gathering sheep for Marking

This was the first gathering of the year on many hills, and for the new crop of lambs it was their first handling, and it takes very little imagination to guess how they reacted to this strange experience. A long, cold, late spring, would mean that the ewes on an open hill would have had a hard time, and their lambs therefore would not be as hearty, but in a good year the lambs were full of vigour, and often shot off in gangs of about a dozen or so at a time, and they took a lot of turning back into the flock, and while a few men, and many dogs had concentrated their efforts on getting these back, another lot were making good their chance to escape. Trials and tribulations, leaving men and dogs exhausted.

Some hills lend themselves well to this operation inasmuch as the sheep enter an area from which it is difficult to escape, but others were notorious for being difficult at this first gathering. Sometimes there were rocks, or broken stones, into which the lambs could escape, and make it virtually impossible for the dogs to turn them back. Some did escape, and would try the same trick at the next gathering, giving the dogs a run for their money. One of the tried and tested strategies of these first gatherings was to try to handle smaller lots, and most important to try not to disturb too much of the flock, therefore keeping the lambs with their mothers. Once they lose contact with each other, they start to mill around looking for each other, instead of moving on in the desired direction.

Once they had been put into the yards, the sorting out began – all by hand in years gone by – and you would inevitably get stray ewes with lambs, and unless somebody like Ned Rees, with a keen sense of observation, had seen them together, it was a long, drawn-out process to try to pick out the estranged couples. The solution to this was to smear marking fluid on the stray ewe's belly, in front of her udders, and turn her in with the unmarked lambs, in the hope that her lamb, in the act of suckling, would rub itself in the raddle, and be easy to pick out. The lamb would then be ear-marked the same as its mother, and both put in with the other strangers.

The flock lambs would then be ear-marked (reference will be made to this later) and the male lambs castrated, except the ones which were deemed to be good enough to be kept on as stock rams. Most everybody involved would have his say about the young ram's characteristics. One would say his ears or tail was too long, another would say his coat was too loose, or his nostrils not black enough, but it was always wiser to err on the side of caution, because there is nothing worse than to see a magnificent type of lamb later on in the year, but without his credentials, bearing in mind that castration is an irreversible operation!

On one memorable occasion, when I was at Ty-llwyd (in the late sixties), we were all busy at ear-marking and castrating the lambs, and a neighbour, Alun Morgan, Pentre, Cwmystwyth was there to help with the gathering. He always had a tale to tell, and was

■ Group of shepherds at a gathering near Llyn Rhuddnant. From the left: Morgan Griffiths, Nanty; Alfred Edwards, Ty-llwyd; Alun Morgan, Pentre; Tom Williams, Pwllpeirian; Ifor Edwards, Pwllpeirian; Tom Griffiths, Ysgubor fach.

renowned as a leg-puller of the highest degree. Alfred Edwards was the butt of many of his jokes and bantering, and Alun kept us all in stitches with his ribald comments. At the end of one particular lot of sheep, Alfred asked him, knowing full well what the outcome of his question would be 'How many lambs did we mark Alun?', and got the reply 'Two hundred and thirty five', which was exactly how many there were. Through all the constant patter he churned out, Alun was able to concentrate, and count each lamb that left the hands of two people ear-marking. To me (who hasn't got an ounce of a mathematical brain) this was quite a feat.

Alun, unfortunately, left us far too soon (1929–1995) and he would have been to me today, a most valuable source of information with his recollections, and his anecdotes of the past would have been a lot of grist for my mill. We can only be grateful for small mercies, as he was one of the characters that I, and many others, were pleased to have known and befriended.

John Davies (1885–1966)

For our next shepherd we cross the Ceredigion boundary, but only just, towards Llangurig. John Davies was known as 'John y Bont' because of his home of Bont-rhyd-galed (bridge of the hard ford), Llangurig. He was a big man in more than one sense, certainly the tallest of the shepherds mentioned here, six foot seven in his stockinged feet.

I believe he was born at a place called Mynachlog in the Llangurig area. His father Owen Davies was buried from there in 1903 aged 61, and was born possibly at Nantydnerth, near Mynachlog. His mother, formerly Martha Owen, came from Brithdir, Hen Neuadd, and died on September 1st 1920, aged 76.

John worked as a young man at Nant-iago lead mine, and used to go there on horse-back with food to last him a week carried in a pillow case. This was the norm for many people of that era, and they stayed in barracks near the mine during the week, and went home at weekends. The living conditions were very harsh, and the safeguarding of their week's rations was a big problem. Two of their worries were rats, and hungry dogs that sometimes roamed from nearby farms. There is one story of miners staying at the barracks near Esgair Hir lead mine near Talybont, who were regularly plagued by a cunning dog which broke in and ate their supplies. This was very serious business, and eventually the dog was caught, but for all their pent-up feelings not one of them could bring himself to kill the dog, so it was decided to tie a stick of explosive to the culprit with a short fuse attached. The dog was then let off, but as can be imagined, his new-found freedom was short-lived!

John Davies started to work as a shepherd for Captain George Bennett Evans in 1912, and according to a statement made by Mrs Bennett Evans in the Western Mail (9th of June 1973) she said 'When my husband came home after World War 1 he found that his shepherd John Davies had built up both stock and money in the bank', and further described John as 'a wonderful man, who was brought up in an isolated mountain cottage, and most of his education came from Sunday School. He was a great Bible reader'. I believe it was James Hogg, the Ettrick Shepherd that said 'Thus interested in the business of his employer, the shepherd enjoys a position superior to that of hired servants generally' and this was certainly true in the case of John Davies. There was a rumour that John and the Captain had tossed a coin to see which one of them would go to the First World War.

In the same article it said that when John and Capt. Bennett Evans started in 1912 the total stock of sheep was 2,000 and no cattle. This changed after a period of years, and accumulation of more land, to carry a stock of nearly 10,000 sheep and 250 head of cattle. However, the relationship between John and the Captain did not run smoothly

■ John Davies in his latter years, with Martha on his left and his niece, Mrs Mary Jane Morgan, Llanidloes.

at all times. In 1933 they had a big difference of opinion (over wages possibly) and the outcome was that John left and went to work for David Lloyd, Y Glyn, as a shepherd at Rhyd-y-bennwch. This was a situation probably regretted by both parties, but was resolved in about two years' time when the Captain persuaded John to return to his old job.

Captain Bennett Evans was a pioneer of hill land improvement, and was awarded the O.B.E. for services to agriculture c.1955. He died in 1972 aged 85. His family still farm the area where he made such changes so many years ago. When Capt. Evans lived at Peithyll, Capel Dewi, he proved himself to be a very capable organist at St. John's Church at Penrhyncoch. In 1932 he hit upon the idea of selling meat directly to the house-wife, cutting out the middle-man whom he deemed to be making too much profit. Today, 70 years later, many organisations are doing the same thing. What's new in life!

When the sheep were sent up from Peithyll in the spring to Bont-rhyd-galed, especially if the weather was inclement (not many fences around at that time) the sheep often headed back whence they had come from, and John had very often to go down as far as Bwlch Nant-yr-arian in Ponterwyd to turn them back.

Several years ago I received a note from Miss Mary Davies, Dyffryn, Aberhosan – taken, I believe, from a sale catalogue of the estate of Watkin Williams Wynn, Wynnstay, c.1919, and referring to Bont-rhyd-galed it states: 'In the occupation of Mr G.L. Bennett Evans at the rent of £75. Tithe rent charge commutation £8–5–4 paid by the Landlord. The tenant is allowed to keep 1,650 sheep. Sheepwalk 955 acres. Total acreage 1,040. Price £8,100'.

Cefn-brwyn, a neighbouring sheepwalk, was also offered for sale about this time, and became (and still is) incorporated in the lands that the Bennett Evans' farm. Again I quote from Mary Davies' note: 'This magnificent farm is let to Mr Thomas Jervis at the very low rent of £60. Total acres 1,992. The tenant is allowed by agreement to keep 2,300 sheep on the sheepwalk'.

I am indebted to people like Mary, who has done, and still does a lot of work for posterity, for passing on information about things that are of interest to me.

The main owner of land in this area was Sir Watkin Williams Wynn. His boundary stones are still visible, marked W.W.W., and as the Captain accumulated more land he earned the nick-name 'Syr Watkin Bach' (little Sir Watkin).

Sarah, a daughter of the Jervis family of Cefn-brwyn, had married a Richard Thomas, who was the shepherd at Cefn-brwyn. Their son Thomas became a well-known shepherd at Perfedd-nant, in the Tywyn, Meirioneth area. In the early twenties (1924?) the Captain called on John one evening and said 'I've found a new man to shepherd Cefn-brwyn'. 'Oh' said John 'and who is he?'. 'A man called Abel from Cwm-belan' was the reply. 'Huh' said John, drawing on his Biblical knowledge 'Cain was there before' making a jocular dig at Richard Thomas.

Charles Abel (1890–1963) came to Cefn-brwyn and remained there till 1947. He had a few sheep of his own, kept two cows, a pig and usually had about four dogs. He and his wife Margaret Jane had two daughters – Doreen and Maglona. Mrs Abel passed away circa 1936 when the girls were aged 13 and 11 respectively. I am very grateful to Miss Maglona Abel, Llanidloes, for a lot of information, and a photograph of her father (cover photograph). Directly in front of Cefn-brwyn house there is a very steep hill called Y Foel. Charles had a white horse, and he would ride this horse right up to the top of the Foel without dismounting!

Charles Abel was a quiet unassuming person, known as a capable shepherd, who afterwards moved to Hendre-aur Llangurig, where he passed away on the 26th of December 1963 aged 73. He died at the house he had been born in.

Returning to John Davies, he married Martha Griffiths in the mid-twenties. She was the eldest of the five girls of David and Martha Griffiths, Cilgwrgan, Llangurig. David Griffiths had to have an operation for appendicitis, and this was performed by a doctor from Llanidloes on the kitchen table, and he charged £16 for his work, and the Griffiths' had to sell two cows to cover this expense.

I believe they got married in Newtown – 23 miles away – and have heard that that was the furthest that John had been from home till that day. They went there by pony and trap. Martha had been working at Glan-gwy near Bont-rhyd-galed so that is probably where they met. Martha was a short rotund lady and was renowned for her laughter, and little wonder, because John had an exceptional sense of humour, and she would shake from head to toe when caught in these laughing bouts.

With reference to this sense of humour which many of these hill people had, I would like to note that there is a different humour between hill and lowland people. It is very difficult to put a finger on it or describe it, but I believe it may stem from having to live in isolated, difficult, circumstances, where being able to see the lighter side helps to overcome the harsh reality of life. I came across a reference that a Dr Duff, a Scotsman, had written an article (pre-1876) referring to the differing humour of the Highland and the Lowland. I should have liked to have seen it to know what an obviously educated man had to say on the subject, but alas, even though I have made several enquiries, it has eluded me so far.

Food was an all-important matter in Bont-rhyd-galed, and Martha (or Matt as John called her) always had a warm welcome for all and sundry, and would conjure up a meal in a twinkling. Alun Thomas, Eisteddfa Gurig, a neighbour, would regularly cycle down to see them as a young lad, and John's first remark would be 'How's the belly situation boy bach?', and then almost before Alun could reply he would say 'Cups and saucers, Matt!'. John was a fast eater, and was very fond of tea, and when Martha sometimes gave him a small cup he would laugh and say 'Is this a cup or an egg-cup?'.

In the early years John did not have a wireless, and often went to his neighbours, Edward and Alice Ann Jones, Bont-isaf to listen to their set, especially to some of the great preachers of the time such as Phillip Jones of Porthcawl. There was a shy side to this big man when out of his domain, as when he went to Chapel (Capel Uchaf). He would quietly take his seat in the back, dressed in his best suit with its skin-tight trousers.

Evan, the son of Edward and Alice Ann Jones, had been asked to go to a shearing at Nant-rhys as a young lad, but didn't know the way, and John gave him the loan of an old pony with only a halter, and told Evan 'She'll take you there' to which Evan replied 'How does she know the way?'. 'She watches the clouds' John said with a laugh. The old mare had been there many times before, and she, like many of her contemporaries of the time, deserve a lot of credit for leading men lost on the hill, especially in mist, for using their 'horse-sense' to get them home.

At one time a new shepherd had come to work for James Edwards, Nant-stalwen, and at the new man's first gathering there was a thick mist, and he had no idea as to where to go, but James Edwards put him on an old pony, and said, 'Give her her head, and when she stops, wait there'. He did as he was told, and the pony stopped at a certain spot and after a while he heard the other shepherds, so he was able to join in the gather at the exact place he should be, thanks to a knowing pony.

John Davies was a tip-top shepherd and had a wonderful memory for sheep ear-marks. He was also a good shearer, and was renowned for his exceptionally wide swaths, and the shears creaking under the strain in his big hands.

Peat was their main source of fuel, and John thought that the world was a much better place when the Captain, or 'Cap' as he referred to him, bought a Caterpillar tractor which meant less labour to carry the peat home.

John, as already mentioned, was a very tall man, and made an imposing figure with his red 'kerchief around his neck. He was able to step easily over a seven-wire fence, and it was almost laughable to see him lift his leg and mount his horse. He was reputed to keep one good dog, and then several others of varying capabilities to make up a team. John Owen, who worked with him in 1946/47, always had a mental picture of John having sent his dog away a good distance, and wanting it to go a certain way, he would take off his hat, making a big sweep in the required direction, and shouting 'He-e-e-ere Quin'.

Another man that came into John and Martha's life was Evan Rees. He was born at Staylittle in a house called Brwyn (rushes) one of four boys of John and Elizabeth Rees. Evan married Ann Lloyd Blaen-hafren, and they lived at Lluest-dduallt, Staylittle, a small-holding, big enough to keep two cows, for which the rent was £10 a year. Ann had gone into service when she was eleven years old, and her wages were £4–12–6 a year. She was renowned for her memory of local history and genealogy, and on her 90th birthday said that she had not been to Llanidloes for 40 years!

Evan Rees was the last to work at Nant-Iago mine, and it would have been most interesting to have been a fly on the wall to listen to John and Evan reminiscing about their times at Nant-Iago. Mr Anslow, the owner, had come to visit the mine one day, and John, wishing to create a good impression, was putting quite a lot of effort into his work, and Mr Anslow told him, 'John Davies, I want you to work so as you can work tomorrow!' He had seen it all before. Anyone interested in the history of the mine would be advised to turn to David E. Bick's book on *The Old Metal Mines of Mid-Wales* part four, page 57.

One of Evan Rees' jobs was to maintain the leet running from the dam near Cerrig Llwydion, about half a mile from the source of the River Wye, to the mine at Nant-Iago. Martha, his daughter, used to take food for him once a week, and stay overnight, and then go home the following day. I am honoured to have met Mrs Martha Davies (his daughter) of Cemmaes, Machynlleth, in August 2002 (when she was aged 92), and am indebted to her for sharing her reminiscences with me. She was the last of seven children. One day she went on her usual trek to Nant-Iago, and her father said to her 'Right, I want you to come with me to buy some clothes' and off they went – to Ponterwyd!

Evan's bosses decided that he should not work on his own amongst all the machinery, so his son Edward (Ted) worked there with him for a period. There once was a row of houses at Nant-Iago, with the mine Captain living in the end house. All the local shepherds called with him regularly, so he caught up with all the news from them.

Evan Rees, on finishing at Nant-Iago, came to work with Captain Bennett Evans and lodged with John and his sister Maggie (who later became Mrs Pugh of Upper Delfarch) and later with John and Martha. Evan Rees was of a very tough constitution, continuously getting soaked to the skin. He seldom if ever wore a coat, and was partial to chewing tobacco, and yet he lived till he was 86. He died in 1963.

Returning to John Davies and his quick wit, some of the following stories which I have heard from people who knew him well will probably testify to his sense of humour. As with many country stories some may have been stretched in passing from mouth to mouth.

■ Evan Rees.

John had a young dog at one time and he had put one leg in its collar to slow it down. When somebody remarked upon this, John replied, 'There's still enough down to match what is upstairs!' – meaning that the dog was a bit brainless! Another time, when he was in his late teens, John was taking a horse to be shod. More often than not you would get a cup of tea and a bite to eat from the blacksmith's wife, but this particular smith was renowned for not giving anybody any food. On seeing John arrive he said 'My, you've grown into a big strong lad!' to which John replied 'Well yes I have, but no thanks to any food that I've had here!'

The Captain and his wife had four children Jane, Ann, Richard and Simon. Jane, who has spent most of her life in Kenya, was a great favourite with John, and he used to call her *Shani*, the Welsh equivalent of Jane. Richard had been away to study at Cirencester, and when John saw him coming, he used to say jokingly, 'Ho, here comes Oxford!' Mrs Evans was being troubled one day by a dog that insisted on coming into the house, and she asked Richard to send it out, which he did, in very strong language, to which John said 'Too much education!'

One of the problems they had years ago, when fences weren't so good, was to keep the rams away from the ewes in the autumn, so as to delay the lambing till the beginning of April, when it was hoped that the weather would be kinder. The Captain came home one day and said 'John, I've had a new idea, what if we started to give the rams a bit of food to keep them more settled?' 'Well, I don't know,' said John, ' – they must be different to me when I was young, the more food I had, the more women I wanted!'

John once had an armful of lambs that had been deserted by their mothers, and he said 'I know where I can find their fathers, but I don't know where the hell their mothers are.' John's comment about a shepherd in the vicinity, who was not very enlightened in the job, was 'I don't think he would recognize his mother if he saw her away from home!'

Another time John had sold two bullocks in Llanidloes for the very good price of £16. Meeting somebody on the street who congratulated him on the price, John's reply was 'I suppose it was a good price, but I'm taking one of them down to Dafydd Owen now.' David Owen was a feed merchant, and the bullocks had eaten a lot of bought-in stuff to get them into good condition.

The Captain had taken some rather poor ewes to be sold in Llanidloes, but had refused to sell them having been offered a low price, and John's view of this was 'Not a good situation, you haven't got any money, nor sheep (alluding that they were bad specimens), nor a lot of dog food either!'

After a funeral in Llangurig most of the men had gone into the Blue Bell pub for a little liquid feed (*Claddu'r meirw, dewch at y cwrw*). John, a good while later, went to the toilet, and found one of the leading lights of the Chapel lying on the floor, much the worse for drink. In stepping over him, John said to a friend 'This is one of Jesus' disciples here!'

Just in case any lady reader feels a bit put out in this mostly male-dominated subject, another person came into John's life – a shepherdess called Patience Bissett, and her story is worth relating.

She was born in 1929 in Buckinghamshire and spent her childhood travelling between England and Malta because her father was a naval officer. In 1940 she went to Canada because of the war, as her mother was Canadian. In her last year at or after school she went to work at Chillingham in Northumberland, and then attended Wye College. During this time she worked for a period at Llanwrda in the Carmarthen hills. She then rode over Mynydd Mallaen, slept at Cerrig Cyplau, Elan Valley, and then on towards the Pumlumon Range. She was hoping to see Captain Bennett Evans to try to get a shepherding job, but he was in London at the time. She then rode her pony down the Wye Valley, through Hereford and over the Malvern Hills, and across the Cotswolds to her home in Buckinghamshire. It was a distance of 300 miles and took her two weeks. She slept rough in barns and it cost her 10 shillings in food!

In the autumn of 1952 the Captain then offered her a job as a shepherd for a 6 month trial, and she was paid £4 a week. She had first been introduced to sheep in 1944 in Scotland, after her return from Canada. In holidays she had worked on her uncle's hill farm called Inversanda, Ardgour, near Fort William. The farm extended to 70,000 acres, and Scotch Blackface sheep were kept there. She still remembers that it was here she first saw the devastating effect that maggots have on sheep.

She moved into Cefn-brwyn where there was a windmill for electricity, but the batteries were not very good at holding their charge, so she needed a gale to read by! Otherwise it was a pressure-lamp or candles. In winter it was so cold the water froze in the cottage and water had to be carried up from the stream in buckets. To a girl brought up in an urban environment, this must have been quite a change to come to live at Cefn-brwyn with very few modern conveniences, and to be quite fair to her, this was not a flirting short-term romance with the hills, for she stayed and worked there till 1958.

One of her first jobs there was to go in the company of Goronwy Evans, another worker/shepherd, to get sheep back from Hengwm-annedd, a place that is very near to my heart. She spent the first winter staying with Tom Emanuel and his family at Bont Isaf, and again in all fairness, she must have been doing her job well because old John Davies thought a lot of her. John taught her quite a bit of Welsh, and with his sense of humour, you can bet she was taught a few things that would not be printable! She well recalls how John, when tying gates with string, would tie knot upon knot upon knot, to make doubly sure that they could not be opened easily.

■ Patience Bissett at work with her dogs. Photo by Dr T. Ifor Rees.

Most of her shepherding was done on horseback, with her four dogs, one of which she had from Tom Emanuel. He was a brown dog called 'Celt' and he would jump up on the pony's withers to get a lift. He had a slight eye, and she recalls him, because of his colour, being quite difficult to see in the distance, especially in the autumn.

Many times during the long winter nights she would visit John and Martha, riding down in the dark on her pony, who knew the way after a time, and Martha would be hovering around tending their every need, yet not eating herself. This habit has led many a visitor to Wales over the years to come to the conclusion that farmers' wives never eat!

Patience (or Pay as she was known), was impressed by John's vast knowledge of sheep ear-marks, and that always entered his conversation at one point or another. Another topic with John, and many others who had witnessed the calamity, was the snowstorm of 1947. He often spoke of the volume of snow, and the total silence on the better days, no sound of water or birds, just total silence, and it was in this silence that 'his' flock was decimated, about 3,000 of them having perished, leaving only about 64 lambs the following spring. John Owen, who worked with John Davies during this storm, often said that he remembered John Davies, this giant of a man, crying like a baby, and sobbing 'I hope it will come better just once more.' It was hell upon earth for man and beast. A caption below a photograph from a press cutting at this time read as follows: 'This man is a shepherd – his name is John Davies. He has been with Captain Bennett Evans since 1912, but can never recall such disaster in the hills. We found him skinning

110

sheep. He was so moved by the tragedy around him, that he could not look at the camera – in case you saw his tears'.

A gentleman called George Grant came to visit the Bennett Evans farm to buy Welsh Black cattle, and got an even better bargain inasmuch as he met Pay, and they eventually got married, and both went to live in Gelli-graean, in Pennal, Meirioneth. They lived there for a year in 1958/59, but then decided to move to Wiltshire to farm. They have three sons – Willie, Tom, and Joe.

Pay is now (if I may reveal) in her 76th year, and remarkably fit for her age, still working hard on the farm with her son Joe, and has recently been to Outer Mongolia (1999) and Patagonia (2002) for riding holidays. On the farm, sadly, the horse has now been replaced by the quad bike. Pay and Joe buy sheep at Builth Wells as ewe lambs, and after the sale they go up to visit Simon Bennett Evans at Glan-rhyd, Llangurig. Cefn-brwyn house was demolished a few years ago, but the area still brings happy memories to her.

She featured in two articles c.1958, one in *Woman's Mirror* and another in *Farmer and Stockbreeder*. John Davies was asked how the new girl was shaping up, and his answer was, as he always said when things were going well, 'Champion!'. I am very much in her debt for sharing with me her recollections of what was for her, a very different way of life.

In 1931 there were 89 shepherds and one shepherdess in Cardiganshire. There was a total of four shepherdesses in Wales at this time. In 1851, for comparison, there were 119 shepherds in the same area.

Eisteddfa Gurig

Moving back into Cardiganshire, adjoining the land of Capt. Bennett Evans we come to Eisteddfa Gurig (Curig's seat). This was once referred to as Eisteddfa Village – there being, as well as the farmhouse, five other houses built by the Company that ran Esgair Llu lead mine. The fact that many children in the area did not have a proper education prompted this letter from the 'Plinlimon Mining Company Ltd' dated the 23rd of April 1878:

> *It is simply a shame and a disgrace to Christianity that so many children should be kept in the state they are in here, running wild like a lot of sheep.*
>
> *John Garland (Mine Captain).*

It was about this time that a school was opened in Cwmergyr, and was attended by about 48 pupils, including my great-grandmother, Mary Ann Rees, Glan-yr-afon, born on the 17th of March 1869.

A man called William Williams and his wife Anne (nee Morgan) lived at Eisteddfa, he being the shepherd there from 1817 to 1821. A John Thomas, born 1795, was a shepherd at Eisteddfa in 1822. He had married a Dinah James on the 26th of May 1820. She was the daughter of Benjamin and Ann James, Aber-nant (Cwmystwyth?). She was baptised on the 21st of September 1801. John and Dinah first lived at Ty'n-y-maes, near Llan-eithyr. They had six children: Mary, 1821; Ann, 1825; John, 1828; Benjamin, 1831; Jane, 1834; and David, 1837.

Benjamin married Margaret James (born 1840) from Nant-y-moch (a sister to William who lived there) and they lived at Camdwr Mawr, and had eight children. One of the children, James, married Mary Ann Morgan, Hengwm-annedd, who was from a branch of my family that had moved to Hengwm from Cwmystwyth in 1874. They had nine children. James became a shepherd at Nant-llyn, and Maesnant, Ponterwyd, in the early 1890s. James and Mary Ann were overtaken by a very tragic experience during this time. They had a little boy, Isaac Richard, who was two years and eight months old. James had gone to the hill with his brother-in-law, and Mary Ann was outside about her chores. Isaac was left playing in the house, but unfortunately must have gone too close to the hearth and his clothes caught fire. He ran out of the house virtually a ball of flame. This was at about 11.00 o'clock in the morning, and one can only imagine the horror of such a happening in such a remote spot, and nobody there to help the distraught Mary Ann. James and her brother came back, and somebody went to fetch the nearest doctor, who was at Machynlleth, nine miles away. I was told many years ago that this doctor had a very good horse, able to jump most obstacles, and that he reached Nant-llyn without dismounting. Even then it was about six o'clock when he arrived, and due

■ Jim and Mary Ann Thomas, Eisteddfa Gurig, with their son Emlyn.

to the severity of the burns, little Isaac died at about 11 o'clock that night, which was the 30th of January, 1900, and was buried at the Chapel at Nant-y-moch.

James Thomas' family moved from Nant-llyn to Eisteddfa Gurig in 1907. (The rent paid to Aber-mâd by James Thomas for Eisteddfa Gurig in 1913, was £40 a year.) James' brother William then replaced James at Nant-llyn as shepherd (with their sister Dinah keeping house for him) for about two years. After William came Hugh Griffiths (already mentioned) who was followed by Richard Price Humphreys (originally from Forge, Machynlleth) who was shepherd at Nant-llyn for the James family of Pwll-cenawon, Capel Bangor, for 10/– (50p) a week.

Records show that wages paid (per week) by the Pugh family of Aber-mad, Llanilar to their shepherds in 1902 were as follows: James Thomas, Nant-llyn 15/– (75p); John Morgan, Hengwm 15/–; William Burrel, Eisteddfa 15/–; Simon Davies, Llaneithyr 17/– (85p). The shepherds were paid every four or five weeks.

Richard Price Humphreys lived at Nant-Llyn till 1919 when he moved to Bwlch-styllen. His adopted son, Edgar Humphreys, Talybont, is still alive, aged 94, and has a clear retentive memory, to whom I am indebted for many stories of yesteryear. They were the last family to live at Nant-llyn. My great-grandfather David Mason, Glan-fedw, Devil's Bridge, carried the timber for the re-building of Nant-llyn and Llechwedd-mawr in 1885. He was given the contract by Sir Pryse Pryse, Gogerddan. There are references to a holding having been at Nant-llyn in 1592.

A friend, Cledwyn Fychan, Llanddeiniol, who has taken a great deal of interest in this area came across a story that a set of triplets had been born in Nant-llyn: 'A daughter of William Williams of Nant-llyn was brought to bed of three female children at a birth'. This was in 1750.

During the Thomas' period at Nant-llyn, a young lad of about twelve or thirteen, from Ponterwyd, called John Michell was employed there as a servant. He was taken there at night, and next day felt very home-sick, and was contemplating running away, and asked one of the family which was the way to Ponterwyd, and he responded by fibbing that he did not know where it was, as he had never been there!

This psychology of taking new servants to some of these isolated holdings at night, or when there was thick mist was one that was played on quite often. Many of them were home-sick, but after a few days settled down, and sometimes spent years in their new environment. A classic story was the one of Abraham Davies, Lluest-gadair (Claerwen Valley) who had gone down to Pont-rhyd-fendigaid to find a servant girl. Having found a suitable candidate, they set off for Lluest-gadair. Whether true or not, it was stated that they called in Nant-y-beddau (by the Claerwen dam) and talked for hours, he as if waiting for it to get dark. They reached home after dark, and as there was only one bed there, the girl slept in the hay by the cattle. This lasted only for two nights as there were mice running about in the hay, as well as other creepy crawlies. She would have made for home, but in the thick mist that lasted for days she had no idea as to which direction to take. The long and the short of it was that they eventually got married. Where and when did they marry? Any descendants?

When James Thomas lived at Nant-llyn, a John Mason lived at nearby Drosgol, and when there was a thunderstorm and the children were frightened, James and his wife would console them by saying that it was John Drosgol creating a rumpus, and all was well. Likewise when a new calf was born at Nant-llyn and the children wanted to know where it had come from, they would say that John had brought it there the previous night.

Probably during this period John Mason had attended a shearing (I can't remember where) and they had mustard there to accompany the midday meal. This was something totally new to John, and he wanted to know what it was. The other shearers took full advantage of this fact, and told him that it was the pudding! John hurried his dinner and the 'pudding' was given to him, and no more need be said as regards the outcome of his curiosity. From that time on, mustard was known in this area as *pwdin John Drosgol* (John Drosgol's pudding)!

This story was told to me by James' son, Emlyn Thomas, Talwrn, Ponterwyd. He died on the 19th of January, 1989, aged 84. He also told me that there is in the river in Cwm Gwarin, behind Hengwm-annedd, a pool called *pwll Sion ceffyl Ifan* (Sion's pool – Ifan's horse). This pool is sided by a very smooth rock at an angle, and the story behind it was that a Sion had borrowed a horse from Ifan and that this horse had slipped down the rock face and drowned in the pool. I often wonder at what period this happened, and I often ask how many more interesting stories like this one have gone to the grave with people like Emlyn Thomas.

Emlyn was a light boned man, very sharp, and a fast runner in his youth. He had a peculiar light-stepping gait when he walked, and would cover distances quickly. He owned Blaen-peithnant, Ponterwyd and one way he had of getting to the upper end of his sheepwalk was to cycle to Eisteddfa Gurig, and then walk the mile or so onto his land. A likeable individual, with an acute sense of observation which made him an accomplished shepherd. He had an agreement with the Jones family of Aber-cwm-dôlau, Capel Bangor inasmuch as they sent a number of their sheep up to his hill during the summer, and he in winter would send some of his sheep down to them. A totally amicable agreement that suited both parties well. Emlyn, full of mischief in his early teens, would go into his parents bedroom every night, kneel by the bed to say his prayers, and at the same time put his hand in his father's coat pocket – to get some tobacco!

After moving to Eisteddfa, James Thomas was known to all as 'Jim 'Steddfa' (the 'Ei' in Eisteddfa being lost in everyday talk). Everybody I have talked with described him as a good sort, a good neighbour, always ready with a favour. He was a man who kept himself tidy, and always wore leather leggings and breeches. These leggings, or at least his better ones that he went to town in, shone like glass. I asked an elderly gentleman what he remembered about Jim Thomas, and his answer was 'Not much, but I remember his shiny leggings!'

He was described as a leading sheep farmer, a competent judge at shearing competitions, and a very faithful member and deacon of Cwmergyr Chapel. Four of his children were made deacons: David and Emlyn in Cwmergyr Chapel; Benjamin was a deacon in Rhiw-felen Chapel for nearly 50 years; and Mrs Lois Jones, Maen-arthur was a deacon in Maes-glas Chapel, Ysbyty Ystwyth. He had spent the whole of his life on the Pumlumon range.

One of his specialties was castrating male lambs, and he went about various farms doing this work. He used hot irons. The scrotum was cut open with a razor-sharp knife and the testicles drawn out. Then a special clamp was used to hold the cord, a blob of green ointment was then put on the clamp, and the testicles were seared with the hot iron. The smell of this antiseptic green ointment being burned was absolutely unique. One of the unmistakable smells of the past.

Castration of male animals was from early times seen as a way of curbing male aggression, especially in bulls and stallions, and also as a way of getting the castrated stock to fatten quicker, and as a means of getting better breeding stock. Another method prior to irons, or for those that did not possess them, was that the scrotum was cut open, the testicles taken out, and then a piece of wood, usually willow, about the size of a man's thumb 3½ inches long, split down the middle, with each half being put on either

115

side of the cord above the testicle, and both ends tied with string to stem the flow of blood. The testicle was then cut, and the piece of wood was left in place for a few days till there was no risk of bleeding, and then removed. Unless this operation was done under fairly clean conditions, there was a chance of infection setting in. These methods may seem rather crude by today's standards, but it should be remembered that they were the only options available at the time. Having said this, I have seen animals castrated by modern methods with almost disastrous results, whereas the irons and green ointment were very efficient, and well proven.

Another method of castrating lambs was that the lamb was held against the catcher's shoulder, while another person cut the tip of the scrotum off, the testes were then squeezed out, and drawn with the teeth. If the operator had been drinking beer the night before the results were not so good, and many lambs died. What it was I don't know, but there must be some degree of truth in it as I have heard of this in several different areas. In 1910 a bloodless castrating pincers was invented by a Dr Napoleone Burdizzo from Italy. It was about 15 to 20 years later that they came to be used in this part of Wales. Even so, the irons were used long after this, especially for bullocks. The other modern method is the elasticated rubber ring, of which I have never been a big fan, except in very young animals.

Jim Thomas was an enlightened character, and he had one of the first wireless sets in the area. Somebody asked him what the wireless had said for the weather forecast for the following day, and Jim said 'Rain all over the world!'

One of the notable facts about Eisteddfa was that the place took a lot of sheep and lambs 'on tack' (keeping) for the summer. In a book of sheep ear-marks written in 1888 by Lewis Jones, Y Bwlch, Llanymawddwy, it is recorded that there were nearly thirty lots of sheep being kept on Eisteddfa over summer. Somebody asked Jim if it was right that he should keep so many lots of sheep on the hill, and his reply was (there were very few fences at the time) 'There's plenty of room between here and Dylife!'

This taking in of sheep to graze over summer was a common occurrence in most of the hill areas. There was an abundance of food on the hill at this time of year – somebody said that on these hills it was 'feast or famine'. As a small example there were in 1926 fifteen lots in Hengwm-annedd, seven lots in Nant-llyn, and nineteen lots in Bugeilyn. In Blaen-myherin about 400 sheep were kept as tack (1916) on top of their 1500 flock. The price for their keeping at this time was 2/– (10p) per ewe, and 1/6 (7½p) per lamb. This can be compared with the following, when, in 1896 there were 25 lots in Cefn-brwyn; 13 lots in Bugeilyn; 25 lots in Blaen-hafren; and 10 in Llwyn-y-gog, Staylittle.

These lots took a great deal of settling, and had to be regularly shepherded, especially when they came up for the first time, and they would stay on their own particular part of the hill. Some of these parts would be called after the sheep that grazed there. There is on Bodtalog a piece called *clap defaid John Hugh* (the hillock of John Hugh's sheep) and on Blaen-peithnant a spot called *pant defaid Lisa* (the hollow of Lisa's sheep).

Some difficult lots of first timers were hobbled, and these hobbles (*tyrch*) were made out of molinia grass, strengthened by pieces of cotton grass. They used an adapted bucket handle for the job of turning the grasses into a rope. The hobble was made in the shape of a collar, put around the sheep's neck, and the ewe's front leg was put in this collar, and this would serve to curtail their movement until it was established that they were to stay on a specific part of the hill. In 1901 a case was made against a Capel Seion man and his son for cruelty when 'four sheep were seen with hobbles of straw bands, the bands being around the neck and right leg'.

Lowland farms as far away as Lledrod brought sheep up to Eisteddfa, and they would walk them up as far as Devil's Bridge, and the shepherd from Eisteddfa would come down to meet them, and take them the rest of the way. The same journey was undertaken in reverse order when the sheep went home in the autumn. Each hill had a half-way meeting point, as did my family who lived in Gelli-uchaf (Quick). Their lowland sheep were brought to Rhos-yr-hydd in Trisant (where members of the family lived) and were duly collected from there.

These patterns of moving sheep were kept up for many years, and times kept religiously. One example of this was that the sheep of Richard (Dick) James, Ty'n-pwll, Goginan were moved up on the second Wednesday in May to Nant-y-moch year after year, and John James, Nant-y-moch came to meet them at Rhyd-y-gaib, Bwlch-styllen. There was no prior communication, that was the day, and that was it!

This long-standing way of life came to an end in Eisteddfa in 1970, when the sheepwalk was taken over by Alun and Eluned Thomas (Jim's grandson and his wife). The charges then were 10/– (50p) a head. At this time, there were thirteen different lots grazing on this upland farm that reaches from the A44 road to the summit of Pumlumon, 2468 feet above sea level. All the sheep that came there on tack, not only had their own distinguishing marks, but also were branded with the letter 'S' (for 'Steddfa) – a big one for the ewes, and a small one for the lambs, so that if they happened to stray, everybody would know where to return them to.

Jim Thomas and Mary Ann were an enterprising couple, and since they lived right on the A44, they set up a business making teas, especially for members of the Cycling Club, and they had a sign showing that cyclists were welcome, and it must be said that hardly

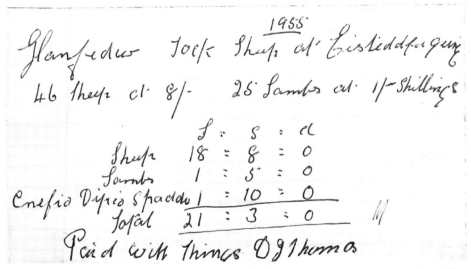

■ An original bill for the sheep of Glan-fedw, Devil's Bridge, on tack over summer at Eisteddfa Gurig, 1955.

117

anybody passed Eisteddfa without being invited in for a cup and a bite to eat. They were well set up for staff, having Edith, Eunice and Nell, their daughters to help. They used to buy big slabs of cake from a shop called the 'Star' in Llanidloes at 4 (old) pence a pound. This cake and other necessities were often brought to them by their neighbour, Mrs Edith Morgan, Eisteddfa-fach. She was a car driver at a time when not too many ladies took to the wheel.

Jim would go down to Ponterwyd regularly to do the weekly shopping on his pony, and the format this journey took was as follows. He would take a short cut along the side of the hill, along a route called *Llwybr glas* (the green path), and head straight for a farm called Bryn-glas where his friends Dei and Blodwen Howells lived. There were very few fences at that time. He would enjoy a meal with them, and have a chat to put the world to rights, and then set off to do his shopping. This was not done in a hurry, depending on whom he met on the way. He would then start his way home (4 miles) along the A44 and call in at Gelli-isaf and have a meal and a chat there, enriched this time by any glad tidings he had heard in the village. There was a quality of life in this era, time did not press as it does today, and neighbourliness was very high on the list of priorities. The following week this route would be reversed, variety obviously being the spice of life.

In the mid-twenties Jim bought three low-lying farms – Cwmnewidion Uchaf, Gwar-ffynnon, and Glan-dwgan – all in the Trisant area. His son Benjamin moved there to manage the places, with his sister Lois to keep house for him. Ben later married Hannah Lewis from near-by Pen-rhiw-cae-gegin. They moved from there about 1942, when, for some reason, the farms were sold, to live at nearby Llwyn-ynwch, and afterwards to farm Nant-arthur, Devil's Bridge with their son Windsor. Ben helped neighbours with fencing, and handling their sheep, to supplement his income. Ben died on the 13th of June 1981 aged 89.

The next farm up from Cwm-newidion was Llety-synod (meaning 'a place for keeping asses') and this was taken to farm c.1931 by William, another son of Jim and Mary Ann. William (or Will as he was known) had been a shepherd at Hengwm-annedd c.1920, and it was there that another sad bereavement came into the lives of the Thomas family. Will had married a Mary Evans from Cwm-newidion Ganol, and she gave birth to a little girl called Mary Jane (May) in December 1921. Unfortunately, Mary (the mother) died within days of the birth, aged 29, and when the news reached Eisteddfa, Mary Ann set off in the middle of the night over the shoulder of Pumlumon, and down the very rough slopes to Hengwm. Little May was baptised on her mother's coffin, and she was the last baby to be born at Hengwm. She was brought up by her grand-parents at Eisteddfa, and later became Mrs May Powell, of Erwyd House, Ponterwyd. She died on the 26th of February 1993 aged 71, and was buried at Ysbyty Cynfyn Church.

I am not sure how long Will remained at Hengwm after this tragic event, but he later became a shepherd at Dôl-wen, for Mr Edwards, Dôlfor, Trawscoed, for several years. Will re-married with Elizabeth Oliver, from Ffair Rhos (who first of all became his house-keeper at Dôl-wen). Later, they moved to farm at Llety-synod, staying there till about 1943. They then moved to Bryn-glas in the Llanafan area, with Will working for the Forestry Commission. They moved again later to Blaen-waun, then to Pen-bont and, last of all, to Gwar-geulan, still in the Llanafan area.

Will, like most of the Thomas family was a good dog handler and to name only one instance, in September 1921, he came second in the Plas Machynlleth Stakes (sheepdog trials) with a bitch called 'Hafren'. Like Emlyn his brother, he was a fast runner, and in August 1921 he won the foot-race at Devil's Bridge Sheepdog Trials. He also liked to go out with his shotgun, with rabbits being his main quarry. He was manager of Devil's Bridge mart for a period, a job that must have suited him down to the ground, because he knew everybody from the catchment area, and it was a fine chance for him to meet his old friends from Ponterwyd.

One thing he did not like was thunder, and probably not without cause. One day while on the hill at Hengwm he had a group of sheep and two dogs with him. There came a terrific thunderstorm, and he and the dogs took shelter under an overhanging rock. When the weather cleared a little he saw that lightning had killed six of the sheep. A pretty close call.

He died suddenly on the 19th of January 1969, aged 73, and was laid to rest in Trisant cemetery.

Returning to Jim Thomas – he and Mary Ann moved down to live in Ponterwyd to a place called Erwyd House, which had a field close by for his black pony as well. Erwyd House had been a shop prior to this, and because, amongst other things, meal had been kept there, the first problem the new tenants had was mice. Jim, like many people of his era, had very little English, but this did not bother this good-natured, jokular character one iota, and he got on with life. On his first trip to Aberystwyth after moving, he went into a shop to get mouse traps and asked a bewildered assistant 'Have you got any catches mouses?'

During a very cold spell he went up to Blaen-myherin to see his daughter Lois and her husband Morgan Jones. Morgan was quite poorly at the time, and Dr John Anderson (who died in 1967) from Pont-rhyd-y-groes had come to see him. The doctor could only bring his car as far as a spot called Craig Cath (Cat's Rock) and then had to walk across a field to the house. He had left his wife in the car, and Jim got to know of this, and said 'Bring her in man, she will *starfio gortyn gwd* in car!' Dr Anderson, originally from Glasgow, had said from the outset that Morgan Jones was suffering from appendicitis, but the powers-that-be at Aberystwyth would not agree, and Morgan suffered for a whole year. In the end he was operated upon, and made a good recovery. Many of these country doctors did a very good day's work, considering the circumstances they had to work under.

This reminds me of a farmer with very little English, who had a boy from 'the homes' working for him, and wanted him to go up to the bank behind the house with a scythe to cut bracken, and to take something to keep him dry if it rained, and his orders went something like this: 'Leggings on legs, sack on back, go up mountain, cut feathers!' Another character had gone to a photographer with his wife and son, and asked, 'How much to pull him, she and it?'

Jim was not feeling well one night and asked his son David (Dei) to bring him some water, which he did, in a cup. He drank this, and said he would like some more, in a basin! Another thing that I've heard about Jim is that, on an exceptionally stormy night, he would pop outside the door, come back in, and tell the family '*Jiwch, Jiwch*, it must be rough in high places!' – as if 'Steddfa was low lying!

Many of these characters had words of exclamation that they used in their everyday talk, and in many cases they were exclusive to their users – indeed, you only had to say these words and people would relate instantly to the person associated with them. Jim had two examples of these words – '*Jiwch, Jiwch!*' and '*Pwff, cawred.*' His son Ben said, '*Bugrins!*' and his other son Dei said, '*Go dangro!*' when things were not one hundred per cent right. A list of these words strongly bonded to their users comes to mind, but then I would be straying.

This kind, humorous character Jim Thomas passed away on the 24th of December 1942 aged 79, and his wife, the hospitable Mary Ann, died on the 20th of November 1954, aged 85.

Their son David Jones Thomas (or Dei 'Steddfa as he was known to most people) stayed on to farm at Eisteddfa, and he was one of the last people I remember who regularly wore breeches and leggings. He was of a gaunt, bony structure, a fit man, and an exceptional walker. He had fully inherited his father's sense of leg-pulling, and when somebody was the butt of this leg-pulling, he would give, what I can only call a 'big wink', with the whole of one side of his face moving, to anybody who happened to be in the vicinity at the time.

One of his specialties was counting sheep, and this has been inherited by his grandson Aled. This is not such a simple job as it may seem when great numbers are involved, and they pass by in an irregular stream, with all sorts of distractions, such as people shouting, dogs barking etc. I believe this sheep counting is even made into a competition in some parts of the world. There are many differing techniques used by different people. Some people count in twos – 2, 4, 6, 8, 10 ...; others count up to twenty, keeping tabs of each

twenty with their fingers, say, of their left hand, up to 100, and then keeping count of the hundreds with their right hand, which would take you up to 500. Another popular method is to put a number of small stones in your hand or pocket, and take one out for every hundred sheep counted. The method employed by the late John George, Penwern, New Cross, whereby you handle least figures, was to count them in blocks of five – 5, 10, 15, 20 ... – and he was noted for his exact counting of big flocks of sheep. My former employer, Mr Ieuan Morgan, Glan-frêd, Llandre was an accomplished sheep counter, as was his father, Arthur Morgan, Pwll-glas, Bow Street.

While doing a bit of research at the Library of the Welsh Folk Museum at Sain Fagan, Cardiff, a few years ago, I came across this interesting old form of counting

■ David Jones Thomas, Eisteddfa Gurig.

from mid-Ceredigion. It was recalled by a Mrs Jones, Ty'n-waun, Llwynygroes. She died in 1949, aged 79. I am grateful to the Museum for permission to reproduce this work, and to my neighbour and friend, Dr David Lewis for taking me there and back, and also to the staff for their courtesy and help.

Old method of counting sheep in the Llwynpiod district:

Eini, beini, bari, batri, bim, eithi, ceithi, cari, catri, cing,

einibas, beinibas, baribas, batribas, bymffas, einibymffas, beinibymffas, baribymffas, batribymffas, eica.

Another old method of counting:

Non, ton, pan, peder, pemp, nith, sith, nec, neuf, nega,

Nega non, nega ton, nega pan, nega peder, nega pyffi, non a pyffi, ton a pyffi, pan a pyffi, peder a pyffi, nega.

I was told that it was the 'Irish Paddies' (Irish tinkers) who brought this method of counting to Wales:

En, dor, car, cor, cwi, shich, shoch, nich, noch, dei,

Unde, dorde, carde, corde, cwide, shichdy, shochdy, nichdy, nochdy, dwychdi,

Dorchwi (40), carchwi (60), corchwi (80), quickhwi (100).

The following is another old method of counting sheep and cattle in Yorkshire. It seems that the great-great-grandmother of the person who wrote down this method, had come from Wales.

Yan, tain, tetherer, metherer, pip, ceaser, aser, catherer, orner, dick,

Yan a dick, tain a dick, tetherer a dick, metherer a dick, bunfit, yan a bumfit, tain a bumfit, tetherer a bumfit, metherer a bumfit, gigot.'

Some of these methods can be compared to the Welsh version of counting: *un, dau, tri, pedwar, pump, chwech, saith, wyth, naw, deg, un-ar-ddeg, deuddeg, tri-ar-ddeg, pedwar-ar-ddeg, pymtheg, un-ar-bymtheg, dau-ar-bymtheg, deunaw, pedwar-ar-bymtheg, ugain(20). Deg-ar-ugain (30), deugain (40), trigain (60), pedwar-ugain (80), cant-namyn-un (99), cant (100), chwech-ugain (120), saith-ugain (140).*

Dei Steddfa was a good dog trainer, and on his many travels back and forth with the tack sheep, he would see a young dog with a bit of promise, and make an offer for it. His top price for this sort of dog would be 5/– (25p – *coron*, a crown in old money). This dog, after being trained, or at the end of the season would be sold for two or three pounds, but if it had good potential might be kept for another season.

He had at one time a blue-grey bitch called Juno, that had come from Pen-sarn in Talybont. She was of the Welsh type and was greatly talked about by all who saw her work, and it is unfortunate by now that most of these eye-witnesses have passed away, but I can still recall the tones of admiration in their recounting about her feats. If there were foxes about she would find their lair, run back to Dei, run off a short distance and bark as if to say, 'come on, follow me'.

When Juno had to be put down, Heulwen, Dei's daughter, told me that it was the only time she recalls seeing tears in her father's eyes, and who could blame him after losing such a faithful friend. Dei always carried a small dog-whip in his coat pocket, and Heulwen remembers that when as children, especially if they had visitors, they were being a bit naughty, he would just show a little of the handle of the whip and peace would reign at once, although he had never laid a finger on his children.

Dei, and his father before him, served their community well by castrating lambs and calves when the need arose, and were accomplished in the art, as well as curing sheep that had 'gid' (*bendro*). Gid is caused by tape-worms. These worms are ingested by the sheep as they eat grass, and they form bladders of liquid and eggs, usually in the head of the sheep, thereby putting a lot of pressure on the brain, and causing the sheep to turn round and round, hence the name 'gid' or 'turn-sick'.

Detection of the exact point is made by putting a little pressure on the skull, which proves soft to the touch. A small round incision is made at this point, and the liquid drained by means of a syringe. The membrane on the outside of the bladder is then drawn out slowly and carefully, as this contains the eggs, and once this is achieved the hole is capped with pitch or Stockholm tar. On taking the pressure off the brain, the effect is nothing short of a miracle. The sheep that a few minutes previously had been turning round in the same place, will head off in almost a normal manner and make a full recovery. If ewes that have gid die, and are eaten by dogs this makes the life cycle of the worm complete, as it needs both the dog and sheep as hosts.

Another job Dei had was that of going around farms that kept flocks of Welsh Mountain sheep, and inspecting the rams to see if they were of the right quality. These then would be marked with a green 'A' for approved, or a red 'R' for rejected. Although he was entrusted with this work of inspecting, he was sometimes criticised that he bought rams for himself that were considered a bit 'kind' for the altitude at Eisteddfa.

According to his family, many were the problems Dei had with the family car. He had at one time parked in the crowded market place at Aberystwyth. In trying to get out he had to reverse, and could not work out why the car was so stiff in moving on, but he found that his bumper had hooked onto another car's bumper, so he was in effect towing another car!

Another time they as a family (Mr and Mrs Thomas, Alun, Olwen, Tegwen and Heulwen) had gone to a concert in Ystumtuen. They were to take part as they were well talented in singing and reciting. Shortly before reaching their destination, the car broke down, and all had to get out to push, so that when they arrived at the venue they were out of breath, and their stint was moved on till they had made a full recovery. Small, but genuine memories that are related by his family to bring to mind happy, carefree days in association with a very kindly personality. Dei was a heavy pipe smoker, and towards the end he suffered from lung cancer, and it was sad to see this once very fit man fighting for his breath. David Jones Thomas died in 1981 aged 79, and his wife Minnie Ellen had pre-deceased him by a year. Both are buried in the Chapel cemetery at Ponterwyd.

I would like to record two little known facts about Eisteddfa Gurig. One is that nobody has actually died at Eisteddfa within living memory (that is they had moved from there or died in hospital) and the other strange fact for a hill farm is that no pups have been reared there, that is to reach maturity.

Some people might have noticed in my writings that the name David is shortened to 'Dei'. The definitive line to the usage of this name is the river Ystwyth. To the south of the river the name most often used is 'Dai'.

Hengwm-annedd

For our next shepherds we move to Hengwm-annedd, still clinging closely to Pumlumon, and indeed to the same family, as it was from this family that Mary Ann Thomas (Eisteddfa) came. Hengwm is set at the juncture of the Gelli-gogau and Gwarin rivers. Gelli-gogau means 'the grove of the cuckoos'. There was at one time a lot of trees in this area, especially birch, and their remnants can still be seen, perfectly preserved in the peat of this area. An old story relates, whether true or not, that a squirrel could go from Machynlleth to Pumlumon without putting its feet on the ground.

In the early 1870s a John Morgan and his wife Elizabeth (she was a sister to my great-great-grand-mother) moved from Cwmystwyth. He had been working in the lead mines there, and the work affected his health to the extent that he was advised to move to a healthier job. The job that he took was as a shepherd at Hengwm-annedd, with his children to help him. This meant moving about fourteen miles, with friends and neighbours helping out with carts and horses with the move. Their own horse had not crossed a ford before, and when they came to Ponterwyd they had quite a performance to get it to cross the ford there. Anybody familiar with the area would know that by the time they reached Hengwm the horse would have got very used to fords.

John, unfortunately, died on the 24th January 1881, aged 45. There was a heavy fall of snow at that time, and about fifteen of his ex-workmates walked from Cwmystwyth past Llyn Rhuddnant, Blaen-Myherin, to Eisteddfa Gurig, then over Pumlumon to Hengwm. The coffin was then taken to be buried at the Chapel at Nant-y-moch. There was such a lot of snow in some places that the coffin had to be dragged on the surface. After the service his friends walked down to Ponterwyd, and back to Cwmystwyth via Devil's Bridge, which speaks volumes for their comradeship under atrocious conditions. John was the second to have been buried at Nant-y-moch Chapel (Blaen-Rheidol) according to dates on the grave-stones. Within two years the family received another blow when their four year old daughter Sarah Ellen died on the 20th of January 1883.

Three sons of John and Elizabeth – William, John and Richard – became first class shepherds and dog handlers. William Morgan had worked in the South Wales collieries for a period, but the attraction to his natural calling was too strong, so back he came to Hengwm. He was a recognized expert on sheep ear-marks. He was a sheep man through and through, with very little to say to other farm work, and with an almost intense dislike of cattle. His dogs meant a great deal to him, and he usually had three – two heading dogs, and one driver/barker. When John Howells was at Cwmergyr, William and his brother John used to go there for a week in July, to help with the gathering and shearing, and as both families came from Cwmystwyth, one can rest assured they had plenty in common to talk about.

William was of a fine natured personality, and everything he did was done meticulously – even when lacing his boots, there were no twists in the laces. One day he did not feel too well, and crossed the river to Lluest-newydd, where his nephew Tommy Morgan lived, to get a bottle of soda water. Having got the bottle, he was on his way back, and on the middle of the foot-bridge (no longer there) by Hengwm house, he must have felt unwell, put the bottle down, and he died there, on the 10th of January 1920 aged 62. I have heard a story that his brother had gone down to the Police Station in Goginan to report the death, and that the officer there did not feel like traipsing up to Hengwm (11 miles) and told him that it seemed that his brother had died in Montgomeryshire and that he should report the matter to Machynlleth. Whether this is true or not I do not know, but it seemed a very hard line to take at what was a traumatic time for the family.

John, William's brother and shepherd at Hengwm, suffered very badly from asthma, and in all probability this made him a more irritable personality. He took more interest in the cattle and arable side of things at home. It was stated that his dogs were even better than William's, and that was quite a compliment by anybody's standard. There is a saying that it is the lazy shepherd that has the best dogs. John was not lazy, but it was his asthmatic condition which dictated that he could not move a lot to help his dogs. Once he had mounted his horse he would very seldom dismount as he would have great difficulty mounting again.

■ Hengwm-annedd c.1960 showing the foot-bridge (no longer there) where William died. Photo by Ann Lawrence, Llanidloes.

During a heavy fall of snow one winter John Evans of Lluest-y-rhos and his son Charles had gone down to Machynlleth through rough weather, and the first person they met there was John Morgan, and knowing about his condition they asked him how he had got there, to which question he did not reply but asked them 'How did you get down?' and they replied that they had walked there, and his dour response was 'You're very lucky you can walk'!

John was very fond of reading, and I have in my possession his Bible, as well as a rush candle holder that had been in use in Hengwm. Both would have many a tale to tell if they could speak. After the death of William, John went to live at Lluest-newydd (just across the river) with his nephew Tommy Morgan and his family.

It was about Hengwm-annedd that I was thinking when the following poem was written in 1986.

THE RAVEN

High where steep the valley lifts
Its head, with crags of granite crowned,
Where man has failed to leave his mark
Tis where the raven can be found.
Glistening in the morning sun
His feathers show a brilliant hue,
Sparkling, dancing, in the light,
As diamonds countless on the dew.

From black satanic eyes he sees
The valley spread beneath, and lo,
A ruined cott and crumbling yard
Where children played so long ago.
The raven's life has little changed,
His care for brood and nest
Are as the ravens of the past,
When children in the cott would rest.

The day awakes, the raven flies,
Majestic in the morning air
An omen dark of death, his call,
Its harshness seems to say, 'Beware,
I gleaner of the bones of fate,
Chosen guardian of the Tower,
Do know how thin the threads of life,
Sentry in my rocky bower.'

King of the crags and upland heights
So proud, aloft upon your throne,
Long to continue may you reign
O'er all your kingdom, wild, – alone.

Tommy Morgan

Tommy was the son of John and William's sister Elizabeth. She later went to live in Minneapolis, U.S.A. She died in 1938, but thankfully still has descendants in that part of the world.

Tommy Morgan married Sarah Jane Jones, in 1909. She was the daughter of Thomas and Margaret Jones, Bugeilyn, which is about three miles upriver from Hengwm. They lived at Bugeilyn for about a year, and in that period they had a little boy that was still-born, and Tommy made a small wooden coffin for him to be buried at the Chapel at Nant-y-moch. He was quite adept at making things from wood. Tommy and Sarah were at Lluest-newydd by the Autumn of 1910, as he is named as having won third prize in a sheepdog trial at Devil's Bridge in September 1910, for running a dog that had not won before.

In 1911 they were blessed with a little girl called Maggie. Their shopping was done in Ponterwyd, which was five and a half miles away.

Tommy was a very good shot with a gun, as were many of his contemporaries. This was a very important element, as a target missed was a meal missed. One old man from the Pont-rhyd-fendigaid area used to work for a farming family there, and as workers, all they had to eat was salted meat day in, day out, and he often said if he hadn't been a good shot they would never get any fresh meat. Tommy once shot a heron that was being a nuisance inasmuch as it was taking fish from the river, which was a valuable addition to their diet. This heron was taken to a man called Hutchings in Aberystwyth to be stuffed, and later took pride of place at Tommy's cousin's home at Nant-cae-rhedyn, Ponterwyd, and is now with a branch of the family on Ynys Môn.

Tommy and his family moved from Lluest-newydd in 1921 so that Maggie could attend school. She was now ten years old, and had had no formal schooling, but had learned to read and write at the Sunday School at Nant-y-moch, and learnt to count by playing rings at home. This stood her in good stead when she started school as she always came out top at mathematics. They first moved to a house called Pen-banc in the Uwch-y-garreg area on the outskirts of Machynlleth, and John (the uncle) moved to Maes-dulais, a neighbouring small-holding, with Maggie helping out after school with the household chores. A neighbour and friend of the family, Charles Phillips, said that the house always smelt strongly of Potters Asthmatic Powder.

The house of Maes-dulais was destroyed by fire, and in 1925 was re-built, with Tommy actually making most of the panelling on its inside, which is still there. He had an in-bred interest in woodwork, and amongst many jobs he did for the neighbours, he adapted a horse-drawn cart for his neighbour Richard Jones of Aber-felin when he had his first tractor.

Tommy was very reluctant to speak English, and would keep it to a minimum. Once, when he was shearing at Bryn-llwyd-wyn, Uwch-y-garreg, the owner, an Englishman, brought out for him a very dirty ewe, and all Tommy did was point to her back-end and say, 'Shit!'

They later had the chance to buy Pen-banc and the land attached to it, thereby forming a unit of about 80 acres which served as the lowland for Lluest-newydd. In the moving from Lluest-newydd, Owen Hughes, a neighbour from Bugeilyn, had the most difficult job, which was taking the old sow down to Pen-banc. She was very reluctant to go, and lay down for long periods at a time.

When they went to do some work in Lluest-newydd such as gathering, Tommy seemed to want to spend as much time there as possible. There was to be a cup of tea and something to eat on arrival, then he would say 'We'll have a smoke before going to gather,' and no matter how late it was that evening there was no hurry to leave. He was recalled by Richard Jones, Mynachdy, Aberhosan, who helped him a lot with the sheep, as being the best he had ever seen at cutting bread, probably due to the fact that he had a good edge on his knife, as he had been taught by his father-in-law to kill pigs. This picture of him as a cool personality was not always true, because when things were not going right he was well endowed linguistically, and could be heard from a great distance away!

Three farms used to send their sheep up to Lluest-newydd over summer, namely Pant-styllen, Penegoes; Gelli, Llanwrin; and Maes-perthi, Penegoes. Maggie remembered Tom Jones from Gelli as a kindly soul giving her 2/– (10p) which was quite a sum at the time for helping with the sheep. He died not many years later when his gun went off while crossing a hedge-bank.

People remembering Tommy in his latter years may remember that he suffered from 'entropion' (eyelids turning in) and that he wore strips of elastoplast on his eyes to prevent this from irritating him.

Tommy sold Lluest-newydd to Edward Walter Lewis, Henllan, Uwch-y-garreg, in 1947, and his descendants still farm there. A family called Jenkins moved from Eisteddfa-fach to Lluest-newydd in the late 1890s, and were there for seven years, during which time the peat fire never went out. This was the case in many upland farms. Mr and Mrs Dewi Roberts moved from Wenffrwd to Lle'r Neuaddau around 1930. Dewi Roberts, respecting an old tradition, carried the fire from Wenffrwd in a bucket, and put it into their new hearth, where it continued to burn for another fourty years. The same fire at Wenffrwd was reputed to have been there for a century. The fire at Bwlch-wallter, Pont-rhyd-y-groes, went out on only one day of the year, when the whole family went to the fair at Ffair-rhos on the 25th of September (Ffair Gŵyl y Grog).

Returning to John Morgan. He had gone for a short break to his niece, Mrs Jeanie Williams, Ty'n-wern, Aberffrwd, in the Rheidol Valley (the daughter of his brother Thomas, Nant-cae-rhedyn). He had gone by train from Machynlleth to Aberystwyth and then by the narrow gauge railway to Aberffrwd, accompanied by his niece Maggie. He was not in the best of health going there, but took a turn for the worst, and died on December the 10th, 1927. Like many upland funerals at that time of year, his was thwarted by bad weather, and the hearse was able to go only as far as Ponterwyd because of snow, and thereafter the coffin was taken by horse-cart (*gambo*) to Blaen-Rheidol Chapel, Nant-y-moch, where he was laid to rest, aged 64.

Richard Morgan (Dick Hengwm)

Richard Morgan (or Dick as he was known locally) was a brother to John and William, and probably the most illustrious of the three. He was born in Cwmystwyth on the 1st of June, 1866. When he was about 20 years old he boarded a ship called the 'Vesta' at Liverpool, which was carrying a load of railway sleepers bound for Patagonia.

He had as a travelling companion John Morgan James from Aber-peithnant, Ponterwyd, and they more than likely worked their passage in loading and unloading these sleepers. A Welsh colony was founded in Patagonia, and John Morgan James made his home there, and I am privileged to have met some of his many descendants, down to great-great-grand-children, who still speak Welsh. When unloading these sleepers, John was hit by one of them, causing a deep cut to his face, and from then on he grew a beard to hide the scar.

My information on Dick's life after this is rather sketchy, but in his later years he spoke a lot about Chubut. There is a story that he spent some time on a Portuguese ship, and that he had struck one of the officers, in consequence of which he was imprisoned. He managed to escape however, and found himself on an island where, according to his nephew Tom Morgan, Nant-cae-rhedyn, there were plenty of oranges growing, and he grew quite plump because he ate so many! It was also said that he had been given the job of guarding a stack of tobacco in case somebody set fire to it, but catch fire it did, and Dick had to make himself scarce pretty sharpish!

I am not sure when he came back to this country, but it is almost certain he spent most of his time working in coal mines. He was a 'sinker', that is to say, his work involved sinking shafts down to the coal seam. He had a good and long-standing companion to help him with this work. His name was Thomas Jones from Glan-yr-afon, Ffair Rhos. He was a very colourful character, and somebody ought to make a record of his life and deeds. He was an imposing figure with his red 'kerchief around his neck, and spoke with what I would call a twang, as though he had spent time in America – whether he had or not, I don't know. He was known to most people as 'Rocky' Jones, which probably came from his sinking expertise.

They were working at one stage in Yorkshire, and walked from there to Pentre Ystrad in the South Wales Valleys. Whether it was at this time or not, but once they found themselves stony broke, but Rocky found a sixpenny piece and said 'Three for me and three for Dick,' – mates to the last.

Rocky, in later years, would take a dog up to Hengwm so that Dick could train it a bit, and told someone in passing that the dog needed 'a bit of long oats' (a stick!).

Rocky's wife Sarah used to help out at shearing time at Hengwm, and they would cut quite a dash going up from their home in Ffair Rhos in a spotless small cart drawn by a

■ Richard and Sarah Jane Morgan in front of Hengwm house.

horse called 'Gilbert', dressed in shining harness. A sight to behold so I was told. That cart is thankfully still around, and is kept at the Welsh Folk Museum in Cardiff. Rocky would have been very proud of that I'm sure.

Richard Morgan was back in Hengwm in 1908 as his name is down as the winner of a sheepdog trial in Devil's Bridge in 1909, where he also came equal fourth. It was probably around this time that he married Sarah Jane Jenkins of Wenffrwd, Ponterwyd, and by 1910 they were living at Pant-y-garreg-hir (hollow of the long stone) Cwm-symlog. They also lived at Castell Coch near Sarah Jane's home, but I do not know for how long or what period.

Dick worked for a period at Cripiau Bach lead mine, but did not settle down there, and got a job as shepherd at Lle'r-neuaddau, Ponterwyd. He was there in 1917 as he won a fifth prize at Devil's Bridge sheepdog trials that year. He and his wife moved back to his home of Hengwm-annedd about 1922 with their adopted son, John Jenkin Morgan (Johnnie), working as a shepherd for Mr Edward Pugh, Maesteran, Penegoes, near Machynlleth. One of the sidelines they had at Hengwm, was rearing geese, and they supplied their friends and neighbours with Christmas geese.

As can be gleaned from the last few paragraphs, Dick was an expert at training sheepdogs, and was placed at many local trials, and was consistent in his placings over many years. I have in my possession a silver cup which I believe he won in the Llyfnant valley sheepdog trials in 1925. This cup was given to me many years ago by Miss Maggie Morgan, Maes-dulais, Machynlleth, a gift which I treasure for obvious reasons. On the 25th of October 1879, when Dick was thirteen years old, he competed in a trial in Machynlleth. Since he was of small stature, he could not see the sheep in the distance, and a man lifted him up on his shoulders to give him a better view. In a sheepdog trial at Machynlleth in 1933 he was given a special prize for being the oldest competitor.

He was in favour of the Border Collie type of dog which he found to be more biddable than the local types of sheepdog, and therefore more suitable for sheepdog trials. However, one of the last things that Tommy Morgan, Maes-dulais told me was that they spent longer gathering the hills of Hengwm after the coming of the Border Collies, because they worked in a more careful manner. But when all is said and done, Dick and his dogs were a valuable asset in any gathering that took place on neighbouring hills – indeed the rough terrain of Hengwm hill itself called for a good heading dog, and even more valuable was a good driving/barking dog to oust the sheep from the rocks where they like to shelter, and even hide. It is amazing how canny some of these 'dodgers' are, and their tricks are passed on to subsequent generations. I have often seen them running at full speed, in front of a dog, and then suddenly turn in to hide under some protective rock. You can almost imagine them smiling as the dog shoots past! Hengwm is a testing place for man and dog, and in my opinion it is 'Wild Wales' at its best, but there again I may be biased. The present house of Hengwm, now in ruin, was built in 1857.

Sarah Jane Morgan was reputed to be very good at growing flowers, and one of these flowers, which I believe to be monkshood, still grows there every year. She was also known for her hospitality when they had visitors, but there is little dispute to the fact that she and Dick did not get on very well at times. There may as always be two sides to this story. There were times when Dick showed a little allergy to work, and it was stated that she once threw a bucket of water over him in bed because he would not get up. I am sure that this had the desired effect, but possibly did not do a lot for a harmonious relationship. It was also said that, at times, Dick could be more interested in training a dog, than tending to the hay, which was a very important part of their winter fodder.

This strained relationship between them may have been underlined by his interest in sheepdog trials, as he would go off for long spells, leaving her on her own. He had once saved a little money to go to Llangurig sheepdog trials, but Sarah Jane found out where he had hidden it, and kept the money to put it, to her mind, to better use. Dick however set off for Eisteddfa Gurig, and borrowed some money from his brother-in-law James Thomas, and proceeded on to Llangurig, where he won a prize that enabled him not only to repay his debt at Eisteddfa, but also have a little to spare as well. When he got home, so the story goes, Sarah Jane was said to have poisoned the bitch.

On another occasion his best dog had died under dubious circumstances, with a trial at Borth to which he had intended going, only a fortnight away. Such was his prowess in training that he re-trained what was a barking/driving dog, to get him good enough to run a trial, and not only did he run, but won a cup, and a good sum of money as well. If he had a dog that was a bit spirited for trial work, Dick would feed it a bellyfull of carrion on the morning of the competition in order to slow it down a bit!

While at Lle'r-neuaddau, Sarah Jane had, in order to get her own way over some matter, threatened to hang herself. She had gone up onto a chair, put a rope around her neck, and tied the other end to a beam or hook. Dick was in quite a state about all this. Who happened to come by at the very moment, but John Jones, who lived at nearby Hen Hafod. On hearing what was going on, John, a no-nonsense man, said 'I'll settle this now once and for all – I'll give the bloody chair a kick.' Sarah Jane, on hearing this, unhooked herself, and came off the chair with the greatest of alacrity before John came into the room.

In the early 1930s a man called Ben Davies came to help Dick at Hengwm. I would deem this Ben to be an interesting character, and I would have loved to have met him. He had been in the First World War, was a crack shot, a first class fisherman, and used to act as a guide to visitors coming to the area. His family lived at Dyfngwm, Dylife, and in his latter days he was a postman at Llanidloes. He also wrote on several occasions to the *Welsh Gazette*, one example being in the issue of the 13th of March 1930, where he mentions place-names on Hengwm-annedd.

When Ben was at Hengwm, Dick used to say to him, 'If you hear me talk in my sleep, wake me up.' He was worried in case he might let on that he had hidden his purse under his pillow, and that Sarah Jane might cotton on and find it!

In 1935 Dick and Sarah Jane moved from Hengwm. They were the last people to live there. This move took them to Cae'r Arglwyddes in Talybont. In 1936, while at Cae'r Arglwyddes, Dick had gone to compete at Trefeurig sheepdog trials, and he won the third prize in the Champion Class. On his way home, and probably feeling quite pleased with his achievement, he came to the crossroads by Pen-cwm, in Penrhyncoch, where a taxi from Eglwys-fach ran over the dog and killed it. Dogs and vehicles don't mix very well, and many a good dog has come to grief in this manner. There was one story of a shepherd driving sheep along the road, when a car came along and knocked his dog senseless. The driver came out and said how sorry he was, and was enquiring as to the quality of the dog, and was assured by the distraught owner that he was a good one. The car driver offered to pay for the dog and was in the act of getting his wallet out, when the dog suddenly got up and ran off, and the shepherd later said, 'Bloody dog, he could have stayed there for a few more minutes!'

Dick died by the pig-sty at Cae'r Arglwyddes as he was feeding his dogs, and I often think that he had spent so much time in their company, he was blessed to go from this world in their presence. This took place on the 30th of March 1938. He was aged 71. His body was buried at Talybont cemetry, and his grave is fourteen rows down from the top, and the fifth grave in from the Taliesin side. There is no stone, merely a border of bricks. Someday I would like to put a tablet there to remember a good shepherd, and a top sheepdog handler.

John Jenkin Morgan

John Jenkin Morgan was Richard and Sarah Jane's adopted son. He was a lively, humorous young man, full of energy, and was a shepherd for Major James John Evans (of the Lovesgrove family) at the Old Park, in the upper reaches of Talybont. His girlfriend was Maggie Hughes, the daughter of Owen Hughes, Bugeilyn.

On a hot Sunday morning on the 14th of July 1929, he had been shearing some sheep at the Old Park, and came home in the afternoon and decided to go for a swim. His mother had gone to the Chapel at Nant-y-moch. Johnnie had taken his terrier with him to a pool called Pwll-y-fuwch. The little dog returned some time later to Hengwm on his own, and Dick at once sensed that something was wrong, and went to investigate. He saw Johnnie's clothes beside the pool, and called out 'Jack! Jack!' but to no avail, and, fearing the worst, went on his pony up to Bugeilyn to get help, and Owen Hughes and Ben Davies (who happened to be visiting there at the time) went with him and recovered the body. This was a bitter blow to Richard and Sarah Jane losing their only son under such tragic circumstances. Those who remember Dick said that he was never the same after this traumatic experience.

Johnnie was buried at Nant-y-moch Chapel, but alas there is no grave-stone to mark his last resting place. There are however two very credible inscriptions to his having been at Hengwm, and I am grateful to Mr Gwylfa Micah, Glan-morfa-mawr, Llanegryn (owner of part of Hengwm) and Mr Ken Jones of Cwm-Rheidol for bringing these to my notice.

Johnnie had carved his name on two rocks in the Gwarin Valley: one reading 'John J. Morgan, Mai (May) 1923'; the other, sadly, inscribed only eight months before he died 'John J. Morgan. Tach. (November) 1928'. Could he have carved his name in other places?

I must admit to having carved my name in stone at various places where I have worked, one of them being on a stone gatepost at Nant-llyn. Somebody came across this one day, and was quite excited at having found what he thought was a very old inscription. He told a friend of mine about this find, and this friend merely smiled and said, 'I don't think it's as old as you think, because I know the bugger well!'

There was a stone/rock on Bwlch-styllen land with the letters 'D.E.' carved in it by David Edwards, whose family lived there for a long time. I have walked there several times to try and find it, but so far, to no avail. I am surprised there are so few stones with initials etc. on them. Not being able to write would be one contributing factor, as well as the fact that the thousands of acres that were the stomping ground of so many of these shepherds in this area are now covered by afforestation, making it virtually impossible to find anything. Indeed, I am convinced that there are many pre-historic

■ Probably Johnnie's last inscription. Photo by Gethin Howells.

standing stones and stone circles that have been covered, and will be further damaged when these trees are felled and removed.

Johnnie has a biological brother who is still alive called Edgar Humphreys from Talybont to whom I am grateful for a lot of information. Edgar was adopted by Richard Price Humphreys (already mentioned at Nant-llyn) and his wife Sarah.

After Richard Morgan's death, Sarah Jane married Richard Price Humphreys, and they lived at Talybont. I am sure they would have been an interesting couple to talk to, with all their experience of living in the uplands of Pumlumon, but I never got the chance to know them.

Thomas Morgan, a brother to John, William and Richard, worked for a period in the coal mines of South Wales, but came back to work at Peithyll, a small mansion at Capel Dewi about four miles from Aberystwyth. It was here that he met his future wife Jane. She was the daughter of Mr and Mrs John James, Llain-arthur, Capel Dewi. After they married they moved to an isolated hill farm called Hore, or to give it its full name, Hore Wen. This sheepwalk was situated on the easterly side of Pumlumon. It must have been a tremendous change for Jane to have moved from virtually sea-level to a house so far from everywhere, but she always said that she was as happy as a lark there. Thomas, however, found the place too far from the nearest Chapel, and was in dire straits as time went on to get away from there, although he loved the job of shepherding Hore. They were there for five years, c.1890, and three of their daughters were born there. They eventually moved to Nant-cae-rhedyn (brook by the bracken field) in Ponterwyd, where the rest of their ten children were born. They had two sons, John James Morgan (1898–1995) and Thomas Hywel Morgan (1912–1992). The two brothers were known always as John James, and Thomas Hywel, which made it sometimes confusing for strangers to the area, who thought that their second names were their surnames.

Thomas Hywel was a tall, clean-looking, individual, with a healthy complexion begotten from being in an active, outdoor job. He was thoroughly versed in the art of shepherding, and a good dog handler. When I was shepherding in the Tregaron area I used to come home (to Ponterwyd) every fortnight, and invariably on the Sunday night would pay a visit to Nant-cae-rhedyn, where Tom (a batchelor) lived with his sister, Miss Sarah (Sal) Morgan. One of the first things you noticed was the large pile of library books there, which was a sign that they read a lot. The talk would always be about sheep, sheepdogs and shepherds, and local characters. The welcome that you had was tremendous, with Sal Morgan plying you with food. 'Come on, eat,' she would say, and no matter how much you ate, something else would appear on the table. She used to be a dressmaker in her younger days, and taught several generations as a Sunday School teacher at Ponterwyd. Tom remembered going to school one morning in mid-summer, looking up, and seeing a man on the skyline heading down towards Nant-cae-rhedyn. He went on to school, and when he came home the man was still there chatting away, and he found out that it was Lewis Rees from Blaen-hafren who had come to fetch some of his sheep which had strayed. They then had tea, and Lewis cooly set off for the nine miles it would take him to get home.

Tom never tired of telling tales about his old black and tan Welsh sheepdog 'Roy'. If Roy put up a fox he would follow it till it went to ground, and Tom, with his long legs would not be far behind. Incidentally, Tom was one of the few people I have known who, when sitting down, could cross his legs, and re-cross them again.

Dogs were the delight of his life, and thankfully I still have the descendants of 'Roy' and a dog called 'Lad' which he had in his latter years. He was also an expert hand-shearer. He would cut wide swaths that would curve up in the middle, forming a pattern on the first side of the sheep to be shorn, and they would continue down on the second side, making the job a work of art. His brother John James was also an expert at this craft, as was another neighbour of theirs, Dewi Roberts of Lle'r-neuaddau who lived about two miles up the road from them. Dewi's wife, Margaret, was the daughter of Thomas 'Rocky' Jones, already mentioned. Somebody asked Rocky at one time how he had learned such good English. 'Mixing with the gypsies' was his instant reply. When on a job in South Wales he would hear of another pit being started, and would shoot off to

■ Thomas Hywel Morgan, Nant-cae-rhedyn.
Photo by G.Whittington-Jones, Fish Hoek, South Africa.

offer them his expertise in sinking shafts. One overseer told him, 'A rolling stone gathers no moss, Rocky,' to which he replied, 'A standing post gathers no knowledge!' He was also an expert at making waterproof clothing from calico boiled in linseed oil.

Tom, after the death of his sister Sal in 1976 aged 82, managed the home and farm on his own, and shore most of the sheep on his own for several years, with help from friends and neighbours on occasions such as dipping. He later bought a house in the village of Ponterwyd called Bryn-hyfryd (which also happens to be the house in which I was born) and eventually moved down to sleep there, going to Nant-cae-rhedyn during the day. He had been blighted by a rodent ulcer for a long time, and had treatment, after which it subsided, but it came back again, and he stubbornly refused to have it treated, and for the next twenty years this advancing malignancy continued its ravages, and disfigured this once handsome man. He must have been of a strong constitution to have stood this pressure, and he died at Bryn-hyfryd aged 80 in 1992.

Having mentioned Lle'r-neuaddau, Hirnant and Nant-cae-rhedyn, I would like to point out that these three farms were the last in the area to practice the long obsolete custom called *clytio* in Welsh. Many hill farms had yearling ewes or ewe lambs that were not in good condition in the autumn, and their owners deemed it best that they should not be served by the rams. Not having enough fenced-in fields to keep them apart, the problem was overcome by tying pieces of sacking onto the wool to cover their rear end, therefore ensuring that they could not be served. This novel way of birth control gave them a barren year in which they could grow, and regain their strength. The boot was sometimes put on the other foot when rams were difficult to contain, and a sack was tied about their middle, making it impossible for them to penetrate the ewes. Necessity is the mother of invention.

Returning to Thomas Morgan (the father), he was an enterprising man who bought another farm down in Aberffrwd, in the Rheidol Valley, as a lowland addition to Nant-cae-rhedyn, and according to what I have heard there were not enough hours in the day for him. He was also very musical and a staunch Chapel goer. Unfortunately, when he was 56 years old, he had appendicitis and died as a result on the 4th of March 1918. His son John James Morgan, Aber-ceiro, was a dab hand at handling a dog, and was precentor and deacon at Ponterwyd Chapel for many years.

The following are a few tales about Hengwm-annedd (Hengwm), for posterity. It may be wise, to avoid confusion, to point out that there is another farm called Hengwm Gyfeiliog four miles away, due north.

There was a father, mother and son living at Hengwm-annedd a long time ago. Despite the fact that the son knew little of life outside his own valley, his father decided to take him down to a hiring fair at Machynlleth one May in order for him to get a job. As they approached the town, they saw a group of girls dancing and screaming. He asked his father, 'What are they?' and the reply came, 'Don't take any notice of them, they're geese!' Whether the boy was employed or not I do not know, but at the end of the day his father asked him 'Would you like me to buy something for you to remember this fair?' His reply was 'I wouldn't mind one of those geese!' So he may not have been so dull after all.

Another two young men had started down towards Machynlleth from Hengwm, and they came to the farm of Tal-bont-drain, and as it happened the farmer there had a cart full of swedes. They had never seen such things and asked what they were, and the farmer, seeing that they were quite gullible, told them that they were 'mare's eggs', so they asked if they could have one, and were given one each. On their way up the steep Rhiw-faeniog, they sat down for a rest, and one of them lost hold of his swede, and it rolled downhill into a patch of rushes, surprising a hare that lay resting there. The hare shot off, and one of the boys said, 'Good God! It's hatched already!'

There was a tale that after heavy rains, flood water swept through the house of Hengwm, and took the fire with it. The occupants had no means of re-kindling a fire, but somebody had a brain-wave, and a burning peat from Lluest-newydd was thrown across the river. Needs must when such problems arise.

Up to 1935, Hengwm was grazed by the Pugh brothers of Maesteran, Penegoes, and their rent to the Pugh family of Aber-mâd in 1913 was £64 a year. In 1935 Hengwm was bought by Lewis Micah, Cefn-cyfrifol, Aberhosan for £850.

In the years 1934–35 a lorry from Machynlleth came up to Hengwm to collect the wool after shearing. The vehicle was owned by Williams, The Skinners Inn, and had been adapted by putting half-tracks on it. This caused quite a sensation at the time.

In 1947 a gentleman from Derwenlas near Machynlleth, called W.J. Richards, published a book of poetry called *Dail y Dderwen* (oak leaves). In this book is included a poem depicting his feelings about sheep from Hengwm-annedd that had been taken to graze at Hyde Park in London, and lamenting that they would miss hearing the lark singing, the whistling of shepherds, and the heather of the Welsh hills. This I feel must be connected to the fact that a Mr G. Dale Williams from Glan-y-don, Tywyn, had the grazing rights at Hyde Park. His sheep at Hyde Park were shorn with a machine for the first time in 1935. I would have liked to have more information on this Tywyn and London connection, but I'm afraid time is one of my main enemies.

There is no doubt that at one time there lived in these outlandish places people that can only be described as being rough. Their living conditions were atrocious, as was described in George Lipscomb's book, *Journey into South Wales in the year 1799*. I quote:

> *Here we saw a cottage, or rather a cairn completely formed of turf and covered with the same. A stone served for the window shutter and the door was of wicker work … It appeared to be the common habitation of a peasant's family with their ducks, dogs, and fowls, and gave us no high idea of the cleanliness or comforts of the moutaineers … It serves however to show the strength of attachment which binds men and their native wilds …*

Near the bank of the young Elan river slightly below Llyn Wngu there once stood a house called Bryn-ieir (hillock of the hens). Today its last remaining wall is about to fall into the river. I have often wondered how on earth the family managed to exist, and on what, in such a remote place. There are no visible signs of enclosed fields, although I have not studied it too closely. I have heard only one story about Bryn-ieir, and that came from Tommy Hughes. He had heard that a man living there had come down to Abergwngu, and was in the house for a few hours talking about various things, and one of the household asked him how his father was, and he replied that he had died that morning! What period was this, and where was he buried?

A group of local lads had gone carol singing to Wenffrwd, Ponterwyd, on a very cold night in the 1930s. When they had finished singing they waited till the owner, John Jenkins, came downstairs from his bed. There were so many cracks in the door that they could see him coming down in his long-johns and shirt by candle-light. Tough people.

In 1926 an enquiry was made by the Government of New Zealand for sheep which they called 'Cardies' which grazed the Pumlumon Ranges, with a view of stocking the vast inland area of poor land in the North Island. Did anything materialize from this enquiry? Could this have been a golden opportunity lost?

A man who gave a tremendous amount of publicity to the Welsh sheep was the late Edward Hamer from Llanidloes. He published a booklet *Welsh Mutton, and where to get it*, and I am grateful to Edward Hamer, his grandson, for pointing out these facts to me. There is a paragraph which says 'The Welsh sheep as found on Plynlimon Mountain are a distinct breed of Welsh, and termed the Plynlimon Breed. Like other mountain sheep they are small, extremely active and wild, and delight in lofty situations, especially for summer grazing, the herbage of their native mountains being preferred by them to richer pasture. If enclosed on the lowlands during summer months few fences can confine them, and even when removed to distant spots they will not infrequently escape, and regain their native mountains ... But when removed from their native soil they loose the 'distinguishable delicious flavour' given to the meat by the herbage of their own mountain ... Although small in the bone they carry a good weight of flesh, being thick set and compact in their quarters', and he goes on to mention 'the Welsh flannel which is extensively made in several factories in Llanidloes'. The booklet boasts of supplying mutton 'to four Royal households' and 'to 2000 Noblemen and Gentry in England'.

It is a fact that in the late 1800s suet was of a higher value than meat because of candle making. Sheep carcasses seen hanging in old photographs of butchers' shops have a special stick attached which was inserted in both flanks to draw them back so that the suet was exposed. This was in complete contrast to what is shown today!

Shearing

There was an old saying:

> *You may shear your sheep*
> *When the elder blossoms peep.*

This would not be applicable in every terrain as the main shearing time on the hills was the month of July, and something came to my mind this moment, that a very knowing lady, Mrs Elizabeth James, of Ty'n-pwll, Goginan, used to say that the mountain grazing started to deteriorate after shearing. June is reckoned to be the best month on the hills.

When shearing was imminent there was another job to be done – washing the sheep. They were gathered about nine days or so beforehand, and driven through dammed-up streams, or naturally deep pools in a river. There is a spot in Lledrod called Cwm-yr-olchfa (valley of the washpool) where sheep from the surrounding areas came to be

■ Washing sheep at Eisteddfa Gurig c.1945. David Jones Thomas (in black leather leggings) and Charles Abel behind the sheep. A young Alun Thomas is to the right of the photograph. Eisteddfa fach is in the background.

washed. Two examples of the time lapse between the washing and shearing from the Pont-rhyd-fendigaid area are as follows: in 1924, Berth-goed were washing on the 30th of June, and shearing on the 11th of July; Blaen-glas-ffrwd were washing on the 20th of June and shearing on the 2nd of July.

When this operation was on the go, shepherds had a very busy time, gathering vast tracts of land, for washing and shearing alternately. The purpose of washing the sheep was to remove the grease from the wool, as it then commanded a higher price. Most shepherds were glad when this washing came to an end, and their reasons were two-fold: one, because of the relentless gathering involved, and secondly, because many of the lambs broke their legs in the hustling and pushing involved. Broken legs were usually mended by stripping a birch branch of its bark, and using this light, strong support to wrap around the limb, tied with strips of material.

Many of the hill farms had allocated spots for the washing, and purpose-built walled funnels leading down to the pools. Many of these are still around as monuments to a tradition that has gone into oblivion. As in all aspects of work where many people are involved, there was also quite a bit of fun attached to it, none more so than if one of the shepherds fell into the pool. Often a strong ewe might run between their legs, or a ram could catch its horn in somebody's clothing, and the rest can be imagined!

The last washed sheep that I can remember being involved in their shearing was at Dôl-gors, on the outskirts of Devil's Bridge, in the late 1960s. The one thing I remember is that the clippers were as clean at the end of the day as when I started. Many years previous to this when I was about six years old (we lived then at nearby Ty'n-rhos, Rhos-y-gell) going with the sheep to be washed at Dôl-gors, and Jack Hopkins, the manservant there, catching a trout for me with his hands to take home. I carried that fish home proudly, and always thought Jack to be a very clever man. Prices quoted in 1908 were 3/6 a score (20) for shearing washed sheep, and 4/– a score for unwashed sheep.

This was the time of year that involved the biggest volume of people on these hill areas, and it was also the time of year that friends and family from far away would come and visit, helping out, and also treating it as a holiday. As regards to the work it was mostly exchanged labour, with a few paid helpers, many of these being tramps who called at the same places every year. One old wag described these tramps as 'milestone inspectors'! Some of them went into workhouses for the winter, and came out to work on farms for the spring and summer. One such man called David Evans (known as Dei Fuches) from Cwmystwyth came to light in the area one spring, and the farmer who saw him said 'Dear me Dei, I'd heard that you had died,' and his reply was, 'I've heard that story too, but I didn't believe it!'

Many of the gatherers came to the farm the night before, because they had to start gathering at first light. In Nant-stalwen, in the Tregaron area, the shearing was on a Monday, and as tradition had it, there would be no gathering on the Sunday, and the rule was that the gatherers were given a full meal around midnight on Sunday, and they would then start off for the far-flung perimeters of the sheepwalk. When daylight came they started the gather, and would therefore be back at the farm before the shearers arrived.

Between the shearers and catchers and various helpers at Nant-stalwen there might be about 200 people. A report in the *Welsh Gazette* in 1930 stated that 6000 sheep had

■ Shearers at Cefn-brwyn C.1936. L to R:- John Rees, Lluest Las; Martha Rees, Blaen Hafren; Lewis Rees, Blaen Hafren; ?; Mrs Jane Rees, Blaen Hafren; ?; John Davies, Bont; Ned Rees, Blaen Hafren; Richard Thomas, Nant-melyn. Note that the men shear the sheep standing behind their benches.

been shorn by 165 shearers with perhaps 40 other people tending. This would have been about 36 sheep per man. The number of sheep there might have been subject to a little journalistic licence, unless the lambs that were shorn had been taken into account. In Nant-rhys in 1933, John George of Penwern, New Cross, was reported to have had 140 men at a shearing. Many of these would have been lads tending the shearers with string for tying the sheep's feet, some carrying in, others carrying out. One man would be in charge of the fire for melting the pitch, that would later be used to brand the sheep with that particular farm's mark. This pitch would have to be at the right temperature – too hot and it might burn the sheep, too cool and it would not have the desired effect of leaving a clear, easily distinguished mark on the sheep, which would last till the Autumn when the sheep would be given a 'raddle mark' (*nôd gwlân*). This involves putting a dab, or stroke of sheep marking fluid on different places on the sheep. Each farm has its allocated mark, and the colours used years ago were mostly red, blue or black, whereas today there is a wider range of colours.

There is a specific type of rock that is found in North Ceredigion and up towards Dinas Mawddwy, which, when crushed to powder produces a bluish paste when mixed with oil or animal fat. This was then used to mark sheep. There are two brooks in this area where this type of rock was visible, and both are called Nant-y-nôd (brook of the marking paste) – one is in Cwm Ceulan, Talybont, and the other is on the land of Eisteddfa Gurig.

There was a saying in Mid Wales:

Tri pheth o Fawddwy a ddaw,	*Three things from Mawddwy come,*
Nôd glas, dyn cas, a glaw.	*The blue mark, bad men, and rain.*

The 'bad men' above refers to the 'red bandits' of Dinas Mawddwy that were in the area long ago.

In the period that I am writing about all the sheep were shorn by hand. The underbelly was shorn first, and then the sheep's feet were tied in order to make the work easier, and most importantly, safer. It happened sometimes that the sheep would kick out, and get its hoof into the handle of the shears, sending it flying across the shearing shed, endangering anyone in its flight. With the sheep safely tied, starting at the neck, the sheep's left side was shorn, working from the belly towards the backbone. When that side was finished, the sheep was turned to lie on its left side, and the right side was shorn, again starting at the neck, this time working from the backbone towards the belly. The shorn sheep were carried out, and put down on a bed of rushes. There were two reasons for the rushes – firstly so that the newly shorn sheep would not bruise, and secondly to keep them clean. It was deemed good husbandry that recently shorn sheep should not be hustled, or as little as possible, because they had lost their protective coat of wool.

There would be a man there who would put the pitch-mark on the sheep, and another man or responsible lad would then untie the feet, and at every tenth sheep being let loose, he would shout at the tally man '*Deg dafad!*' (ten sheep). The tally man had a very important job at the big shearings. He would have a long piece of wood, about 20 inches in length by half an inch square, and for every ten sheep he would cut a cross on one of the square sides. On the other sides he would count up the wethers and rams. There was a great deal of secrecy about this counting, therefore only a man of sound character could be in charge of the tally stick. In a report in a local paper about the shearing at Old Abbey, in Pont-rhyd-fendigaid in 1938, there was mention of a tally-stick used there. Wool was priced that year at ten pence per pound, and there were 82 people at the shearing. The price of wool the previous year was sixteen pence.

A gentleman of the roads from Radnorshire had come to the Pont-rhyd-fendigaid area, and in looking for work went to a shearing at Ty'n-ddôl. Since there was a large flock there, and he probably not being used to sheep work, by the end of the day he'd had a gut's full of the work. On the way back to Radnorshire he met somebody who asked him what sort of place he'd had at Ty'n-ddôl, and he said he wouldn't be in a hurry to go back there because it was '*Deg dafad! deg dafad*! All bloody day!'

Another tramp used to come to the shearing at Nant-stalwen as well as other places in the Tregaron area. I believe his name was Brown, but he was known by his nick-name 'Carnera' – probably after Primo Carnera the boxer, because of his immense strength. He often carried a dagger clenched between his teeth, and his clothes were in tatters. He would be given tidy clothes by people taking pity on him, but he would even make holes in these. He would not come into the house to eat, so food was taken out to him – enough to feed two or three normal men – and he would take it to a corner, and then eat in a rough manner, almost growling in case somebody stole it from him. He was always given the job of catching sheep, and a genteel lady visitor at Nant-stalwen had heard about him, and wanted to have a look at him. She was taken to the shearing shed, and saw Carnera catching sheep, his tattered trousers exposing his credentials, and her

■ Mr Rhys Jones, Glan-gwesyn, Aber-gwesyn keeping count on a tally stick at Nant-stalwen C.1940. Photo by R.Cecil Hughes, Swansea.

■ Close-up view of a tally stick. Photo by Ian Sant.

only comment was, 'What an animal!' Students coming to help in carrying the sheep in and out at Ty-llwyd, Cwmystwyth, years ago, who were not used to the work, asked somebody at about half past ten, 'How many more to go?' because they were thoroughly tired, and got the answer, 'Not many now.' By about 4 o'clock, they were too tired to even ask!

It was important at these shearings to be on good terms with the catcher, or catchers in some instances, because some sheep do not lend themselves to shearing as well as others, as their wool has not risen enough, and if the catcher had a grudge against somebody, he could keep him supplied with these, making the day a very tough one for

■ My father, John Byron Howells (right) and John Postings shearing by hand at Gelmast, July 1979.

the unfortunate shearer. We have a name in Welsh – *spralen* – for a ewe that is very ripe to shear, indeed she may have shed a lot of her wool, and the shearers loved to have these, as a change from the full-wooled sheep. In the Elan Valley these sheep are referred to as a 'spral' or a 'sprally ewe'. The only equivalent from other areas that I have come across has been in the Shropshire area, where they are known as 'pell-necked sheep', and this makes perfect sense as one of the first indications that a sheep is ready to shear is that the wool begins to open about her neck.

There was one type of wool that was not popular with hand shearers, and that is what we would call '*gwlân pan*'. I have not heard an English equivalent for this type of wool. It was of a matted texture, like a thick carpet, and virtually impossible to wrap in the normal style. One farm in North Ceredigion was noted because many of their sheep had this wool, and many would have liked not to go there to shear, but this farm kept a bull, and in return for the bull's service they asked for a day's shearing. That farm has for a long time been reseeded, and the wool problem has been done away with.

There were some good shearers at this time, but there were lots of others who shore very few sheep, and could be called passengers. Many old men used to come to these shearings because they had always come there, but their contribution to the workload wasn't a lot. Many of these old wags, if it was not too far from a mealtime, would actually drape what they had shorn over the sheep, and pretend to be clipping away beneath it, so that they would not have to start another sheep before a break! Many of these wags would also spend overlong in sharpening their shears, especially if there were tough sheep. If some of the better shearers saw somebody taking a long time to shear a sheep, they would call over an unsuspecting young lad, and ask him quietly to go outside, and get a handful of grass, and to offer it to the sheep in the hands of the slow shearer, in case it might be hungry!

It should be noted that in many places the lambs were also shorn, and a little clique of old hands would shear these in a different shed. Being upgraded to shear lambs was quite an honour.

Cutting a sheep during the shearing was frowned upon, and there was a cry then of, 'Cut!' A young lad would then appear with ointment to put on it. Some places were worse than others, and one that springs to mind is one where you were not allowed to shear until you had got to a certain degree of proficiency. If you happened to cut more than once, you were asked if you would go and do a stint in the catching pen!

Many youngsters would go shearing to a farm for the first time, and the owner would come over during the day to have a chat and make them feel welcome, and that was the one time, as sure as hell, that you cut a big slice! One of the customs in almost all places was that the owner of the sheep would come around and give out tobacco or cigarettes to those who smoked, and sweets to those who didn't. For some reason I remember that the type of sweets offered were mostly wine-gums.

Very often, towards the end of the shearing, a competition was held at some of the farms to see who was the best shearer. I include this list from 1933 in Ponterwyd that will I'm sure be of interest to the relatives and descendants of those mentioned:

Ty-mawr:	1. J.J. Morgan, Nant-cae-rhedyn
	2. D.J. Howells, Bryn-glas
	3. D.J. Jones, Llwyn-teifi
Nant-cae-rhedyn:	1. J.J. Morgan, Nant-cae-rhedyn
	2. T.H. Morgan, Nant-cae-rhedyn
	3. Emlyn Thomas, Talwrn, and D J Evans, Ceiro.
Bryn-glas:	1. Edwin Howells, Dyffryn Castell
	2. Emlyn Thomas, Talwrn,

Eisteddfa:

1. D.J. Howells, Bryn-glas
2. T.H. Morgan, Nant-cae-rhedyn
3. T. Howells, Gelli, and Emlyn Thomas, Talwrn

Dôl-wen:

1. W. Thomas, Llety-synod
2. D.W. Davies, Ty-mawr
3. J. Edwards, Cae'r meirch.

■ Shearing at Dinas, Ponterwyd in 1896.

After some of the shearings they would hold a competitive meeting of singing and reciting. A very popular part of the event was to find out who could say the best jokes. These meetings would add a lot of fun after a hard day's work, and provided a means of strengthening a full social life in many an isolated area. One place that was noted for such an occasion was Troed-rhiw-cymer, near Rhandirmwyn, where I spent several years of very rewarding shepherding, not only getting to know an area that was completely new to me, but also making a lot of friends in the district. Many of these have passed away by now, but I gleaned a lot of knowledge from them, and will always treasure having met them, and I'm still in contact with their families in the area. A workday combined with a social gathering. It was only at such times that many of them met, coming from different districts, and it was an ideal boy-meets-girl situation – many, as I mentioned, coming to stay the night before, and you can rest assured that not a lot of sleeping went on!

145

I have been told by several people that one of the prime places years ago was the shearing at Nant-rhys. The men slept in one room downstairs and the girls in the other. There was a hatch between the two rooms for serving food, but on these particular occasions there was a lot of to-ing and fro-ing through this hatch – by both parties. Suffice it to say that many inhabitants over the years were born in April!

Whilst on a romantic subject, another story comes to mind. A young lady called Ann Edwards of Ty'n-ffordd, Cwmystwyth, who was an aunt of Alfred Edward, Ty-llwyd, had been sent out to look for her parents' cattle, as they had wandered rather far from home to graze in glorious summer weather. She went in the general direction of Dôl-wen, and in searching for the cattle met William Jones, the son and shepherd of Dôl-wen, who helped her to find the missing beasts. This started off their romance, and it was stated that the cattle went missing on a regular basis after this! As I always say, everybody has to have a hobby! James Hogg, the Ettrick Shepherd (1770–1835) had got it right in his poem *When the kye comes hame*:

> *Come all ye jolly shepherds*
> *That whistle through the glen*
> *I'll tell ye of a secret*
> *That courtiers dinna ken*
> *What is the greatest bliss*
> *That the tongue of man can name*
> *'Tis to woo a bonnie lassie*
> *When the kye comes hame.*

William and Ann moved to live in Gwar-clawdd, Devil's Bridge, where their great-great-grandchildren still live.

A young shepherd was regularly courting a girl in the nearest village, and he almost boasted that nobody heard him come in in the early hours. This was shortlived however, as one night some mischevious hand had put the bread tins on the stairs!

There was a fairly rigid pattern in every district as to when the different farms held their shearing, and it is still the same to a certain extent. Each farm had its allocated day. The following is a general pattern of the Ponterwyd area:

First Thursday in July	Lle'r-neuaddau
Friday	Craig-nant, Bryn-chwith
Saturday	Bont Farm, Erwbarfe
Monday	Hirnant
Tuesday	Aberceiro, Eisteddfa-fach
Wednesday	Ceiro, Gelli, Dinas, Nant-yr-arian
Thursday	Nant-cae-rhedyn, Quick, Botcoll
Friday	Brynglas, Ty'n-ffordd, Hen-hafod
Saturday	Fagwr
Monday	Aberpaithnant
Tuesday	Blaen-paithnant
Wednesday	Bwlch-styllen
Thursday	Drosgol
Friday	Eisteddfa.

■ The last shearing at Nant-y-moch in 1961.

The Jervis family of Cefn-brwyn in Llangurig had a different way of getting their shearing done. They had an allocated week, and 20 shearers would come there, and stay for the duration, sleeping in tents near the farmhouse. There is in Ty-llwyd, Cwmystwyth, a field called 'Cae-main' – a long field that runs between the road and the river Ystwyth. On the shearing days in times gone by, this field was full of ponies that had carried the shearers there. Cae-main was then, and still is, a favourite camping site of visitors to the area.

One year, when the arduous work of the shearing was over, the shepherds and farmers of Cwmystwyth decided that they deserved a break, and a trip was organised. So on the 23rd of August 1927 they went with a bus on a journey that took them to Llanon, Aberaeron, Cardigan, Llandysul, Lampeter and home. They had enjoyed this trip so much that they planned to go on another one in 1928 – to Hereford!

In 1926, Mr Norman Davies (born on the 4th of August 1894) a solicitor from Aberystwyth, who lived at Llwyn-ffynnon in Llanbadarn, installed a shearing machine at his sheep-walk of Cwmergyr, in Ponterwyd. It was a Wolseley system, driven by belts, and a Mr T.J. Bassett was the demonstrator. In a local paper, it stated that the shearers averaged 83 sheep each on the second day. In 1944, the firm Cooper Stewart advertised a hand powered shearer for sale at £7–10–0, carriage paid.

The system however did not catch on, and it was back to hand shearing for many years after. I well remember the first petrol engine shearing unit coming to Fagwr, Ponterwyd, and a noisy affair it was. The owner of this machine was Mr Idwal Hughes, of Wern-Phillip, Comins Coch, and it was only he that shore with it. The older shearers there were totally put out by all this noise, which meant they couldn't talk, and I can recall muttered threats that they would not be coming there again if the engine was there.

Since the purpose of this whole job was to obtain wool I enclose only a few snippets about it, as I am sure enough has been written by other people on this subject.

It was once a very valuable product. I have a note from somewhere that a John Williams driving sheep for a Margaret Vaughan in 1720, was warned not to take wool from them! Around the 1790s a lot of wool from mid-Wales was sold to Russia in order to clothe its army. Greed has always lurked where there are humans around, and it was the same in this era. Some people started to shear their sheep twice a year but the autumn shearing left them bare, and many perished during cold winter periods.

A man calling himself 'An Old Shearer' wrote to the *Welsh Gazette* in 1918 proclaiming that farmers and landowners were making big profits from their wool sales, and he urged shearers to charge their employers 5/– (25p) a day, plus food, for their work. In 1937, the pay for the hired men at Nant-stalwen was 3/– (15p) a day. Tommy Hughes told me many times that he had seen men having two cull (unthrifty) lambs as payment for a day's shearing. A 'cull fair' used to be held at Rhaeadr on the last Friday of July for many years as a venue for selling this type of lamb.

■ Some of the dozens of horses that had carried their owners to this shearing at Nant-stalwen in the 40s. Photo by R.Cecil Hughes, Swansea.

Another aspect that has long gone into oblivion, were the wool gleaners. Cart-loads of able-bodied women came from the south of Cardiganshire up towards the Abbey at Strata Florida. I quote from the journal *Ceredigion* 1. p.29:

> *Within living memory gleaners came from far and near in search of the pickings from the 'wool hills' lying to the rear of the Abbey ruins.*

A lady called Ruth Jones, who was born in the south of Ceredigion in 1856, in her book of reminiscences published in 1939, recalls how she started shepherding when she was eight and a half years old, and later how she and others used to go gleaning on the hills between Tregaron and Abergwesyn. They often slept in the barns of outlying farms. She mentions going to Moel-prysgau, near Pont-rhyd-fendigaid, and then over to Esgair-garthen, and going on almost to Rhaeadr. They would spend nearly a fortnight in this area wool-picking. The wool would then be taken home and spun, and knitted into garments or stockings for the family.

Knitting was a craft that was important in years gone by, and it was done by men as well as women. In a place, now in ruin, called Y Ffrwd (the waterfall) by Nant-y-maen, Tregaron, there was a tale that the whole family would sit down around the fire and knit stockings. Nobody has lived at Ffrwd since 1911. Many adults and children would knit as they walked to and from different places. I have in my possession an intricately made gadget, consisting of two hooks and a swivel, that they used to hang the ball of wool onto a belt or garment.

In the 1871 Census returns a shepherd's wife and daughter were described as 'stocking knitters'. Personal industry was rewarded by Agricultural Societies, such as the Agricultural Society of Cardiganshire in 1789, who gave a Margaret Rees a prize for knitting 161 pairs of stockings, and Carmarthen Agricultural Society rewarded a Jane Williams for having spun – from the first day of January 1801 to the end of the same year – 287 pounds of wool, the prize being £2–2–0, which would at that time be an honourable sum.

In 1870 there were 40 women selling stockings at a fair in Tregaron. Mary Jane Jones (nee Oliver, Ffair Rhos) from Dôl-goch, Tregaron, used to set a target for herself and her daughters, and any girl working there, that they should knit one stocking a day. These would later be sold at a shilling (5p) a pair. There was great demand for stockings for the workers in the South Wales Collieries in latter years, and the local people saw fit to cash in on this need.

The price of wool was so low in the early 1920s that several farms saw fit to keep the wool instead of selling it. It was stated that Dafydd Lewis, Allt-fedw kept five crops of wool. The Raw family of Ty-llwyd kept their wool for three years. It was stored in every conceivable corner. Mr J.E. Raw was up in the attic of the house throwing the wool down for such a long time that he took a chamber pot up with him!

Shearing Food

One of Ceredigion's greatest characters, Lewis Morris (1700–1765), originally from Anglesey (Morisiaid Môn) lived at Allt-fadog, the farm next to my home in Capel Madog. He moved later to Pen-bryn-barcud in Goginan, and in a letter mentioning his shearing there, he wrote that they had 'a feast day such as the Hebrews made when they sheared their sheep'.

In the many talks I have given on local history, I've never missed a single chance to revere the ladies of yesteryear when it came to the subject of shearing food, especially considering the limited facilities that they had – an open fire, a bread oven, boilers, and that was their lot. As already mentioned the number of people that had to be fed were tremendous, and the food had to be of good quality, and the quantity eaten by healthy, vigorous workers was no joke. A relative of the Thomas family of Eisteddfa Gurig, called David Thomas, used to go there, and help them with the shearing. He was a man who had a phenomenal appetite. The family would allow, for a few days' shearing, a loaf for each man, and two for David Thomas!

Many items such as cake could be made beforehand, and I was given a recipe for a shearing cake from 1910 by Mrs Cecilia Jones, of Westralia, Llanarth, herself a descendant of the Roberts family of Pont-rhyd-fendigaid, and they certainly had the experience of catering for large shearing days. The ingredients were as follows:

12 quarts of flour
5 pounds of butter
2 pounds of lard
5 pounds of currants
4½ pounds of sultanas
7½ pounds of demerara sugar
2 oz nutmeg and spice
½ pound of lemon peel
14 eggs
½ ounce of yeast
a glassful of rum
milk

Being a mere man I cannot expand upon how it was mixed, but it was enough probably to make 12 cakes. Rice pudding was nearly always on the menu, and if the farm did not have many cows, milk would be brought in from nearby farms, and this would be repaid when they did their shearing. Large bowlfulls of this would be made in well prepared brick bread ovens. A fire was put inside the oven, and then the ashes would be scraped out, and hot work it was, with an iron handled tool that was called *corlac* in

Welsh, very similar to a dutch hoe. The name *corlac* was a corruption of 'coal-rake'. When the age of the bread oven had passed, I remember my grandfather using it as a scraper to clean out under the pig.

One very useful addition to the menu in later times was jelly, believe it or not, because it meant that much less milk was needed, and it filled a corner of the bowl, despite perhaps being more of a novelty than nutrition.

Meat was perhaps a more valuable, but also a more perishable item. Most meat was home produced, and usually meaty wethers were killed, and in the Tywi valley it was a practice to kill a calf on some farms. Dôl-goch used to buy about one hundred-weight of beef from Aberystwyth which was taken by rail to the station at Strata Florida, and one of the family from Dôl-goch would come down to meet the train, and take the meat, as well as other provisions the eleven miles to Dôl-goch.

Due to the quantity of meat involved, it could not all be put in the oven, so a portion was put to boil, as it was not a good time of year to keep meat. It was a custom with many people years ago to boil mutton, and then later roast it, and I am convinced they knew how to get the best results.

There was a preservative that used to be put on meat years ago that had a devastating effect on the digestive system, and gave those that ate it severe diarrhoea. Such a thing happened at Nant-stalwen and everybody, workers and family, were affected, except the head of the family Mr James Edwards. As he was going to bed one evening, he experienced some internal discomfort, and ordered that his boots be put at the bottom of the stairs in case of an emergency during the night, as the toilet was an outside one. The boots were duly put there, but an unsympathetic pair of hands had tied the laces. Later on that night he had to get up and the vital seconds he took to unlace his boots proved detrimental to his reaching the toilet in time!

Many things happened to upset shearing plans, as can be imagined. The weather was one of the aggravating circumstances, and constant rain or mist could create a big hindrance, especially where the perishable items were concerned. Many years ago it took Bodtalog seven days to try and get the shearing done because of inclement weather.

> Some respite to husbands the weather may send
> But housewives' affairs have never an end.

Accident or misfortune was another aspect. The farm of Goed-ddôl in Llanwrin held the land of Llechwedd-mawr (locally called Llechweddmor) near Nant-y-moch lake, and being a long way off, the family had prepared all the food in advance, and it was taken up to Llechweddmor by trap and pony. However, in crossing the Llechweddmor river which was slightly swollen, the trap tipped over, and all the food was lost. Somebody was then sent on a pony to Talybont to get two sacks full of bread and cheese and cake, which was very inferior to the pre-prepared feast, but was better than going without.

At another farm everybody was busy preparing a shearing meal, and a girl servant who was working there was upset by something or other, and in a huff sat down on the settle and refused to move. The unfortunate thing was that it was in this settle – a high-backed bench to sit about three people, with a storage box as a base – that this family kept the potatoes, and as they were reluctant to use physical force to remove her, they had to go without potatoes that day.

Ceiro in Ponterwyd, farmed by the Evans family for many years, did their utmost to get new potatoes from their garden for the shearing meal. On one occasion they also had a mishap. A dog belonging to Dafydd James, Hirnant, somehow slipped into the kitchen and took the whole joint of meat out with him, so that was the end of that. Dafydd poured oil on troubled waters with his comment 'Good old Prince!'

Another calamity along similar lines took place at a gathering for shearing at Lluest-dôl-gwiail, which was owned by the late Gareth Raw-Rees, Ty'n Park, Llandre. His mother, Annie Raw of Ty-llwyd, Cwmystwyth, had married David Rees from Llandre, on 28th of January 1920, hence the 'Raw' coming into their surname. As well as farming, Gareth also bred turkeys, and quite naturally he brought up a turkey, ready cooked, to feed the gatherers. The house of Lluest at that time was in a pretty bad state, and a dog broke in, having for himself probably the best meal he'd ever had. At this time they were driving the sheep to be shorn at Ty-llwyd, and needless to say, everybody was very hungry by the time they arrived down there. Since the dog had done his deed, and came out of the house undetected, aspersions were cast as to whose dog it was, and the leg-pulling on this score lasted for years afterwards.

To bring this matter of shearing food to a conclusion, hoping to have clarified most aspects of the work, I heartily salute the womenfolk of yesteryear for coping with the mammoth tasks that they undertook in such an admirable way.

Identifying one's property has probably been an issue since humans have been capable of owning anything. The Egyptians used to ear-mark their slaves several thousand years ago – for example, there is mention in Exodus: 21:6 of ear-marking slaves.

With sheep it was very necessary to work out a system of identification, because of their wandering nature, and the fact that fully stockproof boundaries were almost unknown until recent times. Ear-marking was one of the answers to this problem, and a pattern was worked out to give farms and sheepwalks individual ear-marks. Ear-marks were also used to identify mountain ponies.

These different marks were cut on the outer edges of the ear, which is made up mostly of gristle, and when cut into a lamb's ears, will stay there for the rest of its life. In North Ceredigion we call a ear-mark *nôd cyllell* (knife mark), as all these marks were cut with a razor-sharp pocket knife. All these marks had names, and these names vary from district to district. One cut is called a 'swallow fork' – a v-shaped notch cut into the tip of the ear. In the Llandovery area it is called *llysenfforch*; in Ceredigion it is called *gwennol*; in the Machynlleth area it is called *canwer* – a word that goes back to the eleventh century; and in the Caernarfon area, the same cut is called *cnwyad*.

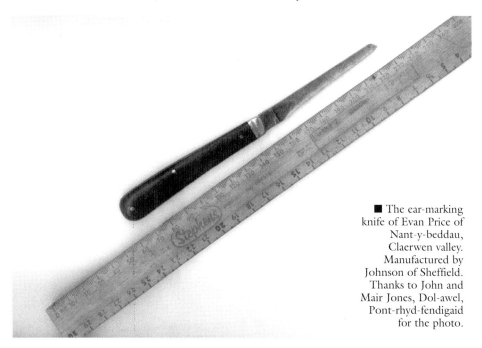

■ The ear-marking knife of Evan Price of Nant-y-beddau, Claerwen valley. Manufactured by Johnson of Sheffield. Thanks to John and Mair Jones, Dol-awel, Pont-rhyd-fendigaid for the photo.

There are ear-mark books going back to the 1820s, and in the National Library there is documentation (*The Leet Court of Glyn-dyfrdwy*) about the settlement of stray sheep and their ownership in the 1600s and the names of the cuts were then as we would use them now.

In describing an ear-mark, the sheep in most areas are looked at from behind, and in the majority of areas the left ear is referred to as the 'near', and the right ear as the 'off'. In Welsh, in this area, the left is called *y nesa*, and the right *y bella*.

I sometimes wonder if certain areas long ago had a definite mark in one ear that would associate that sheep with that particular area. In Bont-goch near Talybont many of the farms have a swallow fork in the same ear. Coincidence? My imagination? Just a thought. In Ponterwyd however, there is positive proof that such a system was employed, but this was to associate the sheep with a family. The James family of Aberpeithnant/Nant-y-moch had a slope with a slit in it under the off, with various marks in the near to differentiate the many holdings. My family, the Howells of Cwmergyr, had a thumb notch above the near, not far from the tip, and as explained above, varying cuts in the off.

■ Nose-branding at Maes-glas, Tregaron in the 40s. Photo: R. Cecil Hughes.

154

■ A rare glimpse of 'nose-burn' irons. Photo by Ian Sant.

Having mentioned pitch marks and raddle marks already, there were two other ways of marking sheep, both of which are no longer used. There was the practice of what was known as a 'nose-burn' (*harn nodi*) where a mark was branded with a hot iron on the sheep's nose. Some of these marks looked ungainly after several years, because sometimes a horny material grew out of the scar. Cases of cruelty brought against landowners a long time ago were lost, because the flock-masters argued that since these sheep roamed up to about forty miles, and similar ear-marks could be found at that distance, it was necessary for identification.

Rhys Jones from Rhiwlas in Ysbyty Ystwyth had a nose brand in the form of a 'T' and it was said that this mark went back to 1750 when the Estate of Hendre-felen owned the place. Hendre-felen also owned or grazed Claerddu around this time.

The other form of marking was a 'nose-slit' (*hollti'r ffroen*) where one or the other of the nostrils were slit. One of the last places to use this mark was Rhiwnant in the Elan Valley, but both these marks were discontinued years ago.

In the Tregaron area three sheepwalks have had their ear-marks put down in verse, therefore making them easier to remember. They are not easily translatable, so I include them in Welsh only:

Moel-prysgau: *Carre fain o dan yr ase*
                      Bylche bawd o war y clystie
                      Dyna'n gwmws nod Moel-prysge

Dôlgoch:	*Nod Dôlgoch ar hyd yr oesau*
	Ydi torri blaen y clystiau
	Tac bach twt o war y nesa
	A'r un fath o dan y bella
Deri-garon:	*Torri blaen y dde yn drist*
	A bwlch tri-thorriad dan bob clust.

The other common method of identifying sheep is the pitch-mark, which was put on after shearing. I have already mentioned pitch marks specific to certain farms. The following are, in all probability, to do with the Hafod Estate, in Pont-rhyd-y-groes. There were five farms in neighbouring areas with numbers instead of the usual letters:

Dôl-gors	9
Allt-fedw	8
Botgoll	7
Ty'n-bryn	3
Blaen-cwm	2.

Were there any other holdings that used the missing figures? I have put feelers out, but had no response to date. The '7' mark used by Daniel Davies, Botgoll was later adopted by Charles Evans, at Cwm-cem-rhiw, Glas-pwll. When the Birmingham Corporation took over many of the farms in the Elan Valley they had to have some extra way of identifying their sheep, so in 1893 they put an extra notch in the ear-mark, and this was called 'the taking notch'. Many of the sheep owned by the Corporation also had the pitch-mark 'B.C.' on them, as well as the farm pitch-mark. Ty-mawr, Cwmystwyth had a small 'B' inside the 'C'.

When Nant-y-moch was owned by Griffith Pugh Evans, Lovesgrove, the pitch-mark was GPE. This mark was later used by Brigadier General Evans, and John James the shepherd, when asked by visitors what it stood for, answered, 'General Protector of the Empire!'

There are 'odd' pitch-marks whose origins are unknown. Llwyn-teifi in Ystumtuen has a mark like a pair of spectacles. Some have a mark which is a circle with a cross below it, similar to the symbol used in medical and biological texts to denote 'female'. Incidentally, without trying to sound philosophical, this was also the symbol for the 'ank' in the name of the Egyptian Pharaoh, Tutankhamen, and was a sign of fertility. Coincidence? Or is it something that goes back a long way? One probably will never know.

In depicting these ear-marks on paper the ears are usually shown like this as viewed from behind:

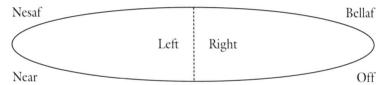

Some examples of the most common marks are as follows:

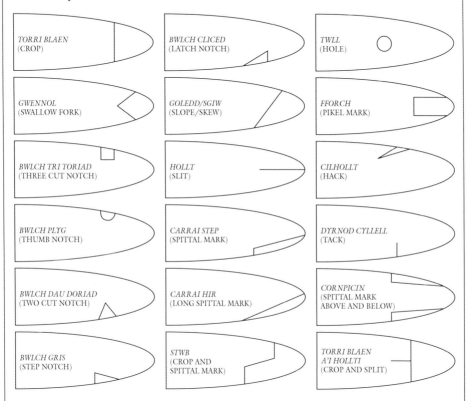

These marks could be cut above or below the ears, apart from the crop, swallow fork, slit and pikel mark. There were various punch marks that could be cut in the centre of the ear. The old ear-mark of Troed-rhiw-cymer, near Rhandir-mwyn involved a punch in the form of a letter 'J' for Jones, the family who had been there for a long time. Some places kept one ear uncut in order to distinguish their sheep. When the ear-mark is put on a lamb, the wool will grow over the sides of the cut, but if an ear-mark is cut in later life, a scar will be visible.

Without knocking modern tagging – because they can be useful, especially the colour coding as regards sheep's ages – they can be cut out, or lost, whereas the ear mark is for life, still very necessary for identification, and without the introduction of a foreign body.

Dogs

Columella wrote in A.D. 42...

> *What servant more attached to his master*
> *What companion more faithful*
> *What guardian more incorruptible*

...and it is as true today as it was then.

To all shepherds, mentioned here or not, dogs are a very important part of their lives. Even Dafydd Lluest-fach (to be mentioned in more detail later) thought the world of his dogs, though they caused him more problems than they solved. Had his dogs been with someone else they might have been the best.

A lot of dog training has to do with a person's attitude and personality, and to put it mildly, dogs vary a lot. Some people are able to make a good dog out of undescribable material, while others if they have, or buy, a good dog, never get the full potential out of it. One of the big advantages of yesteryear with dogs was that sheep were driven long distances, and after a ten mile hike, even the daftest of dogs would be easier to manage, and certainly if his feet were sore there was no need to ask more than once for him to stop. There are many examples of men who are good with dogs, but not so alert with sheep, and some good sheep men, who are mediocre dog handlers. William Cowper, the poet (1831–1900), wrote:

> *My dog! What remedy remains*
> *Since teach you all I can*
> *I see you, after all my pains*
> *So much resemble man!*

I believe enough has been written about dog training, so I'll steer clear of that line, but on a personal note, I am grateful to have had role models in my early years such as Morgan Griffiths, Nanty, Jim Lewis, Troed-rhiw-ruddwen, and my father, who taught me above everything else to keep dogs in good condition, comparing them to a car engine, that if it's well tuned, you get the best out of it. I have always thought of myself as a slow trainer, taking into consideration the old adage we have in this area, that a dog needs 'a year under each foot' to be at his best, and to be relied upon under most circumstances. I use the word dog in general terms, as many people prefer to work with bitches, but they, for obvious reasons such as being on heat, can cause problems especially if you exchange help with neighbours. Because I tend to be always working at different places I have kept mostly dogs for many years, due to the simple fact that you are able to work them throughout the year, but dogs being dogs, I often have to act as a referee at various fights.

■ Erwyd Howells with his dogs on Pumlumon in the early 1970s. L to R: Fly, Jim, Ben and the very special Mag, who was instrumental in keeping the old line of Welsh sheepdogs going.

With a male dog he will either work well, or not so well, as the case may be, and you are stuck with him, but with a bitch you get a 'second chance'. She may work to a certain standard, and not improve as you would wish, but if she has a litter of pups, due to her changing hormones, she will be much more eager to work. Having said that, I will always remember a piece of advice given to me by the late Trefor Evans (T.C. Evans) Pen-lan, Llanfihangel-y-Creuddyn, which was that he thought it unwise to breed from a bitch until she was three years old. He believed that if they bred at a younger age, they were not as committed to their work – he used to say that they had 'two minds'.

There have been for a long time three basic types of dog in mid-Wales. There is the well-known Border Collie, and their feats at sheepdog trials which have made them renowned the world over, and the indigenous Welsh sheepdogs which are sub-divided into two categories – the heading dogs, and the driving/barking dogs.

Dogs came down from Scotland to the Rhaeadr Gwy area prior to 1828, but I don't believe they had the 'eye' of the modern Border Collie – certainly the big black and white dogs (*cwn brith*) that came down to Nant-rhys years later showed no 'eye'. The ones that came down later were referred to as 'Scotch dogs', as in this advert in the *Welsh Gazette* 11th of February 1904:

> *Lost, Scotch collie dog property of Morgan, Glan-gors, Llanio Road (near Tregaron) Colour reddish with white band around neck. Name Moss.*

An article in 'Banner ac Amserau Cymru' in 1886 (under Cwmsymlog) stated that these 'penning dogs' (Scotch dogs) had recently come into the area, which was a novelty for the shepherds, but not so good for the sheep, as they were continuously hassled when the shepherds were training their new dogs. The writer strongly implied that Sunday seemed to be a favourite day for training these dogs, and that the shouting of the shepherds upset the devout worshipers of the area!

The Border Collie has an ingrained instinct to work or herd sheep, and approaches its sheep with caution, as though stalking its charges, and never taking its eye off them, and if they feel challenged by the sheep, they 'set', that is lie down, eyeing them. Too much 'eye' and too much 'setting' can make a very useless dog. In a report on a sheepdog trials in 1926 these Borders were referred to as 'crawlers' since their method of working was so different to local dogs. To my mind a Border that works on its feet, with the right amount of eye is very difficult to beat, giving you a careful, yet practical, sheep-handling work-mate. Today there are thankfully more of this type of dog around than there were years ago, and triallists are pushing to get bigger, more practical courses to test their dogs on, which is a step in the right direction. A classy Border with its pricked ears, and tail set between its legs is a sight to behold when properly handled.

The Welsh dogs work in a totally different way to the Border – tails up, ears down – and have none of their inhibiting characteristics. They are free agents by comparison, with no eye, in fact they are referred to as 'loose-eyed dogs'. One thing I like about them is that when you have got sheep into the yards they go about their own business, whereas the Border collie will be eyeing the sheep under a gate or through a fence, unable to switch off because of their overpowering natural instincts. When the Welsh dogs are under pressure to move their sheep, they bark, and are at their happiest when

■ Toss – my faithful companion for many years. A distinctive type of Welsh sheepdog showing folded ears and pronounced dip between nose and temple.

they are working large flocks of sheep. They have a tremendous amount of energy, and work well in hot weather. Many Borders, especially if they have a thick coat, do not stick heat too well. When there is a large mob of sheep on an open hill, you feel with a few Welsh dogs that you can dictate as to where the flock goes, because of their strong presence. Many people have handled sheep and dogs all their lives, but have no idea of the total cussedness of open mountain sheep or wethers when they want to escape, especially in rough ground or broken rocks, which give them a big advantage in their intentions.

The Welsh Sheepdogs were mentioned in the *Laws of Hywel Dda* c.10th century. He deemed that one 'properly broke in, and trained for conducting the flocks or herds out to the pasturage in the morning, and reconducting them home at night, was considered of equal value to an ox – sixty denarii – while a house dog or sheep was valued at four'.

I quote from a book by the Reverend R.W. Morgan, probably written in 1853 about North Wales:

> *Two kinds of dogs were in ancient times essential to the keeping of sheep; the first corresponding to our modern shepherd-dog had under his charge the sheep themselves; the second, resembling a wolf hound in power and ferocity, guarded them from beasts of prey, but never interfered with the management of the flock …[such a guarding dog] that could prove his blood was rated by the laws of Hywel Dda at the value of one hundred and twenty pence…*

An old Irish law put the value of a dog who guarded the flock, if killed, at 5 cows, plus a replacement of a dog of the same breed.

John Evans in his book *Beauties of England and Wales* (1812) writes:

> *The excellence of these dogs renders sheep pens, in a degree, unnecessary…[The sheep] were driven to a corner, and kept pent up there by one or more dogs. If an experienced shepherd wish to inspect his flock in a cursory way, he places himself in the middle of the field or piece they are depasturing, and giving a whistle or a shout, the dogs and the sheep are equally obedient to the sound; the one flies from him with their swiftest speed, while the other from every quarter, draw towards him in considerable haste, long before the dogs have time to approach them. The stragglers are driven in by the circuitous route of the dogs, which keep flying round from side to side, until the flock be gathered round the shepherd, close enough not only to be seen, but to be laid hold of him, if anything wrong be suspected.*

In his book *A Shepherd's Life*, W.H. Hudson mentions that Welsh sheepdogs were very highly thought of in Wiltshire well over 200 years ago. I would have thought that they would have been taken there by the early drovers, as they took cattle and sheep to the markets of Barnet and Smithfield, or to be fattened on the lush land of Kent. Some of these drovers, at the end of the season would sell their dogs, but some of the more faithful ones would make their way home, sometimes before their owners! Many of the same dogs were sold more than once!

The driving/barking dog was, and still is a very important aspect of a hill farm. They were instrumental in keeping sheep boundaries, driving the sheep back into their own sectors, and also during the summer driving the sheep up from the lower slopes, therefore keeping the growth there for the autumn. Going back long ago before the time of stock-proof boundaries, this type of dog was the only means by which hill farms could keep their hay, oats and green crop from the scavenging sheep. These dogs were kept out day and night, and as soon as they saw sheep within a certain distance, they would give chase. When gathering, they are invaluable in driving the sheep towards the point where they come together, saving the heading dogs a lot of work, and another very important factor, teaching the sheep to get their act together, and move in the required direction. These driving dogs should not be thought of as a race apart from the heading dogs, but a lot depended on how they were initially taught, and many of them after several years of coursing would graduate into heading dogs.

I have always kept Borders and Welsh sheepdogs pure, and feel that they totally complement each other in their work. As Tom Williams said, 'A dog for every occasion.'

A name that I revere in the Border Collie world was that of the late John Evans, Magor, in Gwent (W.J. Evans). I was very fortunate years ago to have had one of the last dogs he sold before he died. A friend of mine Dei Jenkins, Cefn-gweiriog, Taliesin, had bought a pup from John Evans, but was not very pleased with it, and passed it on to David Evans, Tanllan, Llancynfelin, who also did not find the dog to his liking. When he was four and a half years old he came to me, and in a very short time I knew that this dog, Lad (111242), was something very special. At the same time I had a bitch called Gwen (12603) who's breeding also went back to John Evans' Roy (7696), and this is the breeding line I have stuck to, and now have the fifth generation down from Lad and Gwen. I've always felt that John Evans knew exactly what he wanted in a dog, and many people including myself have benefitted from his sterling work. John Evans, with Roy (7696), won the Supreme Championship at the International Sheepdog Trials in Cardiff in 1953. Roy also was the father of Roy (15393) that belonged to Alan Jones, Pontllyfni, Caernarfon, who also made a name for himself on the trialling scene.

My Welsh dogs started in earnest with a mostly black bitch called Mag, which my father had bought from David Jones, Rhos-y-rhiw, Pont-rhyd-y-groes, in 1967, and she was a little gem, honest as the day is long. She was crossed with Lad, one of John Lewis Ty-mawr's dogs. John's other dog Roy had been crossed with Meg, a slick coated black and white bitch that had come from the breeding lines of Morgan Griffiths, Nanty, going back to a slate-grey dog he had bought for a pound from a farm called Cwm-dewi in Brecon. Meg was owned by Jim Raw, Ty-llwyd, and she would move any amount of sheep. The outcome of the mating was Lad, who spent his life at Ty-llwyd.

He was crossed with a coursing bitch owned by Clifford Pugh, Bodtalog, resulting in a dog called Pip. At this time I had a blue merle bitch called Scot from Islwyn Jones, Llwyn-teifi, Ystumtuen. She was descended from an old line of dogs from Fuches-gau, Ponterwyd, and I took her to be mated with Pip from Bodtalog. It was from this crossing that I had Tip, a very strong, black and white dog, who was a no-nonsense sheep mover. He was a clever dog in many respects. If I lost him he would always find his way home. He came with me to a sheep sale in Machynlleth (on a Wednesday) and he probably went on a romantic errand. On the following Wednesday I was on Llechweddmor, the hill of Glan-frêd in Llandre, where I worked for seventeen years, and Tip came to me pleased as punch after his 'holiday'. He was able to climb up and down

■ Ben (216303) – probably the best Border I have had the good fortune of owning. A direct descendant of John Evans' Roy (7696). Photo by Tom Jones Rees.

ladders, as well as opening the latch of the shed he slept in, which thankfully I have on video, as well as a little of his work with sheep.

During Tip's time I had a dark merle little bitch called Meg, whose breeding went back to the dogs of Ochor-rhos, in Devil's Bridge. She was a total pleasure to work with, full of vim, always willing to please, and would work till she dropped. She will always feature in my mind as being the most instrumental in the breeding of true-to-type Welsh Sheepdogs. Having been mated to several different dogs, she helped retain some bloodlines that otherwise would have been lost.

In 1987, Mr E.J. Evans, Pant-anamlwg, Nebo, brought his bitch Fan, whose lineage went back in his wife's family for a long time, to be mated with Tip, resulting in his dog Wag. In the meantime he had bought from me a daughter of Meg called Floss, which he in due time crossed with Wag, and their offspring have pleased me no end, and I will always be grateful to him for his part in helping to preserve a very valuable part of our heritage, which I've always striven to promote, even sending a Welsh bitch to Holland in the late 1980s.

About two years ago, I was able to oversee a mating that in effect, virtually brought together most of the different lines of Welsh sheepdogs I have worked with. This was thanks to my cousin Gwylon Davies, Gors-las, Llangwyryfon, who had kept one line going that I'd lost. I was very lucky to have been at the right place at the right time years ago, and from what was then only routine breeding, the genes of some of the best Welsh dogs around this area at the time have been preserved.

Border collies are predominantly black and white, but I prefer those with a little tan in them. Welsh sheepdogs can be any colour – black-and-tan, blue merle, brown, brindle, black and white, grey, and some are black with flecks of white in their coats (*ci bwrw eira* – a 'snowstorm dog'). There was hardly a farm in years gone by that did not have a black-and-tan, or blue merle, in the yard. A society was set up in 1963 to promote the Welsh Blue Merles. This was more to do with colour than purity of lineage, as in looking at a photograph taken at that time, I see some that have Border traits, and deem them to be 'crossers'. The instigator of this society was the late Gwilym Williams Edwards (1923–1974) who was then the Secretary of the Welsh Black Cattle Society, and in his travelling in connection with his work, to every corner of Wales, he found many of this type of merle, or Cambrian Sheepdogs, as they were sometimes called. The interest and enthusiasm regarding these dogs was strong, but probably due to administrative problems, plus the untimely death of Mr Edwards, the society sadly went into decline.

In 1902 there was a 'muzzling order' for dogs – what this involved I do not know – and in 1906 there came a new law as regards dogs that were straying. This notice is from the *Welsh Gazette* on the 28th of February 1907:

> *We are selling large quantities of dog collars from 1/6 each – Griffiths and Co. Machynlleth.*

Free enterprise at its best!

In the same way as they hound (pardon the pun!) motorists today, one of the favourite pastimes of the police years ago was to look for dogs out at night. The first cases of prosecution I have seen were at Llanbadarn court on the 6th of April 1933 when eight farmers were fined 5/– (25p) for the error of their ways.

A very common name for a male dog in Wales is 'Pero'. The curious thing about this name is that 'perro' is the Spanish word for dog. At what juncture did this name come into Wales? It would be most interesting to find out. Another term that has set me thinking over many years is the word '*pisto*'. This word is used south of the River Ystwyth for a young pup, and I have heard it pronounced '*bisto*'. Thanks to Mr Emrys Williams from Aberystwyth, an ex-member of the staff of the Natrional Library, who pointed me in the direction of the *English Dialect Dictionary*, in which I came across the word 'pishty', a word for an un-named pup or strange dog used in Gloucestershire and surrounding areas. Which way did this word travel? Had the early drovers anything to do with it? Perhaps somebody will find out one day.

While on the subject of pups, picking a pup was an important matter. Some people liked to have a pup with the top of its mouth black. Others would move the pups away from the spot where the bitch had them, and she would carry them back. This would be watched closely, and many would keep the first pup that she carried. Some people liked to keep the runt of the litter, and I remember one case where it worked well. There was a litter of pups at Bodtalog, and Gillian, Bill Pugh's grand-daughter, insisted on keeping the smallest, probably against Bill's wishes, and she called it Rupert. Rupert grew into a big handsome dog, and was an excellent worker.

Apart from certain markings or colour, others would look for dew-claws, or indeed lack of them in some cases, especially for dogs that worked land with a lot of heather, as these dew-claws get caught in the heather, and sometimes made the dogs lame. Some dogs have double dew-claws, which is an indicator of a rugged, strong dog who would be a tireless worker. Everybody to his fancy. Some would pick the pup that came to them first, probably indicating that it was not shy. The guideline I have used on several occasions is to pick the pup that sucks the rear teats, as they contain more milk, hoping that is the pup with a bit of thinking power. All I can say is that it is very much a hit-or-miss business.

Working and breeding these dogs over many years has given me an enormous amount of pleasure, and through this interest I have made many friends throughout the U.K., in Europe, and beyond. One of my favourite sayings is, 'There are very few strangers in the world – they're friends you haven't met.'

Sheepdog Trials

Having dealt with dogs, and their work, I would like to deal with the lighter side of their work, not only for them, but for their handlers as well. A local sheepdog trial meant a day off, and a chance to meet friends from further afield. I will confine myself to Ceredigion, and even then mostly to the North of the county.

Almost certainly the first trial in the county was held at Ysbyty Ystwyth in 1886, with 12 dogs competing, and this was followed by one held in Llangybi in 1887. In 1911 the Ysbyty Ystwyth trials were held on Ty'n-pompren land, with the course 500 yards in length. At the end of the day there was a dinner to celebrate at the Star Inn. The Judges were Sir Edward W.P. Pryse, Gogerddan; Mr Tom Jones, Claerddu; and Mr Tom Howells, Gelli-uchaf (my great-grandfather). Also in 1911, a trial was held at Bont-goch near Talybont, on the land of Llety-ifan-hen, but some people were disgruntled because there were alchoholic drinks for sale on the field!

A trial was held at Pont-rhyd-fendigaid in 1901, but according to one report there may have been one there in 1896. Cilcennin, Tregaron, Aberaeron, and Penuwch trials started in 1926, and in 1925 a sheepdog trial was held at Eglwys-fach, with the Machynlleth Brass Band entertaining the crowd.

A trial was held at Devil's Bridge in 1908, and the course was where the 'mart' premises are today. The competitor had to climb up into the box of a horse-cart, and work his dog from there. One competitor who had slightly over-indulged, had to be helped into the cart. Once he had steadied, he asked his helpers where the dog was, and they, jumping at the chance to have a bit of fun, told him to send it further, stop him, call him in, stop him, and while all this was going on, the old dog was lying stretched out under the cart!

Some of the obstacles they had to contend with at this time included taking the sheep through the iron hoop of a cartwheel, and then there were three parallel gates, and they had to manoeuvre the sheep through one gap, and then through the other which was slightly narrower. In Pont-rhyd-fendigaid trials in 1908 the pen was described as being triangular, with one corner open so as to allow only one sheep in at a time. Recent new rules have even scrapped a six-foot gate, insisting on an eight-foot one instead! New Row village trial started in 1933 and ran till 1939. It was re-started in 1958, and is still going strong.

The names that came to the forefront in these early trials were: Mr Rhys Roberts, Ty'n-cwm, Pont-rhyd-fendigaid; Mr Richard Morgan, Hengwm-annedd; Mr Elias Bonner, Ochor-rhos, Devil's Bridge; and Mr William Hopkins, Llaneithyr, Devil's Bridge. These hill men, although they had good dogs, had another trump up their sleeve in the fact that they understood sheep, and this was to their advantage by comparison to their lowland counterparts.

■ John Jones training 'Spot' in front of Dol-goch house. Spot was one of the first Border dogs to come to the area. He came from Northumberland.

Rhys Roberts was a keen competitor and regularly came into the prize money. In 1924 he and his dogs had gone by train to a trial in Mynachlog Ddu in Pembrokeshire. He won the first prize of £10, shared the second prize of £5 (£2–10–00) and had £1 for coming into sixth place out of 42 contestants. Added to this he won second prize of £2 for working two dogs, and a special prize of £1 for the best handling of two dogs. I'm sure after going all that way, he was quite pleased with his day, and his dogs. He once said that he won enough money at these sheepdog trials to pay a man and girl servant at Ty'n-cwm. Rhys was taken to many local trials by Tom Evans, Wellington House, Pont-rhyd-fendigaid, who was the local Registrar, and also ran a taxi service in the area. Rhys Roberts passed away in 1932. The prize money offered years ago was very high, even if compared to today's standards. A sheepdog trial in Rhuthin in 1882 had a first prize of £10, a second prize of £5, followed by a third prize of £3.

Richard Morgan, already mentioned, was a very consistent winner. Elias Bonner and William Hopkins had some of the first Scotch dogs in the area. William Hopkins had his in 1926, when two pups were ordered from Scotland, costing £1 each. They came by rail to Aberystwyth, and then by the narrow-gauge railway to Devil's Bridge. The other pup went to Richard Morris at Rhos-y-rhiw, Pont-rhyd-y-groes. William Hopkins was frequently asked to judge at these trials. In mentioning the Railway, a notice appeared in local papers in 1902 stating that 'rams now conveyed at a charge as for two dogs – 2/– (10p) each ram'.

In the early years most of the dogs used were of the Welsh type, but with the coming of the Border Collie, which worked in a calmer manner, their days were numbered as far as sheepdog trials were concerned. There is one report in 1887 of a John Jones from Ty'n-lloft, Silian, and his black bitch Fan 'who worked wildly and noisily, and scattered the sheep from the field!'

A trial was held under the auspices of the Collie Club at The Alexandra Palace in 1882, and I quote: 'Most of the dogs, and all the best performers, came from the Welsh moors and mountains' and it goes on to say that some dogs seemed bewildered by seeing so many people, as indeed they might, coming from places where people are few and far between. In Bala in 1899, there was a trial which they declared was 'Open to the World', that is inviting competitors from anywhere. Little did they imagine that one hundred and three years later (2002) that there would indeed be a 'World Trial' there.

I have many references to people in years gone by working their dogs noisily with a lot of shouting and swearing. One man who changed this was William Wallace who worked in a trial at Otterburn in Northumberland, in 1874. He worked his dogs in a quiet manner, and by his example, many took to this new way of working their dogs.

In reading many reports of these trials of long ago, there was a chance of winning several types of competitions, for instance there was a prize for best command, best conditioned dog, and best type of dog. Some places had a shearing competition and others had foot races. I saw in one report that a competition was set up for two men to pen the sheep without a dog! So all in all they had a day out, with healthy competition, and a bit of fun thrown in for good measure.

Ponterwyd sheepdog trials started in 1910. In a report in 1916 there were 15 competitors, with Mr G.E. Jones, Nant-y-fyda, Aberhosan, and Mr Abram Morgan, Ty-newydd, Cwmystwyth, acting as judges. The prize list was as follows: 1. Elias Bonner, Ochor-rhos; 2. J.A. Evans, Ty'n-rhos; 3. J.W. Jones, Claerwen; 4. Morgan Morgans, Ty'n-bwlch, Ysbyty Ystwyth.

In the second class the first and second prize was divided between Edward Hopkins, Prignant-isaf and J. Lewis, Claerwen. The remaining winners were placed as follows: 3. William Hopkins, Dôl-wen; 4. T. Oliver, Pengraig; 5. Tom Meredith, Pantglas.

Afterwards they had a tug-of-war competition, for men and women, and after that a foot-race for men and women, with twenty men, and twenty-two girls competing in each sector. At the end of the day, it was disclosed who had won the 'guessing the weight of the ram' competition. All profit made was spent on buying presents for those from the area who were fighting in the First World War.

The nearest neighbours of the Morgan family of Hengwm-annedd lived right across the river at Lluestnewydd ('new sheepwalk') and we find the roots of our next shepherd there.

A man came there as a shepherd c.1880. His name was Charles Evans (1824–1896) and his parents were John and Mary Evans of Llety-synod, in Trisant. John Evans was born in 1780 and Mary his wife in 1790. They had 16 children, Charles probably being the twelfth.

Charles, as mentioned, was born at Llety-synod, married a Margaret Oliver and lived in the Llanafan area, and worked at Fron-goch lead mine. He was a strong man, but had massive hernias on both sides, and probably had been affected by the working conditions in the mines, and had been told to find a healthier job, hence his coming to Lluest-newydd. He had a big white beard, and was said to have 'a princely appearance'.

Charles and Margaret had (as far as I know) four children – Mary, Margaret, Lewis and John. Did Mary marry a Blackwell and live in South Wales? A Richard Hill Blackwell came to Maesnant in 1883, with Charles Evans paying 10/– towards his keep; little problems like this one were probably sent here to make me think. Margaret had a child from William Morgan, Hengwm-annedd, and he was called William Charles Evans, and was baptized on the 16th of June 1885 at Machynlleth. He lived in South Wales, and had a son called Charles Aneurin Evans, and my information peters out there. Lewis married an Elizabeth Morgan fromYsbyty Ystwyth, and many of their descendants are around this area.

The remaining son – John Evans – married Margaret Jones who was born at Hafod Wnog, which is towards Machynlleth from Lluest-newydd. She was the daughter of Elizabeth Jones, whose family had been in that particular area for a very long time. The only other relative I have heard of, however, is her brother called Rowland. Margaret's father was Humphrey Hughes, from Lluest-y-rhôs. He had been married several times, and was known to have fathered twenty three children. He was a deacon at Tabor Chapel and died on the 11th of July 1893 aged 78. He was buried at Penegoes, Machynlleth. John Jones, Pen-rhiw, Ystumtuen, was a brother to Margaret, and many of his descendants are still around in this area. They had another brother, Tom, who was a very astute shepherd with Thomas Jones, at Bugeilyn, but died a young man.

When Elizabeth Jones (Margaret's mother) had become an old lady, and not able to do a lot, she used to go to the nearest bed of rushes, gather, peel and cut them to size, then she would sell them – as many as she could hold between her index finger and thumb for a penny – to make rush candles. Everybody had to contribute something – from the youngest to the eldest. Others used to collect the cotton grass on the surrounding bogs – these were used for making pillows and cushions. Life was hard.

John and Margaret Evans lived at Lluest-newydd for a period, and because the sheepwalk was only stocked in summer for the lowland farm of Ty Canol, Llanbrynmair, John's wages were about £11 for the summer months, and he would go down to work in the coal mines of South Wales for the winter – what some people called 'half-shepherds'. Margaret would then look after the family and their own stock. This great responsibility which fell on her shoulders called for great strength of character and trust, and couldn't have been the most satisfactory of arrangements. Times were difficult and this was the only way to make ends meet at the time. The outcome of this was that they left Lluest-newydd, and went to live in the South Wales valleys for about a year or so. Margaret Evans had always lived in isolated hill places, and found it difficult to cope with the busybody comings and goings, with very little privacy, and declared one day that she wanted to go back to her native hills.

They then moved back to Dôl-wen, a big hill farm near Devil's Bridge, and so John became a full-time shepherd for Mr David Edwards, whose lowland farm was called Dôlfor, in the Trawscoed area. It was at Dôl-wen that Charles Evans – the subject of this chapter – was born in 1897. Charles grew up thoroughly taught in the ways of shepherding, and he said that he had inherited from his mother's side a keen sense of observation.

In the autumn of 1911 Mr Edwards Dôlfor had been offered fourteen shillings for his draft ewes, and he had refused to sell. John Evans was then given the task of driving these sheep from Dôl-wen to Machynlleth, while Mr Edwards went by train to meet them. The sheep were sold there for fifteen shillings. After deducting the train fare, and luck money, he had gained only sixpence a head.

Margaret Evans was a fastidiously clean person about the house, and her grand-daughter, Olive Jones, from Commins Coch, Aberystwyth, told me that she had seen her grand-mother do something that was a mystery to her. Margaret would pour the water from the cooked potatoes, put a clean white cloth on top of them, and then the lid back on top. Mrs Katie Lewis, nearing her nineties, who lived a mile from me, said that she had seen some of the 'old people' do this, and the purpose was to soak up the steam, and therefore dry the potatoes.

The conditions of their work at Dôl-wen were that they would look after the flock there, and in return they would have a wage, which was 10/– (50p) a week, and they were able to use the in-by land for themselves. This allowed them to graze and gather hay for their cattle, young stock, and horses. They also kept hens and a pig or two, making them fairly self-sufficient. As an added bonus they were also allowed to keep 25 to 30 sheep of their own. John Evans was also a very keen gardener, which kept them well supplied with vegetables. So all in all it was an amiable agreement that suited both parties very well.

In May 1912, however, they decided to move back to their roots, and moved to Lluest-y-rhos on the hills between Ponterwyd and Machynlleth, the next farm to Hafod Wnog where Margaret was born. When they moved they had three cows with calves, two yearling cattle and two two-year-olds; also two ponies – one strong one for work and the other for riding. One cow had calved that morning, and Charles and his sister Lizzie, who worked at the White Horse, Aberystwyth, stayed behind to look after her.

John came back for the calf in the trap in a week's time, and the cow followed behind. They had failed to catch the cat, and John Evans went back to Dôl-wen in a year's time, and took her then, from William Hopkins, the shepherd who was there at the time.

William Hopkins was a noted shepherd, very fond of singing, and a good hand with dogs. Charles told me that his dogs were of the best type, but always on the thin side, and maybe little wonder, for he also had 12 children to feed. In the late twenties William had one of the first Scotch dogs in the area. He later moved to Llaneithyr, and from there to Melindwr, near Glandyfi.

John Evans also had 25 sheep to move, and it was Charles' job then to settle these sheep in their new environment. They were collected twice a day for about a fortnight, and driven to a certain patch of land to get them used to being there, and to regard that particular spot as their own.

Charles must have been a bit of a business man even then, because he told his father 'I think you owe me something for settling those sheep', and it was agreed that he should have one of the sheep. Meanwhile he had been helping a nearby shepherd, Ned Griffiths, Lluest-y-grafie, who looked after the sheep of Sir Edward Pryse, Gogerddan, and he had given Charles a ewe lamb. That was the beginning. In Cwm-cemrhiw many years later he was shearing 1500 sheep, a self-made man in all respects.

Lluest-y-grafie was owned in the early 1920s by Major J.J. Evans, Lovesgrove. There was a shepherd called John Roberts living there till 1928. Did he move to the Pont-rhyd-fendigaid area? I have failed to trace him so far. His wife was called Jane, and they were at Lluest-y-grafie in 1918. I believe they had a son called Will. Major Evans had a new house built there and stones from nearby Lluest-gotta were used in its building. A man called Morris Nicholas was sent up there to prepare a garden in readiness for a new shepherd called Mr Law, who lived at Salem, Penrhyncoch. However, he did not come to work there, and sheep started going into the house, and making a mess, and the end of the story was that nobody lived there.

John Evans, in moving to Lluest-y-rhos, and working for the Hughes family of Mathafarn in Llanwrin, was able to keep up to sixty of his own sheep, which was an added bonus, and was earning a pound a week. When the First World War came, sheep prices shot up, and this helped John and Margaret by increasing their prosperity.

Charles went to live and work at Hyddgen in 1916, with his sister Sarah (Sal) to keep house for him. They stayed there till 1919. I believe that they were the last people to live at Hyddgen. I believe Charles came back to Lluest-y-rhos, and that, about 1920, John Evans and Margaret moved to a lower-lying farm called Llwyn-gwinau in Cwm Einion.

The sheep from Lluest-y-rhos used to be walked to Mathafarn to be shorn for many years. All the sheep were taken off the hill in the winter, but the wethers remained there throughout. When the family and workers from Mathafarn went up to help with the sheep, and the weather was hot, they had seen Charles going to have a drink of water from the stream, and several of them did likewise, but his system was used to the peaty water, and theirs not, and many of them felt quite sick afterwards.

Many of these hill farms came up for sale in 1922, and were bought by Major James John Evans of Lovesgrove (fondly known as 'Jimmy Jack'), and Charles, being an experienced shepherd in the area, naturally went to work for him. In 1927 Charles

■ This interesting photograph is reputed to be have been taken at Lluest-y-rhos.

changed his employer and went to work for General Pugh, Glan-dyfi, as a shepherd at Cefn-coch, and that year he raised 729 lambs there. I always remember that figure because I believe that I read somewhere that this is the number of steps that go up the Eiffel Tower!

When working with General Pugh, one of the jobs that went on there if the weather was rough was the oiling of harnesses, and the oil that was always used was castor oil. It used to be a custom years ago to buy a pair of boots a year in advance, and hang them under a loft, half-filled with castor oil to help make them waterproof and supple. Charles always used to call shoes 'half-boots'.

On the 7th of May 1924, Charles was riding by Llechweddmor house, and the children of David Griffiths came out, and told him that their father had just passed away, and asked if he would go down to Talybont (10 miles away) to inform the doctor there.

David Griffiths was a big man – in fact they used to call him *yr hen gawr* (the old giant) – but he was very averse to cold weather, and disliked draughts intensely. Llechweddmor house is situated in a very exposed spot with the purpose of seeing a lot of the boundary so that neighbours could not course their sheep, and an added bonus to this was you would not have drifts of snow about the house. Hen-hafod was built on the same principles. All the doors in Llechweddmor were covered in drapes, and there were house rules that you had to close the outer door before opening the inner one. The doctor had been up to Llechweddmor to see David Griffiths, and on seeing the amount

■ Charles Evans' parents, John and Margaret Evans at Ty'n Cwm, Cwm-einion, Eglwys fach.

of clothes on the bed, had advised him that it was unhealthy to have so many blankets on. Charles went, as requested, down to Talybont, knocked at the doctor's door, and told him 'I've come to tell you that Dafydd Griffiths, Llechweddmor has passed away' and got the unexpected retort, 'Oh, what did he do, suffocate?' Dafydd Griffiths was 66 years old. Two of his children, Edward and Blodwen, stayed on at Llechweddmor for about two years, and then moved to shepherd for a Mr Lee of Glan-frêd in Llandre. Dafydd's other children Tom, Ruth and Susannah were shepherding and living in Hyddgen till about 1915.

In 1928 Charles and his brother Humphrey moved to Llwyngwinau, Cwm-einion, which was owned by the Forestry Commission by that time, and their parents moved even lower down the valley to Ty'n-cwm. Charles did well for himself by shepherding at various places, having his own stock and working for the Commission.

In 1942 Charles and Humphrey moved to Cwm-cemrhiw, a farm at the top end of the Glas-pwll valley, near Machynlleth. The previous owner kept about 150 sheep there. Things prospered from there on, and Charles sent sheep up to Lluest-y-rhos, and to the Old Park, by Plas-y-mynydd. In 1953 however, he and Humphrey fell out in a big way, and Humphrey went his own way, moving to Maes-pandy, near Forge. Charles advertised for a housekeeper, and a lady called Maud Tanner from Berriew came there, and life was a lot easier for him afterwards.

While working at Ty-llwyd, Cwm-ystwyth, I had started compiling a book of sheep ear-marks, and had heard of this Charles Evans who was an expert on ear-marks, and an opportunity came later for me to go and work there, and with hind-sight, I regard this period as an honour, but I would dearly like to have him back for an hour and a half, to ask the dozens of questions that I should have asked him at that time.

■ Charles Evans and myself at Cwm-cemrhiw in 1970. Thanks to the Western Mail and Echo for permission to reproduce.

On my first morning at Cwm-cemrhiw, Charles looked at my boots, and said that they could do with oiling, and I, eager to be getting on with something, said that I would oil them that evening, but he insisted that I put some oil on them before doing anything. That was lesson number one.

There were special boots called *Esgid y Bugail* (Shepherd's Boot) around at that time. They had hob-nails, and their toes were very turned up, which was conducive to walking up hills. Flatter boots, because they bend when going uphill, tend to crack at the base of the laces. It was these shepherds' boots that Charles always wore. They were totally waterproof, warm and sturdy. When they were new they had to be 'broken in', and worn for a few hours at a time, till they became more supple. I have worn this type of boot for many years, but their price kept going up to a point that I had to change to a cheaper type of boot.

One of the drawbacks of these shepherds' boots was seen when you were walking in snow. This snow would accumulate in a big 'clog', and till it fell off, you were going about like an astronaut! Charles Evans had never worn wellingtons.

He sent sheep up to the Old Park, which had been at one time under the jurisdiction of the Pryse family of Gogerddan. By today Gogerddan is the home of the Institute of Grassland and Environmental Research (IGER). The gathering on the Old Park took place on a Wednesday, in conjunction with other farmers from the Talybont area who also sent sheep up there. On my first three gatherings there was mist every time, where all you could do was make as much noise as you could, and follow the sheep. On each of these occasions the weather was clear on the Tuesday and Thursday. There seemed no chance to get to know the hill. I felt then that the place had been witched!

Charles, a man then aged about 72, was very set in his ways, and always when we went up to the Old Park we would take food, and a kettle to boil water for making tea. Several times I and others had broached the idea of flasks, but all mention of them fell on deaf ears.

The fire was made inside one of the sheds at Plas-y-mynydd, which had been at one time the summer shooting and fishing lodge for Gogerddan, and as I mentioned, the weather being wet, it was difficult to find kindling, and wet wood causes a lot of smoke. By the time the kettle had boiled, my insides were so full of smoke that I felt there wasn't a lot of room for food. But that was the way things had been, so there was no change to be.

It was at Cwm-cemrhiw that I last slept in a feather bed. You jumped into the middle of the bed, and it would close in around you, to give you a wonderful feeling of snugness. There was an outside toilet there, but I was told that it was to be used only by Maud, so every morning it was a 'country shit', in a field of my choice, depending on where the wind was.

Another thing that I saw at Cwm-cemrhiw was shaving with a cut-throat razor. Charles never shaved with anything else, and what a performance it was. Special shaving soap, a brush to lather, a mug of hot water and pre-cut strips of paper, as well as a mirror. I forget on what other nights he shaved, but he always shaved on a Tuesday night in preparation for going to Machynlleth for the shopping and market on Wednesday.

It was quite a long, drawn-out process. The brush was put into the hot water, then rubbed in the soap, this was then rubbed into the face to produce a thick rich lather. The razor was dipped into the hot water, and then the shaving began. The scraping sound I can still hear, as it cut through the bristles, and after doing a patch, the foam and bristles were wiped onto the strips of paper, and so the procedure went on till he finished, with a very satisfactory end result. Then everything was cleaned and put by for next time. The razor would be re-sharpened on a leather strop (belt), and it was Charles Evans who told me that you could use the dried flat fungi that grows on trees for the same purpose. This was probably the 'birch polypore', or 'razor strop' as it was called.

He might sit down for about an hour, and then came curfew time at exactly half past nine. He would look at his watch, and that meant it was time to go to bed.

They were idyllic, carefree times in that era compared to the idiotic bureaucracy that is around today, when farmers are dictated to by ill-informed people who produce nothing themselves – *and* get well-paid for it to boot, come rain or shine.

One evening after supper Charles gave me the ear-marks of every place from Aberhosan and the Machynlleth area down to Talybont, one place after the other, totally from memory, and to this day I haven't seen one of them to be incorrect. This was quite a feat, but in all probability only taxed a fraction of his vast knowledge on ear-marks.

Charles was not a driver, but he had a tractor and a small lorry, and these were driven by those he employed. In the autumn he followed most markets from Llanybyther to Dôlgellau, and he was pretty shrewd at selling. He had, over the years, been tacking (over-wintering) sheep and lambs over most of South Cardiganshire, and he knew every back road and short-cut from one place to the other, so my geography was brought very much up to date in his company.

He kept two riding ponies there for whenever he or I or both went to the hill. There is no better way to shepherd sheep. When I used to go onto the hill in the morning, I could be back around midday, or it might be three or four o'clock before I made an appearance, and it was almost uncanny how Maud would have food waiting for me, with no sign of it having been re-heated, and delicious it was too, and I can testify that every single morsel of food that she produced was cooked to perfection. Maud looked after Charles Evans well, making sure that he was warm, that he did not stay long in wet clothes, and he was certainly well-fed. There was always a roaring fire there, and Charles said of her, 'Once Maud gets a fire going, she'd burn anything on it, even if they were logs from the river!'.

There was a television there, and it was owned by Maud, and she was in control of it. It was switched on about six o'clock, and Charles and I would watch some topical news programmes in Welsh (Maud did not speak Welsh). If she had been outside, a little longer than usual, I might have started to watch a following programme, but then she would march in, say to whoever might be talking on the set at the time 'Fiddlesticks to you!' and switch it off. End of story. The only exception where she would allow a programme to go on after the Welsh one was on a Thursday, when *Top of the Pops* was on, and that was allowed to run its course. Why? It will always remain a mystery to me. Maud died on the 28th of November, 1974.

Charles had a mannerism of drawing in a breath through the side of his mouth, producing a 'll' sound before he said anything, and yet when he spoke he was unable to pronounce the '*ll*' sound in a word. He would always say 'Machyntheth', and '*Twth*' for *twll* (hole). To those from across the border who have difficulty with this sound, I advocate putting your tongue on the roof of your mouth, and hissing like a gander.

Another good friend of mine who helped me a lot with the ear-mark book, and had the same impediment to his speech was John Lloyd, Y Gorn, Llanidloes, yet he like

Charles had a wonderful retentive memory. In mentioning John Lloyd, I have introduced to you the three 'kings' of ear-marks around Pumlumon – John Lloyd, John Davies, Y Bont, and Charles Evans. If one of them had a stray ewe that they could not sort out, they would write each other a letter, depicting the type of ewe and ear-mark, and between them they didn't miss much. The welcome at the Gorn was always warm and genial. John Lloyd died in 1971.

Charles was a typical dog and stick man, his whole life had revolved around sheep, and very little else came to interfere in his life. When he had lived at places like Lluest-y-rhos, it was inevitable that he would go down-country to find sticks, and he was of a nature to emphasise many points, or solve matters with the use of a stick. One story from his youth underlined this. He had gone to a fair at Tre'r ddôl where a number of youths had ganged up against him. He offered no resistance, but ran away into a nearby field, and they followed him. Unbeknown to them, he had left his stick and his coat inside the gate. He was the only one who came out of the field unscathed.

Charles' brother John who lived near Pennal, Machynlleth, featured in an article in 'Country Quest' (October 1985) about sticks, and he, like Charles, was very well versed in the art of shepherding. He was a typical example of 'the small dark people' that have been around for such a long time. Light boned, but as tough as they come. He started working first of all for a William Jones, Cwm Rhaeadr, Glaspwll, who was born at Brwyno, above Glan-dyfi, and then spent a while at Ty'n Llechwedd Bach in Llandre working for Henry Hughes, who would have been his mother's cousin. He then probably went back to Lluest-y-rhos to work for Major Evans and was earning £32 a year.

■ Mr & Mrs John Lloyd, Y Gorn, Llanidloes.

He then went to work in a farm called Y Grofft whose northern boundary would have been the river Dyfi. Here the boss called them at ten to five in the morning and they had to be about their business by five. His next move was to Perfeddnant in the Tywyn area, and he started on £1 per week. He was there for 19 years, and in 1941 took on the farm of Dysyrnant, in a valley called Cwm Maethlon, that has the English name 'Happy Valley' (which bears no meaning with the Welsh name). He paid £1–12–6 for the sheep that were on the farm. He proudly said that he had paid for the place in about seven years, which was an achievement for someone who'd had no education at all. Further to this farm he bought Cefn-cynhafal, Tyddyn Gwilym, and Pant-yr-onn, proving if there is a need to do so, that there was nothing wrong with his business acumen.

John was married in 1924 to Sarah Catherine Pugh, from Llanfihangel-y-pennant. They had eight children, but unfortunately Sarah died in 1940. From there on there followed a catalogue of tragedies to plague John that would have been enough to thwart many a saint. Shortly after his wife, a little boy, Eifion Wyn, died aged two months, and worse things were to follow.

In 1944 the soldiers from Tonfannau Camp had been practising with mortars, not far from Dysyrnant, and on a Sunday morning, the 7th of May 1944 three of John's children – Charles Oliver, Idris Meirion and Christmas Wyn – had gone for a walk, and came across one of these mortars, and the three were instantly killed. This must have caused grief beyond description, and I remember John Evans, even in his eighties, with tears in his eyes when he recounted this horrific loss. Unfortunately this was not the last tragedy fate had to throw at him – his son and namesake John Henry, was killed in the War in April 1945. There are no words I can put on paper to describe the trials and tribulations that hit this one man.

On a positive note, he has eight grand-children, and probably a dozen or more great-grand-children, whom I hope will never forget John Evans' achievements, and the anguish that befell him in his life. John died in 1990 aged 88.

Returning to Charles, I mentioned that his forte in life was sheep ear-marks. When he moved to Lluest-y-rhos in 1912 the first stray sheep he saw was the pet lamb of Dafydd Jones, Dôl-carne, Ponterwyd, which is where my parents live now. Although he had only seen it once, he still remembered the mark when I was with him in the early 1970s, and thanks to him that is the mark I still have on my sheep. Many years later I came across a book of ear-marks, written in 1888 by Lewis Jones from Llan-y-mawddwy, and found in it that the next place up from my parents house – Craignant-bach – had the same ear-mark, but in a different ear. Dafydd Jones had lived there before he moved to Dôl-carne, so he had kept the same ear-mark but switched ears to differentiate. Dafydd Jones' claim to fame was that when he was in Dôl-carne, he was plagued by crows eating his potatoes. The drastic solution he thought of was to mix bran with slivers of glass, and he killed almost every crow in the area.

Since that time in 1912 Charles' keen sense of observation had been working to memorize possibly hundreds of these marks, and over the years he had been instrumental in finding out to whom countless numbers of stray sheep belonged, and getting them back to their rightful owners. There was a shepherd on the Hiraethog mountains called 'Ifan Bwlch Du' who was credited with being able to remember over 1,500 different ear-marks.

It was mostly by word of mouth that this information on stray sheep was relayed. One special place at which many hill people met was Wards Café on Great Darkgate Street, Aberystwyth, on a market Monday. David Thomas from Eisteddfa, Charles, and others would meet there, and many strays were sorted out there over a cup of tea. Towards the end of the 1700s, it was stated that in the Church of Llanddewi Abergwesyn, the local shepherds came there to worship, told each other about stray sheep, and after the service they would go to fetch them – a matter that did not please the clergy at the time (*Cymru* 66).

Prior to, and during Charles Evans' time, stray sheep from a vast area of Pumlumon were brought to the Star Inn in Dylife. Picking out strays could be thirsty work! This gathering of strays, in our area, was called a *shett* or *shett Dylife* which is a corruption of the English word 'escheat', which refers to the return of property to its rightful owner. This event took place four times a year, with the first meeting being held on the third Friday in June, the second on the third Tuesday in July, the third on the second Friday in October and the fourth on the second Friday in November. Charles Evans, John Lloyd y Gorn, John Davies y Bont, Lewis Rees, and John Pugh, Cwm-mawr, Dylife were some of the leading lights there in their period. One of the most noted for his knowledge of ear-marks (prior to his death in 1920) was William Morgan, Hengwm-annedd. He would spend quite a bit of his time in the Star Inn if the weather was cold, and if a dispute arose in the sheep pens, it would be taken in so that William could put his judgement on the matter, and I was told that he rarely failed to find a solution.

Considering the venue, and taking into consideration the fact that many of these shepherds were not used to alcohol, many of them over-indulged – some started for home with their own, and neighbours' sheep, and lost them every one; others fell asleep en-route, and were surprised next morning to see the dogs still in charge of the sheep, but happy in the knowledge that they would escape the ridicule that they would suffer if they had lost their sheep.

At one time, John Davies (y Bont) was on his way home from Dylife with some companions and a bunch of sheep. They were all fairly well oiled and John, at one stage, fell on his back and one of his companions said jokingly, thinking of his height, 'John, if you had fallen forwards, you would have reached home!'

This long-standing tradition at Dylife came to an end probably in the late 1940s, more than likely due to the vast amount of fencing that took place after the War. A similar *shett* used to take place at Hafod-y-rhyd in Pont-rhyd-fendigaid on the first Saturday in April.

Charles Evans enjoyed a sense of humour, and we had many a laugh about the characters that we both knew and their escapades, but he also had a stern side to his personality, and had to be handled with kid gloves at times.

While there one day on a visit, and seeing that he was getting older and his health not getting any better, I ventured to say that it might be better for him if he moved to a small-holding – something to keep his interest, without a lot of responsibility – and his immediate reply was, 'It's got to be hundreds of sheep or nothing!' And nothing it was. He bought a house in Machynlleth. After several bouts of deteriorating health and a spell at Bryn-tegwel nursing home in Aberdyfi, Charles died on the 4th of July 1978, aged 80. He undoubtedly took with him to his grave a wealth of shepherding history that has been lost forever.

David Richards, Hyddgen

Whilst visiting Miss Maggie Morgan (1911–2000, daughter of Tommy Morgan, Lluest-newydd), at her home in Maes-dulais, Uwch-y-garreg, she showed me a photograph of a cairn of white stones that was near a place called Lluest Forgan, not far from Hyddgen. She said that they had been placed there by local shepherds in memory of a man called David Richards, who was a shepherd at Hyddgen, and had collapsed at this spot on the 28th of March 1901, aged 46, and subsequently died.

I was curious as to where this cairn was, so off we went in my car, and she showed me where the spot was. There was not a trace of it to be seen. It had either been disturbed by the work of the Forestry Commission, or had been carted away by someone making a rockery. I felt it was sacrilegious to the memory of David Richards that the cairn was no longer there, and also a slight on the efforts of the shepherds concerned. I made a promise to Maggie Morgan there and then that I would do something about it.

Very soon after that, I contacted the Forestry Commission, and they readily agreed to my request for a big white stone that no-one could remove in a hurry. Meanwhile, a Welsh television programme called *Hel Straeon* (Collecting Tales), was interested in the story, and it was to be filmed the following spring (1996) when the weather got better. As the plans were being thought out, I was made aware that a grandson of David Richards lived in Aberhosan, and that he was the obvious choice to unveil the

■ The cairn of white stones to commemorate David Richards, Hyddgen. It has now been replaced by a big white stone.

commemorative stone. Unfortunately, I found out that the grandson, Mr Eilfed Richards, was not a well man, and so with the co-operation of Aled Thomas, the Forester, the plans were speeded up, and the stone, which had come from the Llechwedd Quarry in Ffestiniog, was unveiled on the 19th of December 1995 by Eilfed Richards, assisted by Miss Maggie Morgan. There were several of David Richards' descendants there as well as other interested parties, and thankfully all this was filmed for *Hel Straeon*, to act as a permanent record. Eilfed passed away on March 25, 1996, aged 63.

A very good friend of the area around Pumlumon, Simon Harries from Romsey in Hampshire, has kindly put a brass plaque on the stone.

The team filming the event were so taken by 86-year-old Maggie Morgan, that they came back to make another programme on her, which was a double bonus for posterity. She took Keith Davies, who interviewed her, back to Lluest-newydd where she spent her childhood.

Many false facts were put in local papers at the time of this filming about David Richards, so I include a summary of the inquest:

INQUEST ON DAVID RICHARDS, HYDDGEN
WELSH GAZETTE 4th of April 1901

Mr John Rowlands held an inquest at Hyddgen on Monday into the death of a shepherd called Richards of Hyddgen. The first witness was Richard Evans, Hengwm [Gyfeiliog], who said deceased was a shepherd and farmer living at Hyddgen. The last time witness saw deceased was on Wednesday when he accompanied him home from Machynlleth. It was a cold night, snowing and freezing hard. They were on the best of terms and very friendly. Witness promised to bring flour belonging to deceased to him on Thursday morning. When parting on the road, it did not strike him that it was impossible for deceased to reach home that night. The distance from the place where they parted to deceased's home was three miles including a long strip along Rhiwfeinog mountain.

It was about 9.30 a.m. Dr A.O. Davies said that he was called to see deceased on Thursday morning. He was lying on the bed. He had his eyes open, and his body was quite stiff. He saw no marks of violence. His opinion was deceased died of exposure. David Richards (13), son of the deceased stated that he found his father's wallet on the ground on Thursday morning. He told his mother, and they afterwards found his father a little lower down. Jane Richards, wife of deceased said the farm was situated about eight miles from Machynlleth. Deceased had gone to Machynlleth for flour and other things for the house, and she expected him to return the same night. She found him on the mountain near Lluest-forgan. He was lying on the road, face downwards resting on his hands. Deceased was taken home on a sledge drawn by a horse. He did not say anything. She gave him some warm tea and whiskey, and sent for Dr Davies. He had had no serious illness. He had resided at Hyddgen for ten years and had eight children.

A verdict was returned that deceased had died from exposure.

Nant-y-moch

It is wise sometimes to go with the flow, and if we follow the valley downstream from Hyddgen we would come to Nant-y-moch or at least today, to where it once stood. More on that later...

Old John James from Nant-y-moch would not acknowledge the 'y' in the middle, and he always called it 'Nant-moch'. '*Moch*' means 'swift running water' in old Welsh, and there are many examples of 'Mochdre' in Wales. In Aberhosan, there is a farm called Esgair-foch-nant, and there is the famous falls in Llanrhaeadr-ym-mochnant near Oswestry. One strange thing is that there are three streams called Nant-y-moch in the Ponterwyd area – the one mentioned above, one in Ystumtuen, and one on the land of Dinas farm.

There is an old reference in 1667 to a Lluest-yn-aber-nant-y-moch (the place at the mouth of the Nant-y-moch brook) which was then associated with the farm of Cefn Coed (now known as Cyncoed) in the Capel Bangor area. In later times a Rowland Rowlands, Cyncoed was still in ownership of Nant-y-moch.

This period was the era of a system known in Wales as the *Hafod a Hendre* – a period of transhumance – whereby the people and animals moved according to the seasons.

■ Nant-y-moch.

They moved up to the Hafod during the summer, and then down to the Hendre for the winter. This system I believe is still practiced in places like Switzerland, where the lush growth of the summer is taken advantage of. There are many place-names containing 'Hafod' in the uplands of Wales. Lluest is a fairly common name in mid Wales, mostly associated with upland sheepwalks.

Also around this time, sheep were milked on the hills, and there remain many examples of milking folds. Several place-names also remain to remind us of this era, such as Cwm-nant-ffald (valley of the fold by the brook) on Aber-glan-hirin land. The sheep would be gathered in very early in the morning before the lambs had a chance to suckle, or they would be put in late at night, and the lambs taken out so that their udders would fill up by morning.

A Mary Jones from Sychnant, Ystumtuen, who was born Mary Isaac, in 1848, at Geufaes, Ponterwyd used to milk sheep when she lived at Bryn-brâs in Ponterwyd. They were milked in a fold on the common land across the river Rheidol from the farm of Bryn-chwith. This milk would then be used to make cheese. The Rees family of Dôl-fawr in Pont-rhyd-fendigaid would get up at three o'clock in the morning to milk their sheep, and after their mid-day meal, the whole family would go to bed for a few hours. The word was spread locally that no one was to call there during this period of siesta. This would have been around 1750.

■ An old fold, still reasonably intact, which could have been used for milking sheep on Nant-llyn, Ponterwyd. Photo by Ken Jones.

■ L to R: John James, John James Thomas and Jim James in the doorway of Nant-y-moch.

I have heard very little reference to cheese making in the areas that I am interested in, but it must have been common practice at one time. In Cwmerfin there is a small holding called Llety-caws (Cheese-house). Rennet was added to the milk in the preparatory stages, and I was interested to hear Mr Edward Morgan, Bow Street, calling it in Welsh *bol llo* (calf's belly), as it comes from a calf's stomach.

There had been four generations of the James family living at Nant-y-moch. James James (1813–1879) had moved there from Aber-paith-nant, a farm lower down the valley, where it is believed that the James family had been since the 1600s. He married Jane Jones of Rheidol House in Devil's Bridge and they had nine children – one of whom was William James (1856–1917) who lived at Nant-y-moch. William James' children – John, Jim and their siblings – were also born at Nant-y-moch and John James Thomas (1902–1979), a nephew to John and Jim and the fourth generation of James' to live at Nant-y-moch, came there to help his ageing uncles in about 1946.

Since the nearest place of worship was at Ponterwyd – four miles away for this remote hamlet – it was decided in the early 1860s to build a chapel at Nant-y-moch, with James James being one of the instigators. The chapel was eventually built in 1865 and called Capel Blaen-Rheidol, and it was decided to build a wall around the building to form a cemetery.

When I think about this building, the first thing that comes to mind is the labour of love that must have been put into its being. Admittedly there were plenty of stones in the area, but they had to be carried from long distances, by horse cart or rough sleigh. Many of them then had to be dressed on the spot, or the corner stones could have been carried from the Hafan Quarry, not so far away. There was no wood in the immediate vicinity, nor slates for the roofing, and if it's taken into consideration that there were only about forty adults resident in the catchment area, apart from the workers at Camdwr Mawr lead mine, it seems everybody had to put their full effort into the project. The chapel contained seventeen pews, and was lit by two lamps. In an old insurance document I saw a few years ago, it said that there was no form of heating.

This meeting place then became the focal point for this isolated community, and as well as the obvious Sunday sermons, the chapel was used for social evenings and Eisteddfodau (competitive meetings). Many preachers from far and wide came there over the years, and as was cited in the case of Maggie Morgan, many children in these outlying farms benefited from the education they received from Sunday school at the chapel. Ironically or otherwise, James James was the first to be buried at Nant-y-moch chapel.

William James (his son), as already mentioned, was born at Nant-y-moch, and the house in which he was born was probably built in 1777. This dwelling was turned into a stable around 1880, when the house that is now remembered as Nant-y-moch was built. William was a man who had a lot to say about horses, and he was an expert at peat cutting. He married a Mary Powell from Llywernog and they had seven children – Elizabeth, Hannah, Ann, John, James (Jim), William and Daniel. Elizabeth married a W.R. Jones from the Rhondda Valley, and when she died, her body was brought back to be buried at Nant-y-moch. Hannah married a close relative, John Thomas, Camdwr Mawr, and they had one son called John James Thomas. Ann remained single, and stayed at home to look after her parents, and later, her two single brothers. She died on the 2nd of May 1946, aged 59. William married, but had no children. Daniel also married, had three children, but they left no issue.

■ Miss Maggie Morgan (1911–2000), Maes-dulais, Uwch-y-garreg.

As the farm could not support them all, William, went to seek an independent living, and it can be said that he found a solution that got him the best of both worlds. As mentioned, the farm had connections with the Capel Bangor area at an early date, and into recent times still remained attached to the same region. For a long time it was held by John Pugh Lewis, Llwyn-iorwerth-uchaf, and William was offered a job there, therefore getting a living, and yet when there was work with the sheep at Nant-y-moch, he would have a perfect chance to see his family there. William Thomas, Llwyn-iorwerth-isaf was also in shares with Nant-y-moch.

When he finished at Llwyn-iorwerth, William was employed by the 'War Ag.', or the War Agricultural Committee to look after nearby Cefn-llidiart farm. His staff were Land Girls and Italian prisoners of war. William was a fine-natured person and a dedicated and conscientious worker, but his staff were not as obliged in their thoughts, and mocked William because he was so particular, with the end result that on Boxing Day 1943, he took his own life – the untimely end of a real gentleman. He was 61 years old.

John and Jim James remained at Nant-y-moch. Jim, unfortunately, had an injury to his knee when he was about 15 years old, and was taken to a hospital in Liverpool where, sadly, his leg was amputated, so he spent the remainder of his years on crutches, and after the death of their sister Ann (1946), he was predominantly in charge of the household chores in the home.

He was a very genial person, had a ready welcoming smile for everybody who came to visit, was very well read, had an excellent handwriting, was an accomplished poet and wrote articles to local papers from time to time. In the late fifties my father had a bee in his bonnet that he wanted some hen's eggs from Nant-y-moch to put under a broody hen we had, and off we set on his motorbike on a Saturday afternoon. We were invited in for tea, and Jim, clasping the loaf to his chest, was slicing the bread. As always one of the household cats was perched on his shoulder, and every now and then this old cat gave a sneeze! We enjoyed our tea, and both my father and I lived to tell the tale!

Another time, some of the local farmers had been after foxes near Hengwm and called by Nant-y-moch on the way home, just as it was getting dark. John had been to Aberystwyth that day and brought back with him some kippers for supper, and these friends called as they were eating. The Nant-y-moch cats must have thought that Christmas had come early since there was such a feast and they were anxious to get their share. John and Jim, in poor light, were trying to sort out fish from bone and at the same time, were trying to keep the cats off the table – a total pantomime! The consensus was that the visitors got little sense out of the James brothers that evening.

One thing that happened at a shearing in Nant-y-moch is still remembered by a few remaining souls, although they are getting fewer by now. The tables had been set for tea, laden with crockery and food, and suddenly two of the dogs decided to have a fight, upsetting the tables and breaking most of the crockery. Jim, in an attempt to stop them, was thrown flat on his back. It was all hell let loose there.

In mentioning the shearing, another story comes to mind. When the two Llwyn-iorwerth farms were shearing, the food and men were brought up by horse-drawn vehicles, but this changed in 1925 when a lorry driven by Tommy Roderick Davies (1906–1981) from Goginan went to Nant-y-moch for the first time. Having gone through quite a bit of water on the way up, which had affected its brakes, the lorry

186

gained speed all the way down the rather steep hill that led to the house, and stopped literally feet from the chapel wall.

John James – the older brother – was a more abrupt character and very often asked people visiting there where they came from before asking how they were. No matter where they came from, John knew something interesting about their home area, and if they were fairly local, he would know about their family. He had read a lot and, more importantly, had remembered what he had read. Papers or monthlies that they bought, often featured articles on certain areas and he had stored this information since long ago.

About one hundred years ago, John, with his cousin Abraham James (1849–1916) from Llwyn, Cwmerfin, (who bought and sold livestock), drove sheep from Nant-y-moch to Anglesey. They started on a Monday morning, staying the first night at Braich-goch farm in Corris, and arriving on Anglesey on Friday afternoon – the sheep then being sold to various farmers there. What a film that journey would have made if today's technology was around at that time.

John was not renowned as a dog man, and somebody who knew him well said that John could take sheep anywhere – as long as he had a fence on one side! The James family produced very few good dog handlers. He was a good man with a scythe, and when Llwyn-iorwerth held Nant-y-moch, John also had to cut a stack of peat for them, which they then carted down country. It was very much against the grain to see his labours disappearing down the road, and there was nobody happier than John when that era came to an end.

John, like many of the hill people, would go down to the shop in Ponterwyd about once a month with a horse and cart to get the bulky items such as flour and Indian corn meal for the pigs and dogs, plus items for neighbours – a favour that would be returned when they went down.

When he reached the shop his horse would be put in the stable and fed, and John was taken into the house for tea while the goods were put into the cart. On one occasion, there was damson jam for tea, and every stone that John had in his sandwich, he spat out into the nearby fire. The two girls working in the shop had a good laugh about this, and hit upon a plan for the next time John came down. On John's next visit, they had moved the table as far as they could from the fire, and put as many damson stones as possible in the jam dish. They were well rewarded by John's antics during his meal there.

During John's time he saw Nant-y-moch being held by several different owners other than the two farmers from Llwyn-iorwerth already mentioned. Two of these were Major J.J. Evans, and his brother Griffith Pugh Evans, of Lovesgrove. In the 1940s, Mr Bill Davies, Pentre Farm, Capel Bangor, took over the place and in 1947, Humphrey, Major J.J. Evans' son, took on Nant-y-moch for a number of years. Then came Brigadier General Lewis Pugh Evans, again of Lovesgrove. Much could be written about each place of ownership but I will restrict myself to the Lovesgrove period, which was the most colourful era.

Brigadier General Lewis Pugh Evans (1881–1961) had spent most of his life as a military man, and was described as the most decorated soldier in Wales – having received, amongst other awards for gallantry, the Victoria Cross. I remember him coming to ask my father if he would come to the shearing at Nant-y-moch, and it used

■ Brigadier-General Lewis Pugh Evans, Lovesgrove (sitting) counting the shorn sheep at Nant-y-moch in 1953.

to tickle us children no end to see this man in knee breeches and white stockings. Little did we know what a brave man he was.

A very short man, he was also famous for something else – car driving. When you saw him coming, all you would see was a steering wheel, a cap visible above it, and a face with a moustache within the wheel. He had gone up one morning from the mansion – where he lived with his two sisters, Miss Bridget and Miss Gwyneth – to the Lovesgrove farm, where he and his staff had a discussion, and it turned out that something was wanted from the Farmers Co-op in Aberystwyth. 'I'll get it,' he said and jumped into his car, and in leaving the farmyard, he caught the rear bumper on a roll of netting. Fred Lewis, his farm bailiff, set off after him but it was by the Farmers Co-op that he caught up with him, and I can imagine 'Brig' (as he was familiarly known) saying, after Fred broke the news to him, 'How stupid of me.'

Often, when he turned the car around in the yard in Nant-y-moch, he would hit the wall, and in re-negotiating the manoeuver would hit the same wall again, and you can guess what he said – 'How stupid of me.' When somebody had done something for him, his remark always was, 'Many thanks.' When at the shearing or dipping at Nant-y-moch and a few whole-eared lambs came in with the flock, especially if some were ewe lambs, the old Brigadier would say, 'Aren't we lucky.' These three sayings of his are still used in the Ponterwyd area (even though the conversation is more often than not in Welsh) and are always attributed to him, the great character that he was.

One more car story should be told, although it may not have been so funny at the time. Tom Morgan, Nant-cae-rhedyn, John Owen (the shepherd), and Dewi Roberts, Lle'r-neuaddau, were being driven from Nant-y-moch by the Brigadier in his car, which had a column change gearstick. With a fairly heavy load, the car stalled as it was going uphill and the Brigadier, in trying to find a lower gear, grabbed the gearstick with both hands, shaking it and declaring, 'There's another one here somewhere!' when the whole thing came away in his hands, and they had to walk all the way down to Ponterwyd.

On one of his visits to Nant-y-moch, the Brigadier was met by John, who gave him a wider than normal smile and said, 'I've had my new teeth, Sir.' The Brigadier replied, probably not over interested in John's teeth, 'Very nice John,' and John, not to be outdone, said, 'Oh yes they are,' and promptly fished them out for inspection! Seeing is believing!

As well as shepherding Nant-y-moch, John had taken a part of Drosgol hill, right opposite the house across the river Rheidol, in order to graze his own sheep. Drosgol was owned by his nephew Iago James (son of Daniel), who had been Director of Agriculture in Nigeria for 25 years and came to live in Aberystwyth after retiring. On the initial agreement between them, John was to pay £12.00 a year for Drosgol. This information I gleaned from a visit to Mr Iago James, and his own words were 'I don't remember if John paid that first year, but I'm sure he didn't pay afterwards.'

John's own shearing was a special affair, with the hand-picked staff – indeed, the majority of them were blood relatives. One of the regulars at this shearing was Richard

■ John James, Nant-y-moch's own shearing and the names of the shearers involved. From left to right: Dilwyn Griffiths, Goginan; John James; Stanley Lloyd, Bont Goch; John Jones, Byrdir; Jim Griffiths, Siop Ceiro; Dewi Roberts, Lle'r neuaddau; Albert James, Hirnant; Dick James, Ty'n pwll, Goginan; Lewis Micah, Machynlleth. Kneeling: William Onllwyn James, Aberpaithnant; Glyn Edwards, Dinas; Thomas Hywel Morgan, Nant-cae-rhedyn.

(Dick) James, Ty'n-pwll, Goginan. Dick was a typical example of 'the little dark people' – lightly built but tough, and a good worker. He was also big hearted. He was a heavy smoker, and on a shearing day especially, he would stock up with fags, and he would share these with his friends, and would not take no for an answer. Dick was mostly concerned with the wool wrapping, and after Dick had finished clearing up, you could hardly say that a shearing had taken place.

Dick's great passion in life was fishing, and he would run back and forth to the river at Nant-y-moch all day as time allowed – at breaks and before and after meals – and many times John had to give him a shout to get him back to work. One day, when the sheep of Penlan and Cyncoed (two farms in the Capel Bangor area, whose sheep were sent up there over-summer) were being shorn, Dick caught 99 trout in a day, and that, as explained, was intersected with a busy day's shearing. From what I have seen in similar streams in the area, you would be more than lucky to catch nine fish there today.

During another shearing at Nant-y-moch, Dick was at his usual pastime of fishing and John James had given him a shout, and he came running back, propping his rod by the side of the shed. One of Nant-y-moch's busybody hens came by, saw a nice worn, and swallowed it. Unfortunately, it was the worm that Dick had been using for fishing, and it had been impaled on a hook. What followed was a big commotion, with Ann James hanging on to the rod, and the distraught hen pulling in the other direction! Dick blotted his copy book with Ann for a long time over this affair.

As well as keeping sheep with John James at Drosgol, Dick used to send a good many sheep up to Blaen-peithnant during the summer months to the care of Emlyn Thomas. Dick was very partial to playing dominoes, and when walking these sheep down in the autumn, he would come to the village of Goginan, where there is a pub called The Druid. At this time, he had a spaniel-cross-sheepdog called 'King'. He was a very wise old dog by all accounts, and while Dick popped into the Druid for a game of dominoes, King would take the sheep the mile or so home to Ty'n-pwll on his own. I remember in the mid-sixties Dick spending several days, if not longer, up on a ladder cutting the

■ Drosgol house as it was. Today it is a total ruin.

side branches of the many oak trees on Ty'n-pwll land and it crossed my mind then that he would not see the rewards of his work, but the trees are still there, much the better from having received his unselfish attention so many years ago.

Dick had another specialty at his home at Ty'n-pwll (which he called 'a little goldmine') and that was his field of green crop. He produced a lot of wonderful vegetables, and I remember that growing carrots seemed to be his forte.

He was a genuine person, willing to help anybody. He and his wife Gwerfyl used to go to Welshpool market from time to time and on one particular visit, Dick had seen a man coming towards him with what appeared to be smoke coming out of his coat pocket. Dick started to beat the pocket, saying, 'You're on fire! You're on fire!' It took the bewildered man a few seconds to get over the shock of this sudden attack and then explain to Dick that he had just bought a packet of chips, which were steaming!

Dick was born on the 19th of April 1913 and died on the 20th of August 1979. Dick's father James (Jim) James (not to be confused with Jim James, Nant-y-moch), was the son of John James, Ffos-fudur (1838–1915), who was a brother to William James (senior), Nant-y-moch. One thing that I know about John James (Ffos-fudur) is that he was particularly partial to tea. Many of his descendants remain in the area, whilst some have gone as far as Johannesburg.

A Professor H.J. Fleure, based at Aberystwyth, conducted a survey of the native people in the Pumlumon area, taking measurements of their stature, noting the colouration of their hair, skin, eyes etc., with a view to typifying them, and probably relating them to other nationalities that had come into Britain a long time ago. Enough has been written on this subject so I won't enhance, and his findings would have been relayed to anthropological societies. I believe it was he that had first said that John James Nant-y-moch had what is called a 'Celtic skull', and there was a rumour that a museum somewhere had offered John £200 for his head, but I believe this Celtic skull theory was refuted at a later date, and I'm sure John went from this world intact.

In the mid-fifties, work began on a large hydro-electric scheme, which would eventually involve the drowning of Nant-y-moch farm and chapel in order to build a reservoir to feed a power station at Cwm Rheidol. In 1960, a Welsh television company (TWW) came to make a film called *Cwm Tawelwch* (the peaceful valley), about the drowning of Nant-y-moch. A lady from Anglesey called Myfanwy Howell was the one who interviewed John and Jim for the film and this, as far as I am aware, is the only record of them talking. John was a mine of information, and it is a great shame more people had not tapped into this source, thus, with hindsight, this film was a gem for posterity.

On the 9th of October 1961, John and Jim had to leave Nant-y-moch. This must have been a wrench, to have to leave the only home that they had known and at the end of the film, they depict John and Jim walking up the hill, leaving the place for the last time; I have no qualms about saying that the first time that I saw this scene, there were tears in my eyes. The house, buildings, and chapel were all demolished before the drowning. The only part that is left is the bridge that was between the farmhouse and the chapel. This site has only once come into view, and that was during the dry summer of 1976. I was the first person to stand on the bridge as there were no other footprints in the mud there. Unfortunately a photograph taken by my late wife at dusk did not come out as we did not have a flash at the time. The graves and gravestones at the Blaen-

Rheidol cemetery were removed to the cemetery at Ponterwyd, where a separate plot was allocated for them. A new house and sheep handling yards were built at a place now called Maesnant – a mile or so upriver of Nant-y-moch – to compensate the land owner for the loss of the previous system.

There was an advert in the *Cambrian News* on the 29th of September 1961 for a shepherd to live and work at Maesnant, which read as follows:

> *Wanted, shepherd to look after a flock of mountain ewes. Good house, 4 miles from Ponterwyd, Cardiganshire. Modern conveniences, good road. Motorcycle with side-car, a cow and a dozen hens provided. Reference essential.*
>
> *Apply Brig-General Evans,*
> *Lovesgrove,*
> *Aberystwyth.*

John, Jim and John James Thomas (their nephew) moved down to live in a house in Capel Dewi owned by Lovesgrove. This must have been a bit of a shock to their system, to move from the peace and quiet of Nant-y-moch to living right on the crossroads at Capel Dewi.

Dick and Gwerfyl James had prepared food for them in advance, and Nan Howells from Capel Bangor brought Jim, John and their nephew down by car to their new home. Nan's husband Ceredig (the son of I.R. Howells) was driving the stock lorry that carried their belongings.

John, Jim and John Thomas, when they moved down to Capel Dewi (which, by the way, was once called Tafarn-y-fagl (the tavern of the snare)) found it quite hard to settle down there, and after attending a service at the local chapel, would come outside and then look up the Peithyll Valley towards Pumlumon, and generally allude to their former home.

During the week, John would roam a bit around the area and was told off more than once for keeping the workers of the nearby Welsh Plant Breeding Station talking. One story has it that he had been invited to tea with a local family and, being the visitor, was offered the jam pot first. He helped himself to a spoonful of jam, licked the spoon clean, and stuck it back in the pot! No one else took jam that day, and I believe he was offered the pot to take home with him.

On the 4th of July 1964, the official opening of the power station at Cwm Rheidol was held, and John and Jim James were given an invitation to attend, as they very rightly should. It should be explained that John and Jim had lived in a 'natural' way, and it fell on the shoulders of David Griffiths of Troed-rhiw-nant-y-fran (Dei Troedrhiw), Goginan, to try to titivate the brothers a bit in preparation for the opening ceremony. I reveal no details of the work he did, suffice to say that many have had medals for doing less!

David Griffiths was related to John and Jim, but so far it has eluded me what their relationship was. They arrived at the power station accompanied by Dei Griffiths and were given a warm welcome. John, like many of his age group and background, had spent his life as a teetotaler, but he espied a young lady with a tray with glasses on it. John was a 'Cardi' of the highest degree, and seeing something for free, made a grab for one, and drank it. David Griffiths asked him, 'John, do you know what you've done now?' 'No, what have I done?' replied John. 'Well, you've taken an alcoholic drink', to which John said, '*Diar, diar*, it was very nice too!'

■ Nant-y-moch house.

To explain what a 'Cardi' is… We are reputed to be so mean in Cardiganshire that we make Scotchmen blush, and Jews turn green with envy. We are the sort of people that cast our bread upon the waters – but only when the tide is coming in. It is stated that copper wire was invented in Cardiganshire. Two Cardis at the same time saw a penny on the floor, both grabbed it, and that is how copper wire started! A joke that I claim as my own: 'What is a Cardi's favourite tablet?' 'Bisodol.' (Buy sod all!)

John, during his working life was renowned for remembering figures and when they were handling many different lots of sheep, John would remember the numbers in the different lots without consulting any paperwork. John was very much a 'tail' man when it came to picking out old ewes. The surest way of identifying a sheep's age is by looking at its teeth. It is common practice on the hill to pull out the draft ewes – ewes aged about four and a half to five and a half years old – which are usually sold then to lowland farmers, usually to breed crossbred lambs. This job is usually done in the autumn, hence the 'half' in their age. The purpose of this work is to reduce the numbers of sheep for the coming winter, and to weed out the sheep that might not withstand another winter on the hill. The time from October to the following May can be long, if the weather is inclement. I read somewhere about this very situation – 'For spring comes but slowly up this way.'

There are other indicators that show if a ewe will, or will not face the test. Some of the older ewes will tend to have a bit of a pot belly, and the sure sign is that the tail grows thinner. I am not a television person, but I saw an advertisement years ago stating that 'graded grains make finer flour' and the same applies to sheep.

Many of these older sheep, if kept, would conceive, bring a lamb, and simply walk away and leave the lamb to its fate. They would do this to get rid of something that was draining their strength, wanting no more to do with something that was going to take them even nearer to death's door. That was a sight I saw many years ago, before people started to feed the hill ewes. I imagine that that sort of sight would be rare today.

This sort of ewe would very slowly regain her strength, then towards the end of May/early June, on a good spring, with a fair bit of grass coming, would get into condition fairly quickly and lose most of her wool, therefore robbing her owner of any revenue he would have had for it. But, as the saying goes, 'It's and ill wind...' This old ewe was one of the best friends that the gleaning girls would meet on the hill, and if they found such a ewe dozing in the warm sun, they would try to creep up on it, and relieve it of any wool it had left!

John James lived a long and healthy life. Shortly before his death he was taken to hospital, and after taking his clothes off for the inevitable scrubbing, his pockets were emptied so that he could witness what they found before his clothes were taken away. Every pocket that he had was stuffed full of paper money which, in total, was about £1000. One of the nurses, still alive today, till that day had never seen so much money in one sum.

John died aged 85, on the 7th of March 1966. Jim and John Thomas continued going to the service on a Sunday, but afterwards there was no looking up the Peithyll Valley, and no talk of Nant-y-moch. Jim died on the 11th of November 1969, aged 78, and John James Thomas moved to live with his relatives in Eisteddfa Gurig to spend his remaining days in comfort. He died on the 9th of October 1979, aged 77.

■ The last view of Nant-y-moch before everything was demolished in 1961.
Photo by Ron Davies, Aberaeron.

John Lewis Jones

This man spent most of his life around the hills between Pumlumon and Talybont. He was born at Byr-dir in the Cwm Soar area near Machynlleth. He was the son of Richard and Ann Jones (nee Annwyl from Mwyars, Llanbrynmair). Richard Jones came from Pen-geulan in Penegoes, and had two big passions in his later life – tea, and going to funerals.

John, or as he was known to most, Jack y Byrdir, was one of six children. He had two brothers – William (Willie Byrdir) and Richard, who farmed at Bwlch near Machynlleth, and three sisters – Mary, Elizabeth and Dorothy.

I am not sure whether John worked somewhere else, but I was told that his first job was at Plas-y-mynydd with Mrs Elinor Briggs. She was the wife of Captain Godfrey Briggs of Pen-wern, New Cross, and the daughter of Sir George and Lady Pryse-Saunders, and grand-daughter of Sir Pryse Pryse and Lady Pryse, Gogerddan.

John was a tall, clean-looking man, and these next few years of living in a different way, and mixing with a different class of people left its stamp on John. He always wore a tie, everywhere he went, and if there was a chance to give orders, he was quite quick on the uptake, and if there was a youngster daft enough to catch sheep on his behalf, John would make sure his feet were kept warm.

Of the whole story of the Briggs family, I would not count myself an expert, but they lived at Pen-wern, New Cross, in lavish style during the winter, and they would spend a lot of the summer at Plas-y-mynydd. Plas-y-mynydd was the summer shooting and fishing lodge for the gentry that came to visit the Gogerddan Mansion. The grouse shooting moors around Plas-y-mynydd were called 'The Old Park' and 'The New Park'. In the 1930s they had four female workers at Pen-wern, and a gardener, cowman and chauffeur.

■ John Lewis Jones (Jack y Byrdir)

195

In the late thirties the Briggs' held sheepdog trials at Plas-y-mynydd, and about fifty contestants came from a good distance to compete. To liven up the proceedings, a cask of whisky was taken there, and for those who wished to partake of the hospitality, they were given a basin each. People like Tom Morgan, his brother John James Morgan (a teetotaller) and Dewi Roberts, had walked from Ponterwyd to the trials. Tom and Dewi were not drinking people, but did sample the *aqua vitae* before coming from there, and they had quite a job getting home that night!

One contestant, John Jenkins of Hengwm-gyfeiliog, whose mother Jane was a daughter of John and Elizabeth Morgan, Hengwm-annedd, was a good dog handler, and little wonder, being the nephew of Richard Morgan. However, before competing, he had had a few drinks. He went to the starting post, and sent his bitch off round the sheep, but as she brought the sheep nearer, John fell on his back in the rushes, and was shouting, 'Steady on good bitch, steady on good bitch,' much to the delight of the crowd.

Many years later there was a story that John Jenkins had been down to Machynlleth, had a bit of liquid refreshment, and was walking home. Since he was walking into the wind, he turned round to light a cigarette, forgot to turn around again and walked all the way back to Machynlleth!

Mrs Briggs, after the death of her husband, started a friendship with a John Evans, who was a stonemason (*Jack y mashwn*) and whatever else they had in common, they both liked whisky. In their latter years a friend of theirs asked Jack, 'Do you think it's right that Mrs Briggs drinks so much whisky?' and he replied, 'I'm drinking as much as I can, so that she doesn't get it!' There could have been a rivalry between John Jones and John Evans at one time, but John the Mason won, and he and Mrs Briggs were true to each other till death parted them.

Mrs Briggs moved to Cefn-coch for a period, and then to Gloucester Hall in Penrhyncoch, with John, the shepherd, looking after the sheep there and in nearby Pen-y-berth, as both units were run together. John had what can only be described as a good time during this period and became rather fond of whisky, a passion he kept for the rest of his life. In mentioning Pen-y-berth, a man called Jenkin Hughes (1899–1985) lived there, and he had a wealth of stories about the shepherds on the surrounding hills. Thankfully many of his recollections were put on video by the late Hywel Evans, Rhandir-mwyn, Penrhyncoch, which was a great favour for posterity.

In exchanging labour, John Jones would help Lovesgrove drive their sheep and lambs up to Nant-llyn in the spring. He would go to Lovesgrove in the morning and Tom Morgan from Nant-cae-rhedyn would come there to meet him. They would then be invited into the mansion for breakfast. A man, called Bryn, who was a general handyman about the house, made the breakfast, and perhaps not being the most methodical person, he had left a bit of bacon hanging over the side of the pan, and Tom Morgan used to chuckle in later years as he remembered John leaning forward, putting his stick under the offending slice of bacon, and flipping it back into the frying pan. One of the Brigadier's sisters noticed quite a bit of dust on a piece of furniture in the house and wrote in the dust 'Happy Christmas Bryn.' Bryn passed there a while later, saw the message and wrote below it, '...and the same to you Miss.' The 'real' message hadn't got through.

■ Plas-y-mynydd 1936.

Margaret Angharad Elinor Briggs died on the 11th of August 1970, aged 66, and was buried with her husband near the Pryse family graves at Penrhyncoch church. John Evans wrote this poem in her memory, which I found rather touching, after all the escapades they'd had together:

No one can replace you,
No one ever will.
In life I loved you dearly,
In death I love you still.
The parting came so suddenly
I wonder why?
The hardest part of all is
I never said good bye.

Johnny

John Jones moved to work at Glan-frêd in Llandre, and must have driven thousands upon thousands of sheep up and down from the Old Park (Plas-y-mynydd), the New Park and Llechwedd-mawr to the low lying ground of Pwll-glas and Glan-frêd which were run at that time as one unit. John was fairly sure of getting one of the first lots, as they were stronger and moved better.

At shearing time when the sheep were brought down, the road was full from Bwlch-y-garreg to the gate of Carreg Cadwgan, with the flock being divided into about eight lots for easier management. My late employer Mr Ieuan Morgan, Glan-frêd, told me that only one man had driven two lots of sheep from the hill to Glan-frêd in one day and that was Eurig Richards from Talybont.

John had a keen eye, especially when picking out strays. He was counting sheep at Nant-y-moch one day and my uncle, Gomer James, was standing by his side, and his job was to catch the strays as John pointed them out, and, as Gomer said, you had to be on the ball to keep up with him.

Many years previous to this, John and Lewis Micah, owner of Hengwm-annedd had gone to a shearing at Nant-y-moch and had stayed there the night before. They realized during the day that they had company – other than human company. That evening they walked from there together, and by Nant-llyn it was a total strip off to look for, and destroy, their new little 'friends'. John was living at home at that period, and on relating this tale to his sister Mary, had had to strip again before being let into the house. Lewis Micah was a character in his own right, an excellent hand shearer, and was most vivid and entertaining when relating about his escapades, especially about the times when he went after foxes.

Many times I heard Mrs Annie Raw and Marged Jane of Ty-llwyd say that since they had a lot of people staying there over the shearing, they inevitably had fleas in the house afterwards and that they had quite a task to clear them. They were part and parcel of life many years ago in some places and worse where there was a high density of population. A John Edwards from Blaen-gorffen, Pont-rhyd-fendigaid took advantage of this situation when he attended a shearing at Dôl-wen, Devil's Bridge. He had gone there the night before, and was sharing a bed with some boisterous young lads, therefore could not have the night's sleep he wanted. He started scratching himself, pretending he had fleas, and very soon had the bed to himself!

This next story came from a wonderful lady that came to live in Cwmystwyth from the Resolven area in South Wales. She was Mrs Sarah Thickens of Talwrn. She said that years ago, in her old neighbourhood, somebody had died and a lady relative of the family had come there to express her sympathy. Since she had a good scratch every now and then, one of the family made the comment 'A little flea?' 'Yes' she said, and not willing to admit it was hers, added, 'I recognize a strange flea straight away!'

When I was working at Lovesgrove, and because they had the hill of Nant-llyn, and Glan-frêd had the adjoining Llechweddmor as a hill, it was my job every now and then to go and get John in the morning to help with the gathering. It was a form of habit rather than a contribution to lighten the work-load in John's last years, but he was good company to have around, and because he frequented the local watering holes, there was hardly a scandal in the area of which he didn't know most of the details. He would often complain that his stomach was not very well, and yet it was a standing joke that he would clear every morsel of food that was put before him.

One time while gathering Maesnant and Nant-llyn, John had been placed above Maesnant house near the road going up to Llyn-llygad-rheidol, to stop the sheep going back towards the Nant-y-moch side. This job of acting as a 'stop' is one that involves waiting a long time till the other shepherds have closed in over a large area.

After waiting a long time John decided to go down to a nearby dip to answer a call of nature, and it was at that time that a large party of sheep, seeing nobody there, crossed over, unseen by John. It was a while later before he saw them, and they had spread out a good bit. One of John's outstanding features was his booming voice, and when he saw these sheep, they must have heard him down in Ponterwyd trying to get the dog to fetch them. It is one of those things that can happen on a hill gathering, but hopefully not to you. That episode took a lot of living down.

Jack y Byrdir was a non-driver and a fit man in his time and it would be interesting to know what sort of mileage he would have clocked up in his lifetime. He died at Machynlleth Hospital in March 1976, aged 72.

Dafydd and Mary Ann Owen

This couple deserve to be written about – not only because Dafydd was a shepherd but also because they were unique even in their era. So many stories about their way of life have been handed down in an endearing way that it seems a pity for these to go into oblivion.

Dafydd was born in Ty'n-cwm, a house now in total ruin on the slopes opposite the Dyffryn Castell Hotel in Ponterwyd. I believe his parents were called David and Catherine (Kitty) Owen. He'd had no education and was never able to read or write but he had a wonderful sense of observation and was able to memorize hundreds of sheep ear-marks. Brought up in almost total poverty, he did not have any form of foot-wear until he was twelve years old, yet it seems that this hard upbringing produced a very fit man because, when Dafydd was sixty years old, he was able to out-run and catch a sheep on the hill. Another fact about Dafydd was that he had never shaved in his life.

Mary Ann lived at Shop Ceiro, near Aber-ceiro on the way from Ponterwyd to Nant-y-moch. This was a typical Welsh long-house and Dafydd Griffiths (Mary Ann's brother) and his cow used to go in through the same door – the cow turning to the left and Dafydd going to the right. Dafydd used to say when there was a cold easterly wind that it was coming 'Direct from Siberia'.

Mary Ann was able to read and write and was very well versed in her Bible, but had turns of speech at times that were everything but biblical! I do not know when she and Dafydd were married, but the food afterwards was at Shop Ceiro and I can only imagine that everybody had a good time at such a joyous occasion. Towards the end of the proceedings, Dafydd suddenly got up and said, 'Well, I'd better go now, my mother is at home on her own.' And off he went!

He and Mary Ann later lived at Camdwr-biti, near the Camdwr Mawr mine. When exactly they moved there I do not know, but I have a record of them being there in 1898/99, as members of Blaen-rheidol chapel. Dafydd was a shepherd in that area although I am unsure as to whom he was working for. At the same time, three young men from the Porthmadog area came to work at the Hafan Quarry and their job was to teach local quarrymen how to dress stones for building. These three men stayed with Dafydd and Mary Ann at Camdwr-biti. During their stay there, Mary Ann's only cow died and these three big-hearted young men, who could not have been earning a great deal, clubbed together to buy Mary Ann a new cow, saying it was a gift in return for her kindness. Two of the men returned to their native area but one of them, John Jones, who originally came from Nefyn, stayed in this area. He was a member of Tabor Chapel and one night, at a social evening, a Susanah Jones had come up from Cwmsymlog as part of a quartet, and that is how their courtship started. They were later married and

■ Dafydd and Mary Ann Owen, Lluest fach, Ponterwyd. Two very original characters.
Note that the handle of the scythe is straight apart from being angled near its junction with the
blade. More modern 'S' shaped handles were known as 'american handles' and were much more
tedious to work with.

John was given a Bible as a present from the chapel members. They went to live in
Cwmsymlog and it was their daughter, Mrs Nansi Kenny, Aberystwyth, who told me this
tale.

John Jones, in later years, was afflicted with silicosis and not in good health and Mary
Ann – then living in Lluest-fach – would call by and give the family butter, buttermilk
or eggs, and would refuse any payment, saying that she still remembered his great

kindness so many years ago. These people remained true to their friends through their entire life. I heard a story that Dafydd and Mary Ann might have buried a child, probably stillborn, while at Camdwr-biti; the burial would probably have been at Nant-y-moch.

When Dafydd was a shepherd at Lluest-fach he would have small lots of sheep coming up during the summer months and in going to meet them, would look them over carefully and say, 'I remember that one from last year, such and such a thing happened to her.' He would look at them again and say, 'I don't think that one has been up before.' Dafydd knew his onions when it came to sheep.

Dafydd's shortcoming as a shepherd were his dogs. They were nigh on hopeless and Mary Ann was mostly to blame because she spoilt them silly. There was an art in going to Lluest-fach so I was told. You would go to the house, knock on the door, and then step to one side. The door would then be opened and about three dogs would come hurtling out. Then you had to nip in quickly and close the door before the dogs turned around, in order to have a bit of peace and quiet inside. In the twenties they had two dogs, called 'Somme' and 'Mons', after the famous battles of the First World War.

Dafydd's dogs would follow so closely at his heels that he often tripped over them, going arse-over-tit when he was gathering sheep. He often went down to neighbouring valleys to fetch sheep back. In starting off home with the sheep, he would find that he could not control his dogs. He would then have to take the sheep back to the farm and take the dogs home to Lluest-fach then come back on his own to take the sheep home by running himself, throwing stones at them to keep them in line!

It was a habit of many people years ago, when taking a few unruly sheep (maybe up to five in number) and not having a dog up to the job, to tie the heads of the sheep together so that they were side-by-side and at the other end, tie their tails together, making sure there was to be no escape.

One of the most famous stories about Dafydd and Mary Ann is that they had gone to an Eisteddfod at Goginan and it was quite dark when they set off for home. Somebody, however, gave them the loan of a flash-lamp – something entirely new to them – but they got home to Lluest-fach unhindered. That is when their trouble began – they could not put it out and they thought that if this lamp was left as it was, it might set fire to the house, so, being practical country people – they put it in a bucket of water!

They, like a lot of country people, did not turn their clocks forward or backward, and were often caught out by being an hour late or early for functions in the area.

Dafydd, in his older years, was very prone to nodding off and when they had visitors, Mary Ann, every now and again, would have to say, 'Dafydd, wake up!' and he would oblige, but if he lapsed more than a few times, she would say quite sharply, 'Dafydd, do I have to get a stick!' Not that there was any danger to the old boy, but it made him sit up and pay attention. He would often go to sleep while milking the cow.

When at this stage of life, he would go to the shearing at Bwlch-styllen and would nod off many times during the day. At this time most of the sheep in the area were bothered by 'keds' – blackish insects that were very mobile on the sheep's skin, not to be confused with ticks. We called them *llai defaid* in this area and they are called *hislod* in North Wales. They transferred easily from sheep to shearer, and before a quiet night's sleep could be had, a search would have to be made for the stow-aways. Dafydd had a habit of cutting each ked he saw in half and if there were quite a few of these blood-sucking insects, the sheep looked as though someone had tried to murder it!

Edgar Humphreys from Bwlch-styllen was walking over the retaining wall of the Blaen-melindwr lake with Dafydd one windy night when the wind took Dafydd's hat into the river on the lower side. 'Oh, what a pity,' Dafydd said, 'I've had that hat for fifteen years.'

On moonlit nights, Mary Ann used to go to visit Bwlch-styllen and she would tell tales about ghosts till the early hours. Edgar said that he didn't venture out after dark for about a fortnight afterwards.

Edgar, born in September 1910, used to take eggs, a hundred at a time, each individually wrapped, from Bwlch-styllen to be sold at Jim Evans' shop in Bontgoch. He had a half-penny each for them. When he was about 13 years old he walked to Davies' garage in Tre'r Ddôl to buy a bike for £1. He pushed it all the way home because he could not ride it but in a few days came to master the technique. A few years later he used to go peat cutting for Mrs Briggs at Plas-y-mynydd, staying there for a week.

He was at one stage employed to help drive sheep from Lovesgrove, near Aberystwyth, to Lluest-y-rhos (owned by Major J.J. Evans) in the company of Morgan Oliver, Dynnin (near Glan-dyfi) and Will Williams, Dôl-gelynnen, Talybont. A man with a horse-drawn float followed behind to pick up any sheep or lambs that felt the strain of the journey, which took them through Cwm Ceulan in Talybont. Edgar's family moved from Bwlch-styllen to Rhyd-yr-onnen, Cwm Ceulan, and then later to Pencae in Talybont.

Mary Ann was a trim person who had pride as regards her appearance and her hair kept its colour till she was an old lady – this she attributed to rinsing her hair in her own urine.

They lived in the age of barter and Mary Ann used to take butter, eggs or whatever else was available to exchange for their goods. She had gone to the shop of Mari Roderick in Goginan one day, and Mari looked at the pounds of butter Mary Ann had and remarked that they looked rather small, to which Mary Ann replied, 'They shouldn't be, because I balanced them with the pound of currants I had from you last week!' It was a case of 'Put that in your pipe and smoke it!' There were no flies on some of these old characters.

Mary Ann would go down to Cwmsymlog every Wednesday to meet the baker. She would call in three houses, have a cup of tea in each one, and have another at the shop, where she took eggs as barter for her goods.

The following story that I heard about Dafydd speaks of his beautiful manner. When he had gone somewhere on a visit, after chatting for a while, the lady of the house invited him to have a bit of food, and he said, 'Thank you, with your permission' (*gyda'ch cennad*). This, to me, speaks volumes of a person who'd had no formal education.

Dafydd Jenkins, an ex-National Librarian from Penrhyn-coch and some friends at the College at Aberystwyth used to go walking quite a bit and they enjoyed calling in with Dafydd and Mary Ann and she used to give them bara brith and buttermilk before they left. He said that during a visit there Dafydd had told him, '*Dilyn di natur, ei di ddim yn bell o dy le.*' (You respect nature, and you won't go far wrong.) Somebody once wrote

'Love of nature is an essential part of true wisdom,' so Dafydd wasn't far from the mark.

The old couple had worked out a pattern in life – Dafydd went to the funerals and Mary Ann went to the concerts. They both enjoyed going to the Eisteddfod, associated with the Camdwr Mawr lead mine, which was held at Nant-y-moch Chapel. Mary Ann liked to recite and would often practice at home, with Dafydd adjudicating. If Dafydd let off a fart, even if it was in Chapel, he would say '*Hysgitt!*' after it, as though to send it on its way.

I could go on and on about this delightful and endearing couple but I hope that this will suffice for future generations to keep them in mind 'lest they be forgotten', for they lived a long and honest life. Dafydd once had a cow that was a kicker and only he could milk her. When he sold her, he said that she kicked, and therefore got less money for her.

When they got rather infirm they moved to live with relatives in Bronant where they were looked after in the twilight of their life. Mary Ann died on the 28th of October 1944, aged 88, and Dafydd died on the 3rd of January 1946, aged 89, and both are buried in the chapel cemetery in Ponterwyd. Inscribed on their gravestone are the following very suitable words:

> *Annwyl a chariadus buont yn eu bywyd, ac yn angau ni wahanwyd hwynt.*
> *(Dear and loving were they in life, and in death they were not parted.)*

■ Lluest-fach as it is today. Photo by Seiriol Dafydd.

John Owen

Another Owen who spent most of his lifetime shepherding in the area was the above-mentioned John Owen. Having known John for a good many years and worked with him at Lovesgrove during the early 1970s, this is the tribute that I wrote to his memory. The translation of the original was made by Dafydd Ifans, Penrhyncoch: I have added a few statements for clarity.

A TRIBUTE TO JOHN OWEN 1911–1992

John was a native of Montgomeryshire where he had been imbibed with the richness of that county's dialect, and he had no doubt seen during his long years more change than had been witnessed by any previous generation. He had a marvellous turn of phrase and he would use long-obsolete terms from the world of horses with the greatest of ease. He was enchanted by unusual place-names and he discussed one, *Cwm-llym-wynt* (valley of the keen wind), with me when he was poorly in hospital. He would often mention the hardship which he had encountered in his early years and he would emphasise the pressures on people to make both ends meet. When he began working he earned £14 a year, and only had tea on Christmas Day. He also mentioned receiving only two halves of an egg during one year; eggs at that time were an important source of income for the farmer and every possible egg was taken to the shop and exchanged for goods.

Very often it was decided that it was too wet to take the horses out of the stable, but at the same time the farmer would order the servants out to open ditches. In the days before the invention of the wellington boot and oilskins, they merely had the protection of old sacks around their legs and over their shoulders. A craft that he was well versed in was hedge laying, and he was able to get good results, even from the roughest of them.

John, on his own admission, had a bad memory for some things, and he was often seen to bring his raincoat, but having forgotten his leggings. It is indeed surprising that he kept going without getting rheumatism when one remembers how wet he often was. Mrs Blodwen Howells, formerly of Bryn-glas Farm, had retired to live in Glasfryn in the centre of the village in Ponterwyd. As John was going to a shearing at Bryn-glas, he had offered her a lift as she was also going there. Next day John came onto the square at the appointed time and Mrs Howells, waiting on her doorstep, waved her hand to greet him. John waved back, and shot off, having forgotten all about their plans!

When I remember John, it strikes me about him that he was a man who always made the best of whatever situation he found himself in. He experienced the rough and the smooth paths of life. Possibly the greatest disappointment in his life was the loss of his first wife, Meirwen, when their only daughter Betty was only fifteen months old. Then,

■ John Owen and his dogs
at Lle'r Neuaddau, 1976.

after remarrying, he lost a little girl called Veronica, a sister to Ann and Joan who were born later. They lived at a farm called Cefn-peniarth near Llanidloes and John would sing the praises of this time for they were more or less self-supporting. He often recounted how he would, while feeding the animals, slap the sheaves against the barn wall and the hens would enjoy the oats, and would subsequently lay well, and the eggs were sold in Llanidloes.

Then he moved to Bont-isaf to work for Captain Bennett Evans and with John Davies, the head shepherd, or 'John y Bont' as he was known locally. This lasted for two to three years when he endured the bitterness of the 1947 hard winter when many losses were experienced, with 'John y Bont' in tears, begging to see the return of mild weather and the thaw.

John and his family then moved to Grove Cottage to work on Lovesgrove Farm, near Aberystwyth, and to shepherd Nant-llyn, Nant-y-moch and Hen Hafod (Lle'r-neuaddau had not been bought at this time). The farm and the country house at Lovesgrove were at their prime at this time, employing a gardener, a cowman, and a man to look after the hens, not to mention girl servants and farm workers, with the old Brigadier-General Evans and his sisters ruling the roost. John could have written a book about this period with its fun and troubles concerning the people and work which belonged to a period which is so very different from things as they are today.

John and a friend bought a greyhound from Gypsies who were staying near the Black Bridge – the railway bridge near Llanbadarn – and the understanding was that they would have the use of the dog every other week. As it happened it was the turn of his friend, Jack Davies (Jack Recorder, because he travelled around to record milk) to have the dog for the first week, and he tied it to a three-legged table. The greyhound, however, decided that he was homesick and so he returned to the Gypsy encampment, table and all, towards Llanbadarn, the table disintegrating plank by plank until there was just one leg left tied to the chain. It was adept at catching rabbits, but he would insist on carrying his catch back to the Gypsies!

After the creation of Nant-y-moch dam, the death of the old Brigadier, and his grandson becoming responsible for the running of the farm, a great change was made in the administration of the Estate. Lle'r-neuaddau was bought, and there were as many cattle there as there are sheep on some farms. About 1971 John moved to live by himself at Lle'r-neuaddau, and that is where he remained for the rest of his working life. Lle'r-neuaddau farmhouse was renowned for being cold and for the wind which whistled in through various holes. John, however, was clever at lighting a fire and it is a miracle that the house did not go up in flames with such a stoker! Although the stove was red-hot your back always felt as if it were in Siberia! The welcome however was always warm and I remember one particular occasion which leads me on to one of John's great delights, namely football. Everyone who knows me realises that I haven't the slightest interest in sport, but once, my future wife and I visited Lle'r-neuaddau and received the usual welcome and were shown into the parlour to a grate alight with fire, and a football match on the television. Nothing was allowed to impair the game and I was surprised to learn that he knew all the players' names and their capabilities and habits – 'You watch that one, he's a real old b——d', 'He's a good one for scoring'. John would commentate and get excited, and you were lucky not to be kicked. I have to admit that this was the only game that I have ever enjoyed watching. Singing was another of his interests and he was blessed with a good ear, and a rich bass voice and it was he who introduced me to such solos as *Yr Ornest*, *Brad Dynrafon* and similar songs. He was a member of Melindwr choir under the baton of Mr Felix at one time.

John was often impulsive, and I remember my father telling me that he went down to Grove Cottage one day (some business concerning dogs almost certainly) and John out of natural kindness offered him some new potatoes. He didn't have time to fetch a garden fork but began lifting them with his bare hands! It's obvious that he was a very mischievious youth, and I remember having lots of fun at Lle'r-neuaddau when his contemporaries gathered to recount old happenings. He had an extraordinary gift of being able to laugh heartily until his eyes watered, and he would slap his knee from time to time as if to underline the fun. This jocularity persisted in his character, and if anyone ventured to do anything unusual he would be renamed by John. 'White stockings' was his nickname for the Brigadier because of his knee-breeches. 'The pencil man' was his name for Edward Lewis, Henllan, Machynlleth, because he always carried biros or fountain-pens in his coat pocket. 'The wellingtons man' – that's what he called Ieu Morgan, Glan-frêd as he lived in them day in and day out. John James, Nant-y-moch was nicknamed 'the old boiler' because he was fairly black at times! The list went on and on. His lively humour appeared through the smoke of his 'Woodbines', which he boasted to have smoked since he was eleven years of age.

One of the highlights of John's life was making the film *The Shepherd* – an hour-long documentary shot by BBC2 Bristol – about the work on Lovesgrove Estate, Aberystwyth, whose 3000-acre hill included Hen-hafod, Lle'r-neuaddau, Nant-y-moch, Maesnant and Nant-llyn. It's a good thing that the programme was made as it is a good record of how he was in 1976. His last words on the film were 'I don't want to be a nuisance for nobody.' You never were a nuisance, and many lives were enriched through knowing you.

After the last storm of his eighty-year-long life died down on the 10th of August 1992, he was taken back to Staylittle to rest close to the spot where his life's journey began.

Quarrels

In Robert Burton's *Wales* (1688) he makes reference to the steep hills and deep valleys in Meirioneth, saying, '...so that if the shepherds should fall out in the morning, and challenge each other to a fight, before they can come to each other the day will be spent, and the heat of their fury abated, after they have slept till morning.'

Just in case I have painted too rosy a picture about shepherding life on open hills, I would like to point out that there were many quarrels as regards boundaries and the coursing of neighbours' sheep, which were sore points in many areas – often leading to threats and sometimes fights.

I have heard of one shepherd who did not have a heading dog. He had two coursers and another dog that would kill a sheep on command. Many sheep that were persistent offenders were killed or drowned, some even had their teats cut off so that they could not rear another generation of trespassers. This matter would be abhorrent to most shepherds, but it was a fact that it did happen many times, with some areas being worse than others.

A landowner and his shepherd had rounded up a bunch of neighbours' sheep that were constantly on his land and there was a discussion as to what to do with the ewes. It was decided to let them go but the shepherd said, 'What about the seed?' (*beth am yr had?*) – meaning the lambs – and they were done away with there and then. It is easy to be judgemental in this day and age of this behaviour when most hills are under a stockproof fence, but to keep an open hill under control years ago you had to be quite a strong character.

The isolated sheepwalk of Esgair-garthen, that was also called Pant-y-beudyau (the hollow of the cow-houses) which lies at the top end of the present Claerwen dam, was owned by John Jones of Nant-stalwen, and he was bothered by his sheep being coursed and abused. In consequence to this, in 1867 he had a house built there, probably on the site of an older building, and put a shepherd there. The shepherd was a man called Stephen Lloyd, originally from Ffair Rhos, the son of Stephen and Mary Lloyd, Llether, Rhos-marchnant. He obviously was a good man from his employer's point of view in keeping the boundaries, but the fact of the house and shepherd being there did not please people in the Llanwrthwl area, who sent sheep up to graze neighbouring hills. They decided that some action ought to be taken, and on the night of the 10th of September 1868 about fifteen of them went up to Esgair-garthen, their faces blackened and some with their coats turned inside-out to avoid recongnition. As it happened, Stephen Lloyd was not at home: I believe he had gone to a funeral at Ffair Rhos. They roused his wife Elizabeth, and ordered her and her four-month old daughter, and Elizabeth's ten-year old sister, Mary Morgan, out of the house, and then carried their belongings outside, started to dismantle part of the house, and set it on fire, as well as the haystack and the stack of peat they had for fuel. I believe Elizabeth and Mary went for shelter that night to a farm called Garreg-lwyd. Full details of the ensuing court case can be seen in The Brecon County Times on the 3rd, 10th, 17th and 31st of October 1868.

Stephen Lloyd was living in Lle'r-tai-hirion in Aber-gwesyn in 1881, and in the census his family were listed as:

> *Stephen Lloyd, 45 years old, shepherd; Elizabeth Lloyd, 36 years old, his wife; their children – Stephan (12), Jane (10), Mary (8), John (6), David (4), Elizabeth (3) and Bertha (2).*

They later moved to Newbridge-on-Wye and I was told that when they went there Stephen Lloyd had hardly a word of English. I believe he came to Bwlchgarth first of all, then to Pentre-bach, retiring later to New-hall. He was known locally as 'Styfin'. He died in 1921, aged 87, having lost his sight.

Esgair-garthen house was re-built and a family called Roberts went there. They were the descendants of 'the respected clan of Roberts' from Fron-goch-ar-Deifi. It is quite obvious that the boundary-keeping problem was still there, because one of the family told me that there were three sons there, and in around April/May time when neighbours' sheep came up, they used to go coursing alternately, in shifts – keeping, for a period, a virtual 24 hour vigil.

In 1925 a David Roberts died at Esgair-garthen aged 83, having been a shepherd for John Jones, Nant-stalwen, for 60 years. He had buried his wife Jane (nee Jones) 38 years previously. She became very ill not long after giving birth to their last child, Elizabeth, in January 1887. He went for help and came back to find that his children were trying to wake her up but she had died since his departure. Altogether, they had 13 children who were all able to be at his funeral, except for Margaret, who died when she was 10 years old. I am grateful to Miss Eurwen Roberts from Builth Wells, herself a descendant of Esgair-garthen, for a list of the all thirteen children, and they were as follows: William (1863), Mary (1865), Margaret (1866), Morgan (1868), Catherine (1869), Jane (1870), Rhys (1872), David (1874), John (1876), Thomas (1878), Evan (1880), Margaret (1883), Elizabeth (1887).

There was a story that David Roberts had taken one of these children, who was about three to four years old and had not been from home before that time, down towards Pont-rhyd-fendigaid, and the child said, 'Dear me, they've got big rushes round here.' These big rushes that the child saw were actually trees – something he would not have seen up in Esgair-garthen!

David Roberts, his son (born 1874), was a shepherd at Dôl-goch in Cwm Tywi. He married Elizabeth Jones, the daughter of Dôl-goch, and they went to live at Troed-rhiw in Pont-rhyd-fendigaid. They had twelve children – ten daughters and two sons. He died very suddenly after he had been gathering sheep. He had come back to a tree not far from the house, probably felt unwell, sat down, and died. When he was found, the pony's reins were on his arm and the dogs holding the sheep. He had his birthday on the same day as his grandson, Islwyn Roberts, Bryn-glas, Llanddewi-brefi – on the 12th of March.

John, David's brother, came after him as a shepherd at Dôl-goch, and was there till John Jones (1892–1968) the son of Dôl-goch, was old enough to be a shepherd. John

■ Jane Roberts, Esgair-garthen going down on her faithful horse to a special preaching festival (Cyrddau Mawr) at Pont-rhyd-fendigaid in the summer of 1930.

Roberts was the last shepherd to be employed there. He lived later at Pant-clwydau, Cwm Tywi.

The family dispersed from Esgair-garthen one by one, till in the end only Evan and Jane his sister were left. Jane was described as a 'square' lady, not very tall and on the plump side. She was always said to be chuckling or laughing, obviously a contented soul. Time was something that did not bother them, and they were often not aware of what day it was. They were regular chapel goers and would come down to chapel, either in

■ William Lewis, taken when he was 27 years old, in front of Nant-stalwen house.

Cwm Moiro (built in 1882) or Pont-rhyd-fendigaid, but sometimes arriving on a Saturday morning! On his way back to Esgair-garthen after shopping or such business, Evan often had to sleep in the cart over-night because there was a flood in the river and he couldn't cross. He once carried a piglet on horseback from Nant-stalwen to Esgair-garthen. All these out-lying farms in the catchment area of the Elan Valley dams were paid a sum of money every year by the Birmingham Corporation for not throwing any sewage into the rivers passing their homes.

Some of the ponies from Esgair-garthen were over-wintered at Ffos-y-bleiddiaid in Swyddffynnon and Evan would come to collect them very late in the day, much to the disgust of the occupants, as they had to be collected from a piece of rough ground, and he took them home in virtual darkness. Evan used to have potatoes and a load of corn sheaves from Ffos every autumn. He and Jane would come down to shop in Ffair-rhos at dusk, proving again that they were very much night birds.

Ned Davies (1919–1983) who spent many years as a shepherd at Hen Fynachlog in Pont-rhyd-fendigaid, had been shepherding at Nant-stalwen many years ago. He once had to stay overnight at Esgair-garthen and there was very little food there and he, after a day's gathering, was pretty hungry. The shepherd suddenly asked him, 'Do you like liver?' 'Yes. Yes. I'll eat anything,' was Ned's reply. The shepherd, calling his dog, sent him around some sheep, caught a wether, and set about killing it. You can't get liver fresher than that!

Evan Roberts had gone to a shearing at Pen-twyn, Abergwesyn, and had been taken by the owner, Thomas Hope, to see the ornate church at Abergwesyn. After seeing the church, he asked Evan what he thought of it, and Evan replied, 'It would make a wonderful place for shearing!'

Evan and Jane Roberts moved from Esgair-garthen in 1935 to live in Ty-canol Farm for two to three years, shepherding for the family of Wern-felen. They then went to live at Delfryn, Pen-creigiau, in Pont-rhyd-fendigaid, which was about ten miles from their original home of Esgair-garthen.

Jane died on the 28th of February 1946, aged 75 and Evan died on the 4th of April 1959, aged 78. Both are buried at Strata Florida.

In about 1932, Elizabeth (Bet) Evans from Ffos-y-ffin in Blaen-pennal came to work in Nant-stalwen. At around the same period, Will Lewis (1909–1978), who was born at Cefn-gilfach, Abergwesyn, also came there to work as a shepherd. His father, Thomas Rees Lewis, was a brother to Dafydd Lewis, Glan-hirin, Elan Valley. Will and Bet fell in love, were married in 1935 and moved to live in Esgair-garthen. Two of their children – John and Thomas – were born there and the family moved from there in 1937. They used to keep three goats to supply them with milk. Their belongings were put on three 'gambos' – flat-bed horse-drawn vehicles, used mainly for carrying hay. When they were coming down near Fron-goch, one of the wheels broke and they had to borrow one from Fron-goch. They continued on their way down to Pont-rhyd-fendigaid and a lorry owned by Tysul Ebenezer, Llangeitho, took them and their belongings to Bryn-beddau, Bethania. They were the last family to live at Esgair-garthen.

They had two other children – Morgan and Margaret – and later (1943) moved to Crofft-y-cyff near Tafarn Jem, Harford (between Lampeter and Llanwrda). Will and Bet are both buried at Capel Pant-y-celyn, Abergwesyn, where many of the Lewis' of Pen-cae have found their last resting place.

■ Esgair-garthen in ruins 1968. Thanks to Mrs Margaret Jones, Harford, for the photo. Her parents were the last people to live there.

Tommy Hughes

This unique man is my last subject, but as the old adage goes, 'last, but not least' and in dealing with him, we turn a full circle, and go back to the Elan Valley.

Tommy was born at Blaen-glyn-olwyn, Llys-dinam, near Newbridge-on-Wye, in 1918. He was the son of Harold and Elizabeth Hughes and one of five children. His family from his mother's side had been at Aber-glan-hirin since 1854. His great-grand-father from his father's side, Thomas Hughes, kept the toll-gate at Trympeg-y-mynydd, and his wife Ann Hughes (nee Morgan) came from Ty'n-bryn, Cwmystwyth, and she was a sister to my great-great-grandmother, Elen Howells from Cwmergyr, Ponterwyd.

Harold Hughes and his family moved from Blaen-glyn-olwyn to New Mead, near Newbridge, when Tommy was three months old and with his typical humour, he said he was not allowed to help, in case he might break something!

■ Tommy Hughes in 1961.

After attending Newbridge and Llandrindod schools, he left in 1932 and worked on the family farm, cycling, when the need arose, from New Mead to Aber-glan-hirin, with his dogs following behind. He always maintained that the dogs were very fit, and although the road was rougher then, he never saw them foot-sore. On the 25th of April 1931, he was helping to walk sheep from New Mead, starting at six in the morning, to Aber-glan-hirin. There was a distance of fifteen miles to cover, and it was seven o'clock that night when they arrived, having coped with driving rain most of the day.

William Griffiths, a brother to Hugh Griffiths already mentioned, was a shepherd for Tommy's grandfather, Robert Hughes, at Aber-glan-hirin. After him came Thomas Pugh who was there for ten to twelve years, and then moved to Cilbwth, Pant-y-dwr.

Harold Hughes used to do quite a bit of buying and selling and would go as far as Devil's Bridge mart to buy sheep. Tommy would then take them to Aber-glan-hirin, stay the night, and next day go on to New Mead.

Tommy always used to enjoy relating how in July 1945 he had been in the first car to go to Nant-y-beddau. This car was driven by Malcolm Richards, from the Butchers Arms in Rhaeadr. Arthur Price, Ashfield, and Lesley Davies, Pen-glan-einion, were also

■ Tommy Hughes, Aberglanhirin 1992. Photo by Mrs Veronica Davies, Dyffryn, Rhaeadr Gwy.

passengers in the car. According to Tommy they were stuck more often that they were on the move. Another time, Tommy had been to a shearing at Nant-y-beddau, and bought some lambs there. He then walked them down by the Claerwen river on what is today the floor of the Claerwen dam. At this particular time, the very first pieces of equipment for building the dam had just arrived there.

In mentioning Claerwen, there used to be pie-bald ponies roaming the hills of that area and they had originally been the ponies of Nant-gwyllt (drowned under the reservoirs) but they were done away with around 1965. Seeing a troupe of mares running free on the hill, guarded by a masterful stallion, is a sight to behold, but they

214

are getting less nowadays – indeed, the ponies of Aber-glan-hirin are probably some of the last in the area.

In about 1935 Harold Hughes had taken a farm called Cornel in Llanwrthwl on rent from the Penlan-oleu estate. Tommy (aged about 17) went to live there for a few years to look after the place, with his sister Myfanwy to keep house and to help generally. He moved afterwards back to New Mead where he stayed until he was 25 years old and then the Hughes family moved to live in Stone House, Rhaeadr, where he lived for seven years. In 1947, he married Ellen Ann Lewis, a sister to John Lewis, Ty-mawr, and he and Nell, as she was known, spent a week on their honeymoon with friends in Sarnau, Llanfihangel-y-creuddyn, going to sight-see by bus to Aberystwyth. They moved to Aber-glan-hirin in 1949, when the present house was built, and they had two children – Robert and Elizabeth – both long-standing names in the family. His children and grand-children all called him Tommy.

He was a shrewd judge of character, and it didn't take him long to work out who was genuine, and who wasn't.

Tommy was a man with a sense of belonging. Every acre of his surroundings meant something, or had a tale to tell. His sense of observation was beyond belief. He would see or hear something once and it would always by retained in his mind and, in a twinkling, he could recall these facts from so long ago with great accuracy.

His knowledge of sheep ear-marks in the surrounding districts is a legend and he could see an ear-mark when others could hardly see the sheep! People were of great importance to him. He knew not only them, but of their family background going back a long way and when and where they were born: he was able to surprise many people by telling them facts about themselves that they didn't know, all tied in with an incredible sense of humour. I well remember taking Tommy for a spin in the car one day and I wanted to go to Cwm Dulais, near Llanafan Fawr. While on a narrow road and not totally sure of the way, a man in a pickup came along and I asked him the way. Tommy managed to get an inkling as to who he was, and said, 'You're fifty two years of age,' gave him the day and date of his birth, told him the weather on that particular morning and said he was one of twins. There was a look of total disbelief on that man's face, but every word Tommy told him was true.

Tommy had been blessed with a mathematical mind and it was astounding how he remembered dates of events long ago, birthdays, when people were buried and their ages. He also had a talent of being able to tell you what day it was on any given date, even if it was 150 years ago.

To anybody interested in the history of the locality, Tommy was a true gem, as his in-depth knowledge of the happenings of yesteryear was, to say the least, incredible. I can only say, by modern comparison, that he had a head like a computer. He knew something about almost every farm from Aberystwyth to Brecon, as well as interesting information about the people who lived in them. He compiled daily diaries from 1947 onwards, and these were consulted periodically if there was a dispute about dates or events. Thankfully, his daughter-in-law, Janet, still keeps an account of the daily events at Aber-glan-hirin.

While at the sheep in Bodtalog years ago, Clifford Pugh had been counting the different lots and had put down on a piece of wood which happened to be convenient, the count of the ewes and wethers from each lot. This piece of wood was left out in the pens in torrential rain, and when he went to find it a day or so later, it was totally illegible. He told this tale to Tommy, who had been helping him at the time, and Tommy was able to recall all the figures involved, but not only that, able to compare them with the same figures from the previous year!

He had read a good deal and listened to the stories of the old people he had met in his youth, and he would enjoy relating these tales in his own inimitable way, intersected with wry comments that would keep everybody in stitches.

He had a way of saying things to people without them taking offence. As can be imagined he thought a great deal of Ned Rees, Pen-garreg, and his family, and he told Pat, Ned's daughter, that she had been the ugliest baby he had ever seen – a statement that always makes her burst out in gales of laughter. He used to enjoy a bit of leg-pulling whenever he got a chance. He asked John Jones, Lan-fadog, if there were any whinberries on Dôl-fola hill – a place noted for them – to which John answered that there were a fair few there. Tommy went on to say that he had some big ones behind Aber-glan-hirin and that they had to roll them down and split them with an axe! Anybody who knows Aber-glan-hirin would see straight away that is it not whinberry country at all.

Tommy had been discussing the high cost of funerals with somebody and thinking of his own funeral, in order to save costs, said, 'I'd better go down to Glan-llyn to meet Bernard Lloyd,' (the undertaker). Glan-llyn was six miles nearer Rhaeadr than Aber-glan-hirin!

He had a way of finding things out that was totally uncanny and would put most detectives to shame. I am very indebted to this particular talent of his, as he solved scores of my enquiries over the years. One story that seems to prove the point is this one about Billy and Jean Pugh, The Park, by Rhaeadr. Billy was the son of Tom Pugh, Gwardole. He was born on the 18th of July 1926, on the day of the worst thunder and lightning storms of the century. It went on continuously for twenty-four hours. Billy and Jean set off one morning with a view to going to Troed-yr-aur, which is three miles from Castell Newydd Emlyn, to buy pigs from Tom Evans who was a noted breeder. They went to Pont-rhyd-y-groes, down to Trawscoed, and decided to go across country, ending up on a grassy lane near Llanrhystud, very lost. They saw some men working with the electricity who pointed them in the right direction. All this had made them late and they were afraid of missing the sale but they made it on time. Three gilts were bought and they decided to play safe and come home on the coast road but, en route, they had a puncture. The wheel was replaced and off they went. When they came back to Bodtalog there was a gathering going on and they stopped to have a chat. Tommy came up to them and he knew where they had been, that they had been lost, what they had bought and about the puncture – and all that even before they had arrived home!

He loved his telephone, and I must confess to having that weakness and if I had to pick a hero from the past it would be Alexander Graham Bell, even though he has cost me a small fortune over the years. With his customary, 'How a' yuh boy?' Tommy's next comment would be 'What's news?' and that would set off a long, interesting conversation.

On a market day in Rhaeadr, several men had been counting a sizeable bunch of sheep and failing to agree as to the correct figure. Tommy went to count them and got it right. Somebody asked him how he had done that and, very typically, Tommy said, 'Oh, I just counted their feet boy, and divided by four!'

Another time, a group of men were talking about boots and praising the ones they had and so on. Tommy said – and he was about seventy then – that the best pair he'd ever had were the ones that he was wearing that day. He'd had them since he was in school!

Tommy was not a Welsh speaker, but it was surprising how many Welsh words came through in his conversation. He would say 'The ewe went under the *geulan*' (a bank) and he'd say about a small lamb 'Keep him in, he'll only *nychu* (waste away) on the hill.' Tommy and his friend Anthony Powell were talking one day about warbles in cattle, and they referred to them being caused by a *pry* (pronounced pree) which is the Welsh word for a fly. I have also heard them saying of a small, unthrifty lamb, 'He's a bit of a *cadodwyn*,' which means a runt, or the smallest, in a litter of dogs or piglets. All this I find most interesting.

Somebody had hit one of Tommy's dogs for some misdemeanour and Tommy, not liking this, said sharply, 'Haven't you got any dogs of your own to hit!'

His often curt replies and comments will be things that will live on for a long time, as will be his 'Boy, boy,' which was an expression he often used before making a statement. He often said to Robert, his son, 'You walk by the river, and it's surprising what you'll see.' Tommy's last walk took him upriver from the house and he died as he would have wished, on his own land, with his boots on. After a long search, his body was found by Lyn Lewis of Cwmystwyth, a friend, whose family Tommy knew well, and I am convinced, from the position of his body, that he died even before hitting the ground. Thomas Walter Hughes died on Friday the 21st of February, 2003, aged 85.

To his grand-children, Helen, Christopher, David, Jessica and Gemma, I have this to say:

Your Tommy was the most interesting, amazingly informed individual that I have ever met, and these writings are studded with information which I gleaned from him. He was the last person of this calibre, to have retained these facts and tales and saved them from going into oblivion.

The mould from which this great intellectual country character came was unique and he enriched the lives of many who came into contact with him. One thing is certain, there will never be another Tommy Hughes.

Gone from the bleating of sheep
Gone from the barking of dogs
Gone from the heather and whin
Gone from the shearing of hogs,
Gone to a haven of peace
Gone to the fold of the soul
Gone to the Shepherd of man
Remembered, and loved by us all.

DIOLCH I/THANKS TO:

Rev. Daniel Davies, Llanelli
Mr D.J. Edwards, Llety Llwyd
Mr Clifford and Charles Pugh, Botalog
Mr Tommy Hughes, Aber-glan-hirin
Mr Cledwyn Fychan, Llanddeiniol
Mr William Evans, Llwyniorwerth Isaf
Mr Vincent Lewis, Elan Valley
Miss Rhiannon Evans, Tregaron
Mr Hugh Jones, Pantycraf, Tregaron
Mrs Neva Price, Pantydwr
Mr Morgan Griffiths, Llangurig
Miss Maglona Able, Llanidloes
Mrs Nancy Jones, Llanidloes
Mr David Williams, Llandrindod
Mr Billy Rees, Elan Valley
Mr Islwyn Lewis, Cwmystwyth
Mr Edgar Morgan, Llanilar
Mr Arthur Chater, Aberystwyth
Mrs Jane Rowlands, Hen Hafod, Tre'r ddol
Dr Kay Little, Rhaeadr Gwy
Mrs Ann Lawrence, Llanidloes
Mrs Elizabeth Allen, Devil's Bridge
Mr & Mrs Gwyn Davies, Brenan, New Cross
Mr Rhys Jones, 15, Penllwyn, Capel Bangor
Mr Tom Griffiths, Cwmystwyth
Mrs Nancy Edwards, Tygwyn, Devil's Bridge
Mr & Mrs Jim Raw, Tyllwyd, Cwmystwyth
Mr & Mrs Richard Jones, Llwynhyrddod, Llangurig
Mrs Patience Grant, Wiltshire
Mr Ieuan Rees, Cwm Biga
Mr Simon Harries, Gossport, Hampshire
Mr Granville Ashton, Llanidloes
Mr John Morgan Jones, Llanafan
Mr Sam Evans, Pennal
Miss Olive Jones, Cae Cwta, Commins Coch
Mr Edgar Humphreys, Talybont
Mrs Eirionedd Baskerville, Abermagwr
Mrs Morfudd Clark, Bow Street
Mrs Heulwen Price, Bridgend
Mr Ken Jones, Cwmrheidol
Mr Gwylfa Micah, Llanegryn
Mr Iorwerth Davies, Ysbyty Ystwyth
Mr Aneurin Davies, Lampeter
Miss Eirwen Howells, Caerdydd

218

Mr Haydn Jones, Aberystwyth
Mr Norman Roderick Jones, Devil's Bridge
Mrs Margaret Jones, Harford
Mrs Elin Davies, Llangurig
Mr Goronwy Jones, Talybont
Mr John Jones, Nant-llwyd
Mr Christopher Evans, Hereford
Mrs Betty Davies, Rhaeadr
Mrs Curigwen Griffiths, Talybont
Mr Dafydd Lloyd Roberts, Ciliau Aeron
Mr Islwyn Roberts, Llanddewi Brefi
Mrs Annie Mary Davies, Troed-yr-henriw
Mrs Bertha Jones, Pont-rhyd-fendigaid
Mrs Marina Kenyon, Penparcau
Mr Edward Morgan, Bow Street
Mr Dai Hawkins, Nantmel
Mrs Jennie Timms, Lampeter
Mr David James, Llandre
Mr Gomer James, Ponterwyd
Mr Alun Thomas, Eisteddfa Gurig
Mr Ronnie Hope, Cribyn
Mr Tony Murray, Gelmast, Cwmystwyth
Mrs Gwen Rees, Aberhosan
Mr Aled Rees, Llanbadarn Fawr
Mr Robert Hughes, Aber-glan-hirin
Mr & Mrs Wyn Hamilton, Aberangell
Mr Gilbert Jones, Llandre
Mr & Mrs Merfyn Powell, Commins Coch
Mr Gethin Howells, Capel Madog
Mr Alan Lewis, Cefn-caido, Rhaeadr
Mr Donald Rees, Staylittle
Mr Lewis Griffiths, Ty'n Coed, Rhaeadr
Mrs Eirwen Owen, Glan-wern, Borth
Mr Rheinallt Llwyd, Penparcau
Mr Dewi Morris Jones, Bronant
Mr John Edwards, Pen-y-garn
Mr Howell Jones, Ponterwyd
Mr John Owen Worthing, Carmarthen

DIOLCH ARBENNING I/SPECIAL THANKS TO:

Miss Elen Howells, Llanbadarn
Mr T.C. Griffiths, Farnborough
Mr Ian Sant, Goginan
Mr Owain Hammonds, Bontgoch
Cambrian Printers, Aberystwyth

National Grid Map References
for Selected Placenames

Aber Glanhirin	2887 2723	Aber-felin	2784 2986
Aberbotgoll	2749 2764	Abergwngu	2871 2735
Aber-ceiro	2753 2822	Abermad	2601 2761
Abercoed	2669 2581	Aber-nant	2810 2748
Abercwmdolau	2643 2807	Aberpeithnant	2752 2842

Dolcarne	2747 2811	Glaspwll	2739 2977
Dolchennog	2786 2737	Glyn Hafren	2895 2847
Dolfeiniog	c 2916 2670	Gogerddan	2634 2837
Dolfor	2667 2716	Goginan-fawr Farm	2682 2822
Dolgoch, cwm Tywi	2806 2563	Gorn Farm	2975 2845
Dolgors	2745 2741	Gors lwyd, bog	2857 2753
Dologau	2772 2733	Gwarafog bridge	2956 2494
Dolwen	2777 2787	Gwar-clawdd	2729 2757
Dre-isaf	2709 2674	Gwar-coed	2555 2481
Drosgol	2766 2884	Gwar-dolau	2962 2690
Dyffryn	2753 2684	Gwarffynnon, Ystrad Meurig	2712 2679
Dyffryn Castell	2774 2817	Gwar-geulan	2682 2712
Dyfngwm	2861 2924	Gwern-arglwydd	3154 2598
Dylife village	2863 2941		
Dysyrnant	2650 2996	Hafan quarry	2733 2881
		Hafod Lydan	2887 2782
Eglwys Newydd	2768 2736	Hafod Mansion (Hafoduchtryd)	2759 2733
Eisteddfa Gurig	2797 2841	Hafod, Llanwrthwl	2962 2614
Eisteddfa-fach	2799 2842	Hafod-wnog	2763 2937
Erwbarfau	2749 2784	Hafodyrhyd	2725 2641
Esgair Hir lead mine	2735 2912	Hen Fynachlog (Old Abbey)	2717 2647
Esgair Llu (or Lle) lead mine	2792 2828	Hen Hafod	2758 2848
Esgair Wen, Cwmystwyh	2826 2755	Hendre, Llangurig	2865 2814
Esgairgarthen	2837 2649	Hendre-aur	2952 2799
		Henfaes Uchaf	2898 2807
Fagwr	2782 2817	Henfron	2904 2643
Fainc Ddu, hillside	2780 2880	Hengae	2820 2681
Ffos	2687 2671	Hengwm-annedd house	2797 2892
Ffosyffin, Blaenpennal	2609 2641	Hengwm-gyfeiliog	2781 2948
Frongoch lead mine	2723 2745	Henllan	2775 2986
Frongoch-ar-Deifi	2766 2667	Hirnant, Cwm Elan	2888 2699
Fuchesgau	2767 2808	Hirnant, Ponterwyd	2754 2837
Furnace village	2685 2951	Hore Wen	c 2827 2873
		Hyddgen	2780 2909
Garreg-lwyd	2788 2646		
Garth	2635 2718	Kingsfield (near Upper Lan-fadog)	
Gelli, Llanwrin	2781 3043		c 2936 2655
Gelli-grean, Pennal	2685 3003		
Gelli-isaf	2763 2814	Lan-fadog	2935 2656
Gelli-uchaf (also known as Quick)		Llaethdy	3068 2801
	2785 2827	Llainarthur	2626 2823
Gilfach	2628 2635	Llaneithyr	2762 2772
Glan Gwy	2889 2801	Llannerch-irfon	2836 2557
Glandwgan	2708 2749	Llansantffraid Cwmdauddwr Church	
Glan-fedw	2733 2759		2967 2677
Glan-gors-fach	c 2715 2594	Llanwrda village	2713 2315
Glan-hirin	2865 2716	Llanwrthwl village	2976 2637
Glanyrafon, Ffair Rhos	2748 2702	Lle'r-neuaddau	2758 2849
Glan-yr-afon, near Troed-rhiw	2828 2756	Lle'r-taihirion	c 2887 2558
Glan-yr-afon, Ponterwyd	2782 2817	Llechwedd isaf hillside	2825 2749

Llechwedd-mawr	2762 2889	Nant Tidnerth	2872 2825
Llether	2741 2702	Nant yr Arian farm	2715 2814
Llety-ifan-hen	2685 2853	Nant yr Hafod	2874 2913
Llety-synod	2718 2738	Nantarthur	2743 2748
Lluest Las, Llangurig	2888 2817	Nant-cae-rhedyn	2752 2829
Lluest-aber-caethon	2875 2688	Nant-carreuau	2786 2796
Lluest-dduallt	2892 2905	Nantgwernog	2739 2515
Lluest-dolgwiail	2843 2769	Nant-gwyllt, now under water	
Lluestfach	2718 2834		c 2913 2638
Lluest-forgan	c 2779 2915	Nant-llymysten	2905 2747
Lluest-gadair	2869 2663	Nantstalwen	2805 2576
Lluest-gotta	2753 2905	Nantsyddion	2773 2791
Lluest-las	2888 2817	Nanty	2854 2816
Lluest-newydd	2797 2895	Nant-y-beddau	2853 2662
Lluest-y-broga	2609 2626	Nantyfyda	2810 2962
Lluestygrafie	2752 2914	Nant-y-maen	2762 2585
Lluest-y-rhos	2753 2917	Nant-y-moch, now under water	2763 2871
Llwynderw	2846 2519	Nant-y-nod brook, Eisteddfa Gurig	
Llwynglas	2643 2902		2791 2840
Llwyngwinau	2722 2925	Nant-y-nod, Cwm Ceulan	2702 2904
Llwynteifi	2742 2783	Nant-yr-hydd	2794 2850
Llwyn-y-gog	2875 2918	New Mead	3025 2588
Llwynynwch	2723 2745	New Row hamlet	2728 2734
Llyn Rhuddnant	2806 2784		
Llywernog	2732 2807	Ochorglog	2790 2741
Llywernog lead mine	2733 2809	Old Abbey (Hen Fynachlog)	2717 2647
Lovesgrove	2628 2816	Old Park	2746 2928
Lovesgrove farm	2631 2819		
		Pant y Craf	2714 2614
Maen-arthur	2729 2728	Pantanamlwg	2543 2664
Maes-dulais	2781 2982	Pantclwydau	2806 2531
Maes-glas	2667 2622	Pant-styllen	2788 2998
Maesnant	2774 2881	Pantybeudyau	2837 2649
Maespandy, Forge	2783 2990	Pant-y-garreg-hir	2704 2835
Maesperthi	2782 3012	Pant-y-mawn	2763 2738
Marchnant	2906 2613	Pantyronn	2668 2998
Mathafarn	2807 3045	Parc, Henllan	2363 2419
Melindwr	2693 2963	Parkgwyn	2758 2805
Moel-prysgau	2805 2612	Peithyll	2632 2827
Mount	2750 2808	Pen-banc	2778 2975
Mynachdy, Aberhosan	2788 2955	Penbryn	2829 2753
Mynachdy, Ystrad Meurig	2712 2679	Penbrynbarcud	2683 2810
Mynachlog Ddu village	2145 2303	Pencae-mawr	2894 2557
Mynachlog, Llangurig	2861 2840	Pencefn	2627 2794
Mynydd Mallaen	2730 2450	Pencreigiau	2733 2664
		Pendre	2608 2806
Nant Iago lead mine	2826 2863	Pen-garreg	2912 2676
Nant Iwrch	2793 2855	Pen-graig Isaf	2706 2678
Nant Llyn	2783 2891	Pengraig, Cwmystwyth	2788 2734
Nant Rhys	2837 2793	Penpompren	2734 2708

Penrhiw, Ystumtuen	2737 2784
Pen-rhiw-cae-gegin	2683 2746
Pen-rhiw-lwyd, also Tyrpeg Neli	
	2855 2758
Pen-rhiw-wen, hillside	2925 2709
Pensarn	2670 2910
Pentre Farm, Capel Bangor	2637 2812
Pentre, Cwm Ystwyth	2788 2740
Pen-twyn, Abergwesyn	2855 2527
Penwern	2636 2766
Perfedd-nant	2628 3055
Plas-y-mynydd	2747 2923
Pont-ar-elan	2903 2715
Pontrhydgaled	2839 2828
Prignant, Devil's Bridge	2750 2755
Pumlumon	2790 2870
Pwll y fuwch, Hengwm	2799 2895
Pwll-cenawon	2638 2803
Pwllpeiran	2775 2746
Quick (Gelli Uchaf)	2785 2827
Rheidol House, Devil's Bridge	2736 2769
Rheidol View	2747 2810
Rhiwfaenog	c 2775 2947
Rhiwfelen Chapel, Trisant	2717 2758
Rhiwnant	2895 2616
Rhosyrhiw	2741 2733
Rhosyrhydd	2705 2758
Rhuddnant gorge	2797 2784
Rhydoldog	2942 2679
Rhydybennwch	2857 2869
Rhyd-y-gaib	2730 2853
Shop Ceiro	2752 2822
St. Brides Church, Cwm-dauddwr	
	2967 2677
Star Inn, Dylife	2863 2941
Tabor Chapel	2736 2886
Tai Newyddion, Cwm Ystwyth	
	c 2792 2750
Talbontdrain	2777 2958
Talwrn, Ponterwyd	2746 2806
Tanyrallt, Capel Bangor	2657 2788
Troed-rhiw, Cwmystwyth	c 2827 2755
Troed-rhiw, Gors-neuadd, Tregaron	
	2695 2584

Troedrhiw, Pont-rhyd-fendigaid	
	2763 2662
Troed-rhiw-cymmer	2764 2485
Troed-rhiw-drain	2895 2670
Troed-rhiw-goch	2766 2808
Troed-rhiw-ruddwen	2771 2479
Ty Canol	2781 2650
Ty'n bryn, Ponterwyd	2752 2813
Ty'n Cwm, Cwm Einion	2700 2943
Ty'n Cwm, opposite Dyffryn Castell	
	c 2779 2811
Ty'n Cwm, Pont-rhyd-fendigaid	
	2771 2655
Ty'n Ddol, Cwm Ystwyth	2808 2747
Ty'n Ddol, Ffair Rhos	2767 2677
Ty'n Llechwedd Bach	2606 2864
Ty'n Lloft, Silian	2582 2515
Ty'n Parc, Llandre	2627 2872
Ty'n Rhos, Ponterwyd	2747 2816
Ty'n rhyd, Cwmystwyth	2787 2747
Ty'n y Maes, Devil's Bridge	c 2766 2777
Ty'nbryn, Cwm Ystwyth	2783 2746
Ty'nffordd, Ponterwyd	2755 2797
Ty'nllwyn, Devil's Bridge	2746 2772
Ty'npwll, Goginan	2675 2818
Ty'nwern, Aberffrwd	2675 2781
Tyddyn Gwilym	2648 2993
Ty-gwyn, facing Dolwen	c 2772 2775
Tyllwyd, Cwmystwyth	2823 2753
Tymawr, Cwmystwyth	2815 2747
Tynant, Ponterwyd	2762 2799
Tynewydd, Cwmystwyth	2790 2735
Tynllechwedd	2624 2874
Tyrpeg Neli, also Pen-rhiw-lwyd	
	2855 2758
Tyrpeg-y-mynydd	2871 2741
Tywi	2792 2612
Waun-fyddau	2677 2766
Werndeg	2737 2804
Wern-felen	2723 2648
Y Ffrwd, near Nant-y-maen	2762 2576
Y Foel hillside	2838 2842
Y Grofft	2813 3041
Ysguborfach	2784 2744
Ysbyty Cynfyn Church	2752 2791
Ystradolwyn	2931 2795